S0-FCC-122

DOCUMENTS ILLUSTRATIVE

OF

AMERICAN HISTORY

1606–1863

WITH INTRODUCTIONS AND REFERENCES

BY

HOWARD W. PRESTON

NEW YORK & LONDON
G. P. PUTNAM'S SONS
The Knickerbocker Press
1886

Press of
G. P. Putnam's Sons
New York.

TO

MY FATHER.

PREFACE.

In his inaugural lecture at Oxford, October, 1884, Prof. Freeman declared that the historical professor "must ever bear in mind himself and ever strive to impress on the minds of others that the most ingenious and most eloquent of modern historical discourses can after all be nothing more than a comment on a text." A conviction of this truth was the incentive to this work.

It is hoped that this presentation of a few of the more important documents, the original authorities and sources of our history, may promote in some degree a more accurate knowledge of American history. Should this hope be realized the editor will be well repaid.

Howard W. Preston.

Providence, R. I.
February 13, 1886.

CONTENTS.

DOCUMENTS ILLUSTRATIVE

OF

AMERICAN HISTORY.

FIRST VIRGINIA CHARTER—1606.

The favorable report of the country brought home by the early English explorers, joined to English activity, led to the formation of the Virginia Company, on a plan somewhat similar to the famous East India Company. In 1606 James I. granted the necessary charter, and in the spring of the following year Jamestown was founded.

"The first written charter of a permanent American colony, which was to be the chosen abode of liberty, gave to the mercantile corporation nothing but a desert territory, with the right of peopling it and defending it, and reserved to the monarch absolute legislative authority, the control of all appointments, and a hope of an ultimate revenue. The emigrants were subjected to the ordinances of a commercial corporation, of which they could not be members; to the dominions of a domestic council, in appointing which they had no voice; to the control of a superior council in

England, which had no sympathies with their rights; and finally, to the arbitrary legislation of the sovereign." (Bancroft.)

This charter is of especial interest as the first under which a permanent English settlement was planted in America.

Consult *Bancroft's U. S.*, 1st ed., I., 120; Centenary ed., I., 95; last ed., I., 85; *Hildreth's U. S.*, I., 94; *Doyle's English Colonies in America*, 109; *Bryant and Gay's U. S.*, I., 267; *Cooke's Va.*, 16; *Neil's Va. Co.*, 3; *Stith's Va.; Chalmers' Political Annals*, 12.

THE FIRST CHARTER OF VIRGINIA—1606.

JAMES, by the Grace of God, King of *England*, *Scotland*, *France* and *Ireland*, Defender of the Faith, etc. WHEREAS our loving and well-disposed Subjects, Sir *Thomas Gates*, and Sir *George Somers*, Knights, *Richard Hackluit*, Clerk, Prebendary of *Westminster*, and *Edward-Maria Wingfield*, *Thomas Hanham*, and *Ralegh Gilbert*, Esqrs. *William Parker*, and *George Popham*, Gentlemen, and divers others of our loving Subjects, have been humble Suitors unto us, that We would vouchsafe unto them our Licence, to make Habitation, Plantation, and to deduce a colony of sundry of our People into that part of *America* commonly called VIRGINIA, and other parts and Territories in *America*, either appertaining unto us, or which are not now actually possessed by any *Christian* Prince or People, situate, lying, and being all along the Sea Coasts, between four and thirty Degrees of *Northerly* Latitude from the Equinoctial Line, and five and forty Degrees of the same Latitude, and in the main Land between the same four and thirty and five and forty Degrees, and the Islands thereunto adjacent, or within one hundred Miles of the Coast thereof;

And to that End, and for the more speedy Accomplishment of their said intended Plantation and Habitation there, are desirous to divide themselves into two several Colonies and Companies; the one consisting of certain Knights, Gentlemen, Merchants, and other Adventurers, of our City of *London* and elsewhere, which are, and from time to time shall be, joined unto them, which do desire to begin their Plantation and Habitation in some fit and convenient Place, between four and thirty and one and forty Degrees of the said Latitude, alongst the Coasts of *Virginia*, and the Coasts of *America* aforesaid: And the other consisting of sundry Knights, Gentlemen, Merchants, and other Adventurers, of our Cities of *Bristol* and *Exeter*, and of our Town of *Plimouth*, and of other Places, which do join themselves unto that Colony, which do desire to begin their Plantation and Habitation in some fit and convenient Place, between eight and thirty Degrees and five and forty Degrees of the said Latitude, all alongst the said Coasts of *Virginia* and *America*, as that Coast lyeth:

We, greatly commending, and graciously accepting of, their Desires for the Furtherance of so noble a Work, which may, by the Providence of Almighty God, hereafter tend to the Glory of his Divine Majesty, in propagating of *Christian* Religion to such People, as yet live in Darkness and miserable Ignorance of the true Knowledge and Worship of God, and may in time bring the Infidels and Savages, living in those parts, to human Civility, and to a settled and quiet Government: DO, by these our Letters Patents, graciously accept of, and agree to, their humble and well-intended Desires;

And do therefore, for Us, our Heirs, and Successors, GRANT and agree, that the said Sir *Thomas Gates*, Sir *George Somers*, *Richard Hackluit*, and *Edward-Maria Wingfield*, Adventurers of and for our City of *London*, and all such others, as are, or shall be, joined unto them of that Colony, shall be called the *first Colony;* And they shall and may begin their said first Plantation and Habitation, at any Place upon the said Coast of *Virginia* or *America*, where they shall think fit and convenient, between the said four and thirty and one and forty Degrees of the said Latitude; And that they shall have all the Lands, Woods, Soil, Grounds, Havens, Ports, Rivers, Mines, Minerals, Marshes, Waters, Fishings, Commodities, and Hereditaments, whatsoever, from the said first Seat of their Plantation and Habitation by the Space of fifty Miles of *English* Statute Measure, all along the said Coast of *Virginia* and *America*, towards the *West* and *Southwest*, as the Coast lyeth, with all the Islands within one hundred Miles directly over against the same Sea Coast; And also all the Lands, Soil, Grounds, Havens, Ports, Rivers, Mines, Minerals, Woods, Waters, Marshes, Fishings, Commodities, and Hereditaments, whatsoever, from the said Place of their first Plantation and Habitation for the space of fifty like *English* Miles, all alongst the said Coasts of *Virginia* and *America*, towards the *East* and *Northeast*, or towards the *North*, as the Coast lyeth, together with all the Islands within one hundred Miles, directly over against the said Sea Coast; And also all the Lands, Woods, Soil, Grounds, Havens, Ports, Rivers, Mines, Minerals, Marshes, Waters, Fishings, Commodities, and Hereditaments, whatsoever, from the same fifty Miles every way on the Sea Coast, directly into the main Land by the Space of one hundred like *English* Miles; And shall and may inhabit and remain there; and shall and may also build and fortify within any the same, for their better Safeguard and Defence, according to their best Discretion, and the Discretion of the Council of that Colony; And that no other of our Subjects shall be permitted, or suffered, to plant or inhabit behind, or on the Backside of them, towards the main Land, without the Express Licence or Consent of the Council of that Colony, thereunto in Writing first had and obtained.

And we do likewise, for Us, our Heirs, and Successors, by these Presents, GRANT and agree, that the said *Thomas Hanham*, and *Ralegh Gilbert*, *William Parker*, and *George Popham*, and all others of the Town of *Plimouth* in the County of *Devon*, or elsewhere, which are, or shall be, joined unto them of that Colony, shall be called the *second Colony;* And that they shall and may begin their said Plantation and Seat of their first Abode and Habitation, at any Place upon the said Coast of *Virginia* and *America*, where they shall think fit and convenient, between eight and thirty Degrees of the said Latitude, and five and forty Degrees of the same Latitude; And that they shall have all the Lands, Soils, Grounds, Havens, Ports, Rivers, Mines, Minerals, Woods, Marshes, Waters, Fishings, Commodities, and Hereditaments, whatsoever, from the first Seat of their Plantation and Habitation by the Space of fifty like *English* Miles, as is aforesaid, all alongst the said Coasts of *Virginia* and *America*, towards the *West* and *Southwest*, or towards the *South*, as the Coast lyeth, and all the Islands within one hundred Miles, directly over against the said Sea Coast; And also all the Lands, Soils, Grounds, Havens, Ports, Rivers, Mines, Minerals, Woods, Marshes, Waters, Fishings, Commodities, and Hereditaments, whatsoever, from the said Place of their first Plantation and Habitation for the Space of fifty like Miles, all alongst the said Coast of *Virginia* and *America*, towards the *East* and *Northeast*, or towards the *North*, as the Coast lyeth, and all the Islands also within one hundred Miles directly over against the same Sea Coast; And also all the Lands, Soils, Grounds, Havens, Ports, Rivers, Woods, Mines, Minerals, Marshes, Waters, Fishings, Commodities, and Hereditaments, whatsoever, from the same fifty Miles every way on the Sea Coast, directly into the main Land, by the Space of one hundred like *English* Miles; And shall and may inhabit and remain there; and shall and may also build and fortify within any the same for their better Safeguard, according to their best Discretion, and the Discretion of the Council of that Colony; And that none of our Subjects shall be permitted, or suffered, to plant or inhabit behind, or on the back of them, towards the main Land, without express Licence of the Council of that Colony, in Writing thereunto first had and obtained.

Provided always, and our Will and Pleasure herein is, that the Plantation and Habitation of such of the said Colonies, as shall last plant themselves, as aforesaid, shall not be made within one hundred like *English* Miles of the other of them, that first began to make their Plantation, as aforesaid.

And we do also ordain, establish, and agree, for Us, our Heirs, and Successors, that each of the said Colonies shall have a Council, which shall govern and order all Matters and Causes, which shall arise, grow, or happen, to or within the same several Colonies, according to such Laws, Ordinances, and Instructions, as shall be, in that behalf, given and signed with Our Hand or Sign Manual, and pass under the Privy Seal of our realm of *England;* Each of which Councils shall consist of thirteen Persons, to be ordained, made, and removed, from time to time, according as shall be directed and comprised in the same instructions; And shall have a several Seal, for all Matters that shall pass or concern the same several Councils; Each of which Seals, shall have the King's Arms engraven on the one Side thereof, and his Portraiture on the other; And that the Seal for the Council of the said first Colony shall have engraven round about, on the one Side, these Words; *Sigillum Regis Magnæ Britanniæ, Franciæ, & Hiberniæ;* on the other Side this Inscription round about; *Pro Concilio primæ Coloniæ Virginiæ.* And the Seal for the Council of the said second Colony shall also have engraven, round about the one Side thereof, the aforesaid Words; *Sigillum Regis Magnæ Britanniæ, Franciæ, & Hiberniæ;* and on the other Side; *Pro Concilio secundæ Coloniæ Virginiæ:* And that also there shall be a Council, established here in *England,* which shall, in like Manner, consist of thirteen Persons, to be, for that Purpose, appointed by Us, our Heirs and Successors, which shall be called our *Council of Virginia;* And shall, from time to time, have the superior Managing and Direction, only of and for all Matters that shall or may concern the Government as well as of the said several Colonies, as of and for any other Part or Place, within the aforesaid Precincts of four and thirty and five and forty Degrees above mentioned; Which Council shall, in like manner, have a Seal, for Matters concerning the Council or Colonies, with the like Arms and Portraiture, as aforesaid, with this inscription, engraven round about on the one Side; *Sigillum Regis Magnæ Britanniæ, Franciæ, & Hiberniæ;* and round about on the other Side, *Pro Concilio suo Virginiæ.*

And moreover, we do GRANT and agree, for Us, our Heirs and Successors; that the said several Councils of and for the said several Colonies, shall and lawfully may, by Virtue hereof, from time to time, without any Interruption of Us, our Heirs or Successors, give and take Order, to dig, mine, and search for all Manner of Mines of Gold, Silver, and Copper, as well within any part of their said several Colonies, as for the said main Lands on the Backside of the same Colonies; And to HAVE and enjoy the Gold, Silver, and Copper, to be gotten thereof, to the Use and Behoof of the same Colonies, and the Plantations thereof; YIELDING therefore to Us, our Heirs and Successors, the fifth Part only of all the same Gold and Silver, and the fifteenth Part of all the same Copper, so to be gotten or had, as is aforesaid, without any other Manner of Profit or Account, to be given or yielded to Us, our Heirs, or Successors, for or in Respect of the same:

And that they shall, or lawfully may, establish and cause to be made a Coin, to pass current there between the people of those several Colonies, for the more Ease of Traffick and Bargaining between and amongst them and the Natives there, of such Metal, and in such Manner and Form, as the said several Councils there shall limit and appoint.

And we do likewise, for Us, our Heirs, and Successors, by these Presents, give full Power and Authority to the said Sir *Thomas Gates*, Sir *George Somers*, *Richard Hackluit*, *Edward-Maria Wingfield*, *Thomas Hanham*, *Ralegh Gilbert*, *William Parker*, and *George Popham*, and to every of them, and to the said several Companies, Plantations, and Colonies, that they, and every of them, shall and may, at all and every time and times hereafter, have, take, and lead in the said Voyage, and for and towards the said several Plantations, and Colonies, and to travel thitherward, and to abide and inhabit there, in every the said Colonies and Plantations, such and so many of our Subjects, as shall willingly accompany them or any of them, in the said Voyages and Plantations; With sufficient Shipping, and Furniture of Armour, Weapons, Ordinance, Powder, Victual, and all other things, necessary for the said Plantations, and for their Use and Defence there: PROVIDED always, that none of the said Persons be such, as shall hereafter be specially restrained by Us, our Heirs, or Successors.

Moreover, we do, by these Presents, for Us, our Heirs, and Successors GIVE AND GRANT Licence unto the said Sir *Thomas Gates*, Sir *George Somers*, *Richard Hackluit*, *Edward-Maria Wingfield*, *Thomas Hanham*, *Ralegh Gilbert*, *William Parker*, and *George Popham*, and to every of the said Colonies, that they, and every of them, shall and may, from time to time, and at all times forever hereafter, for their several Defences, encounter, expulse, repel, and resist, as well by Sea as by Land, by all Ways and Means whatsoever, all and every such Person and Persons, as without the especial Licence of the said several Colonies and Plantations, shall attempt to inhabit within the said several Precincts and Limits of the said several Colonies and Plantations, or any of them, or that shall enterprise or attempt, at any time hereafter, the Hurt, Detriment, or Annoyance, of the said several Colonies or Plantations:

Giving and granting, by these Presents, unto the said Sir *Thomas Gates*, Sir *George Somers*, *Richard Hackluit*, *Edward-Maria Wingfield*, and their Associates of the said first Colony, and unto the said *Thomas Hankam*, *Ralegh Gilbert*, *William Parker*, and *George Popham*, and their Associates of the said second Colony, and to every of them, from time to time, and at all times for ever hereafter, Power and Authority to take and surprise, by all Ways and Means whatsoever, all and every Person and Persons, with their Ships, Vessels, Goods and other Furniture, which shall be found trafficking, into any Harbour or Harbours, Creek or Creeks, or Place, within the Limits or Precincts of the said several Colonies and Plantations, not being of the same Colony, until such time, as they, being of any Realms, or Dominions under our Obedience, shall pay, or agree to pay, to the Hands of the Treasurer of that Colony, within whose Limits and Precincts they shall so traffick, two and a half upon every Hundred, of any thing, so by them trafficked, bought, or sold; And being Strangers, and not Subjects under our Obeysance, until they shall pay five upon every Hundred, of such Wares and Merchandise, as they shall traffick, buy, or sell, within the Precincts of the said several Colonies, wherein they shall so traffick, buy, or sell, as aforesaid; WHICH Sums of Money, or Benefit, as aforesaid, for and during the Space of one and twenty Years, next ensuing the Date hereof, shall be wholly employed to the Use, Benefit, and Behoof of the said several Plantations, where such Traffick shall be made; And after the said one and twenty Years ended, the same shall be taken to the Use of Us, our Heirs, and Successors, by such Officers and Ministers as by Us, our Heirs, and Successors, shall be thereunto assigned or appointed.

And we do further, by these Presents, for Us, our Heirs, and Successors, GIVE AND GRANT unto the said Sir *Thomas Gates*, Sir *George Somers*, *Richard Hackluit*, and *Edward-Maria Wingfield*, and to their Associates of the said first Colony and Plantation, and to the said *Thomas Hanham*, *Ralegh Gilbert*, *William Parker*, and *George Popham*, and their Associates of the said second Colony and Plantation, that they, and every of them, by their Deputies, Ministers, and Factors, may transport the Goods, Chattels, Armour, Munition, and Furniture, needful to be used by them, for their said Apparel, Food, Defence, or otherwise in Respect of the said Plantations, out of our Realms of *England* and *Ireland*, and all other our Dominions, from time to time, for and during the Time of seven Years, next ensuing the Date hereof, for the better Relief of the said several Colonies and Plantations, without any Customs, Subsidy, or other Duty, unto Us, our Heirs, or Successors, to be yielded or payed for the same.

Also we do, for Us, our Heirs, and Successors, DECLARE, by these Presents, that all and every the Persons being our Subjects, which shall dwell and inhabit within every or any of the said several Colonies and Plantations, and every of their children, which shall happen to be born within any of the Limits and Precincts of the said several Colonies and Plantations, shall HAVE and enjoy all Liberties, Franchises, and Immunities, within any of our other Dominions, to all Intents and Purposes, as if they had been abiding and born, within this our Realm of *England*, or any other of our said Dominions.

Moreover, our gracious Will and Pleasure is, and we do, by these Presents, for Us, our Heirs, and Successors, declare and set forth, that if any Person or Persons, which shall be of any of the said Colonies and Plantations, or any other which shall traffick to the said Colonies and Plantations, or any of them, shall, at any time or times hereafter, transport any Wares, Merchandises, or Commodities, out of any of our Dominions, with a Pretence to land, sell, or otherwise dispose of the same, within any the Limits and Precincts of any of the said Colonies and Plantations, and yet nevertheless, being at Sea, or after he hath landed the same within any of the said Colonies and Plantations, shall carry the same into any other Foreign Country, with a Purpose there to sell or dispose of the same, without the Licence of Us, our Heirs, and Successors, in that Behalf first had and obtained ; That then, all the Goods and Chattels of such Person or Persons, so offending and transporting, together with the said Ship or Vessel, wherein such Transportation was made, shall be forfeited to Us, our Heirs, and Successors.

Provided always, and our Will and Pleasure is, and we do hereby declare to all Christian Kings, Princes, and States, that if any Person or Persons which shall hereafter be of any of the said several Colonies and Plantations, or any other, by his, their, or any of their Licence and Appointment, shall, at any Time or Times hereafter, rob or spoil, by Sea or Land, or do any Act of unjust and unlawful Hostility to any the Subjects of Us, our Heirs, or Successors, or any the Subjects of any King, Prince, Ruler, Governor, or State, being then in League or Amitie with Us, our Heirs, or Successors, and that upon such Injury, or upon just Complaint of such Prince, Ruler, Governor, or State, or their Subjects, We, our Heirs, or Successors, shall make open Proclamation, within any of the Ports of our Realm of *England*, commodious for that purpose, That the said Person or Persons, having committed any such Robbery, or Spoil, shall within the term to be limited by such Proclamations, make full Restitution or Satisfaction of all such Injuries done, so as the said Princes, or others so complaining, may hold themselves fully satisfied and contented; And, that if the said Person or Persons, having committed such Robbery or Spoil, shall not make, or cause to be made Satisfaction accordingly, within such Time so to be limited, That then it shall be lawful to Us, our Heirs, and Successors, to put the said Person or Persons, having committed such Robbery or Spoil, and their Procurers, Abettors, and Comforters, out of our Allegiance and Protection; And that it shall be lawful and free, for all Princes, and others to pursue with hostility the said offenders, and every of them, and their and every of their Procurers, Aiders, abettors, and comforters, in that behalf.

And finally, we do for Us, our Heirs, and Successors, GRANT and agree, to and with the said Sir *Thomas Gates*, Sir *George Somers*, *Richard Hackluit*, *Edward-Maria Wingfield*, and all others of the said first colony, that We, our Heirs and Successors, upon Petition in that Behalf to be made, shall, by Letters Patent under the Great Seal of *England*, GIVE and GRANT, unto such Persons, their Heirs and Assigns, as the Council of that Colony, or the most part of them, shall, for that Purpose, nominate and assign all the Lands, Tenements, and Hereditaments, which shall be within the Precincts limited for that Colony, as is aforesaid, To BE HOLDEN of Us, our Heirs and Successors, as of our Manor at *East-Greenwich*, in the County of *Kent*, in free and common Soccage only, and not in Capite:

And do in like Manner, Grant and Agree, for Us, our Heirs and Successors, to and with the said *Thomas Hanham*, *Ralegh Gilbert*, *William Parker*, and *George Popham*, and all others of the said second Colony, That We, our Heirs, and Successors, upon Petition in that Behalf to be made, shall, by Letters-Patent, under the Great Seal of *England*, GIVE and GRANT, unto such Persons, their

Heirs and Assigns, as the Council of that Colony, or the most Part of them, shall for that Purpose nominate and assign, all the Lands, Tenements, and Hereditaments, which shall be within the Precincts limited for that Colony, as is aforesaid, To BE HOLDEN of Us, our Heirs, and Successors, as of our Manor of *East-Greenwich*, in the County of *Kent*, in free and common Soccage only, and not in Capite:

All which Lands, Tenements, and Hereditaments, so to be passed by the said several Letters-Patent, shall be sufficient Assurance from the said Patentees, so distributed and divided amongst the Undertakers for the Plantation of the said several Colonies, and such as shall make their Plantations in either of the said several Colonies, in such Manner and Form, and for such Estates, as shall be ordered and set down by the Council of the said Colony, or the most part of them, respectively, within which the same Lands, Tenements, and Hereditaments shall lye or be; Although express Mention of the true yearly Value or Certainty of the Premisses, or any of them, or of any other Gifts or Grants, by Us or any of our Progenitors or Predecessors, to the aforesaid Sir *Thomas Gates*, Knt. Sir *George Somers*, Knt. *Richard Hackluit*, *Edward-Maria Wingfield*, *Thomas Hanham*, *Ralegh Gilbert*, *William Parker*, and *George Popham*, or any of them, heretofore made, in these Presents, is not made; Or any Statute, Act, Ordinance, or Provision, Proclamation, or Restraint, to the contrary hereof had, made, ordained, or any other Thing, Cause, or Matter whatsoever, in any wise notwithstanding. IN WITNESS whereof, we have caused these our Letters to be made Patents; Witness Ourself at *Westminster*, the tenth Day of *April*, in the fourth Year of our Reign of *England*, *France*, and *Ireland*, and of *Scotland* the nine and thirtieth.

LUKIN
Per breve de privato Sigillo.

SECOND VIRGINIA CHARTER—1609.

In the hope of improving the wretched state of affairs the Virginia Company, in 1609, obtained a more specific charter, extending their authority and transferring to the company powers previously reserved to the king. The government now vested in "The Treasurer and Company of Adventurers and Planters of the City of London, for the first Colony in Virginia." The company left no means untried, and the general interest in the adventure is shown by the long list of patentees, numbering over 650 names, together with 59 of the London companies. The social standing of the patentees ranged from the great lords of the realm to the fishmongers. The Lord Mayor is said to have urged upon the great livery companies the necessity of aiding the enterprise, and the indefatigable Hakluyt published "Virginia Newly Valued," to excite interest in the undertaking. The charter was sealed May 23, 1609.

Only the more important provisions of this charter are here inserted.

THE SECOND CHARTER OF VIRGINIA—1609.

JAMES, by the Grace of God, King of *England, Scotland, France*, and *Ireland*, Defender of the Faith, *&c.* To all, to whom these Presents shall come, Greeting. WHEREAS, at the humble Suit and Request of sundry our loving and well-disposed Subjects, intending to deduce a Colony, and to make Habitation and Plantation of sundry our People in that Part of *America* commonly called VIRGINIA, and other Parts and Territories in *America*, either appertaining unto Us, or which are not actually possessed of any *Christian* Prince or People, within certain Bounds and Regions, We have formerly, by our Letters patents, bearing Date the tenth Day of *April*, in the fourth Year of our Reign of *England*, *France*, and *Ireland*, and of *Scotland* the nine and thirtieth, GRANTED to Sir *Thomas Gates*, Sir *George Somers*, and others, for the more speedy Accomplishment of the said Plantation and Habitation, that they should divide themselves into two Colonies (the one consisting of divers Knights, Gentlemen, Merchants, and others, of our City of *London*, called the FIRST COLONY; And the other consisting of divers Knights, Gentlemen, and others, of our Cities of *Bristol*, *Exeter*, and Town of *Plimouth*, and other Places, called the SECOND COLONY). And have yielded and granted many and sundry Privileges and Liberties to each Colony, for their quiet settling and good Government therein, as by the said Letters-patents more at large appeareth.

Now, forasmuch as divers and sundry of our loving Subjects, as well Adventurers, as Planters, of the said first Colony, which have already engaged themselves in furthering the Business of the said Colony and Plantation, and do further intend, by the Assistance of Almighty God, to prosecute the same to a happy End, have of late been humble Suitors unto Us, that (in Respect of their great Charges and the Adventure of many of their Lives, which they have hazarded in the said Discovery and Plantation of the said Country) We would be pleased to grant them a further Enlargement and Explanation of the said Grant, Privileges, and Liberties, and that such Counsellors, and other Officers, may be appointed amongst them, to manage and direct their affairs, as are willing and ready to adventure with them, as also whose Dwellings are not so far remote from the City of *London*, but they may, at convenient Times, be ready at Hand, to give their Advice and Assistance, upon all Occasions requisite.

We greatly affecting the effectual Prosecution and happy success of the said Plantation, and commending their good desires therein, for their further Encouragement in accomplishing so excellent a Work, much pleasing to God, and profitable to our Kingdom, do of our especial Grace, and certain Knowledge, and mere Motion, for Us, our Heirs, and Successors, GIVE, GRANT, and CONFIRM, to our trusty and well-beloved Subjects, Robert, Earl of Salisbury, (and others) . . . . and to such and so many as they do, or shall hereafter admit to be joined with them, in the form hereafter in these presents expressed, whether they go in their Persons to be Planters there in the said Plantation, or whether they go not, but adventure their monies, goods, or Chattles, that they shall be one Body or Commonalty perpetual, and shall have perpetual Succession and one common Seal to serve for the said Body or Commonalty, and that they and their Successors shall be known, called, and incorporated by the Name of *The Treasurer and Company of Adventurers and Planters of the City of London, for the first Colony in Virginia.* And that they and their Successors shall be from henceforth forever enabled to take, acquire, and purchase by the Name aforesaid (Licence for the same from Us, our Heirs, and Successors, first had and obtained) any Manner of Lands, Tenements, and Hereditaments, Goods and Chattles, within our Realm of England, and Dominion of Wales. And that they, and their Successors, shall likewise be enabled by the Name aforesaid, to plead and be impleaded, before any of our Judges or Justices in any of our Courts, and in any Actions or Suits whatsoever. And we do also of our special Grace, certain Knowledge, and mere Motion, give, grant and confirm, unto the said Treasurer and Company, and their Successors, under the Reservations, Limitations, and Declarations hereafter expressed, all those Lands, Countries, and Territories, situate, lying, and being in that Part of *America*, called *Virginia*, from the Point of Land, called Cape or *Point Comfort*, all along the Sea Coast to the Northward, two hundred miles, and from the said Point of *Cape Comfort*, all along the Sea Coast to the Southward, two hundred Miles, and all that Space and Circuit of Land, lying from the Sea Coast of the Precinct aforesaid, up into the Land throughout from Sea to Sea, West and Northwest; And also all the Islands lying within one hundred Miles along the Coast of both Seas of the Precinct aforesaid.

* * * * * * * * * *

AND forasmuch as the good and prosperous Success of the said Plantation, cannot but chiefly depend next under the Blessing of God, and the Support of our Royal Authority, upon the provident and good Direction of the whole Enterprise, by a careful and understanding Council, and that it is not convenient, that all the Adventurers shall be so often drawn to meet and assemble, as shall be requisite for them to have Meetings and Conference about the Affairs thereof; Therefore we DO ORDAIN, establish and confirm, that there shall be perpetually one COUNCIL here resident, according to the Tenour of our former Letters-Patents; Which Council shall have a Seal for the better Government and Administration of the said Plantation, besides the legal Seal of the Company or Corporation, as in our former Letters-Patents is also expressed.

* * * * * * * * * *

AND the said Thomas Smith, We DO ORDAIN to be Treasurer of the said Company; which Treasurer shall have Authority to give Order for the Warning of the Council, and summoning the Company to their Courts and Meetings. AND the said Council and Treasurer, or any of them shall be from henceforth nominated, chosen, continued, displaced, changed, altered and supplied, as Death, or other several Occasions shall require, out of the Company of the said Adventurers, by the Voice of the greater part of the said Company and Adventurers, in their Assembly for that Purpose: PROVIDED always, That every Counsellor so newly elected, shall be presented to the Lord Chancellor of *England*, or to the Lord High Treasurer of *England*, or to the Lord Chamberlain of the Household of Us, our Heirs and Successors for the Time being, to take his Oath of a Counsellor to Us, our Heirs and Successors, for the said Company of Adventurers and Colony in *Virginia*.

* * * * * * * * * *

AND further, of our special Grace, certain Knowledge, and mere Motion, for Us, our Heirs and Successors, we do, by these Presents, GIVE and GRANT full Power and Authority to our said Council here resident, as well at this present time, as hereafter from time to time, to nominate, make, constitute, ordain and confirm, by such Name or Names, Stile or Stiles, as to them shall seem good, And likewise to revoke, discharge, change, and alter, as well all and singular Governors, Officers, and Ministers, which already have been made, as also which hereafter shall be by them thought fit and needful to be made or used for the Government of the said Colony and Plantation: AND also to make, ordain, and establish all Manner of Orders, Laws, Directions, Instructions, Forms and Ceremonies of Government and Magistracy, fit and necessary for and concerning the Government of the said Colony and Plantation; And the same, at all Times hereafter, to abrogate, revoke, or change, not only within the Precincts of the said Colony, but also upon the Seas, in going and coming to and from the said Colony, as they in their good Discretion, shall think to be fittest for the Good of the Adventurers and inhabitants there.

* * * * * * * * * *

AND we do further by these presents ORDAIN and establish, that the said Treasurer and Council here resident, and their successors or any four of them being assembled (the Treasurer being one) shall from time to time have full Power and Authority to admit and receive any other Person into their Company, Corporation, and Freedom ; And further in a General Assembly of Adventurers, with the consent of the greater part upon good Cause, to disfranchise and put out any Person or Persons out of the said Freedom or Company.

* * * * * * * * *

AND forasmuch as it shall be necessary for all such our loving Subject as shall inhabit within the said Precincts of *Virginia* aforesaid, to determine to live together in the Fear and true Worship of Almighty God, Christian Peace and Civil Quietness each with other, whereby every one may with more Safety, Pleasure and Profit enjoy that whereunto they shall attain with great Pain and Peril; WE for Us, our Heires, and Successors are likewise pleased and contented, and by these Presents do GIVE and GRANT unto the said Treasurer and Company, and their Successors, and to such Governors, Officers, and Ministers, as shall be by our said Council constituted and appointed according to the Natures and Limits of their Offices and Places respectively, that they shall and may from Time to Time, for ever hereafter, within the said Precincts of *Virginia*, or in the way by Sea thither and from thence, have full and absolute Power and Authority to correct, punish, pardon, govern, and rule all such the Subjects of Us, our Heires, and Successors as shall from Time to Time adventure themselves in any Voyage thither, or that shall at any Time hereafter, inhabit in the Precincts and Territories of the said Colony as aforesaid, according to such Orders, Ordinances, Constitutions, Directions, and Instructions, as by our said Council as aforesaid, shall be established; And in Defect thereof in case of Necessity, according to the good Discretion of the said Governor and Officers respectively, as well in Cases capital and criminal, as civil, both Marine and other; So always as the said Statutes, Ordinances and Proceedings as near as conveniently may be, be agreeable to the Laws, Statutes, Government, and Policy of this our Realm of *England*. AND we do further of our special Grace, certain Knowledge, and mere Motion, GRANT, DECLARE, and ORDAIN, that such principal Governor, as from Time to Time shall duly and lawfully be authorized and appointed in Manner and Form in these Presents heretofore expressed, shall have full Power and Authority, to use and exercise Martial Law in Cases of Rebellion or Mutiny, in as large and ample Manner as our Lieutenants in our Counties within this our Realm of *England* have or ought to have, by Force of their Commissions of Lieutenancy.

* * * * * * * * *

AND lastly, because the principal Effect which we can desire or expect of this Action, is the Conversion and Reduction of the People in those Parts unto the true Worship of God and Christian Religion, in which Respect we should be loath that any Person should be permitted to pass that we suspected to affect the Superstitions of the Church of *Rome*, we do hereby DECLARE, that it is our Will and Pleasure that none be permitted to pass in any Voyage from Time to Time to be made into the said Country, but such as first shall have taken the Oath of Supremacy; For which Purpose, we do by these Presents give full Power and Authority to the Treasurer for the Time being, and any three of the Council, to tender and exhibit the said Oath, to all such Persons as shall at any Time be sent and employed in the said Voyage. ALTHOUGH express Mention of true yearly Value or Certainty of the Premisses, or any of them, or of any other Gifts or Grants by Us, or any of our Progenitors or Predecessors to the aforesaid Treasurer and Company heretofore made in these Presents, is not made; Or any Act,

Statute, Ordinance, Provision, Proclamation, or Restraint, to the contrary hereof had, made, ordained, or provided, or any other Thing, Cause, or Matter whatsoever in any wise notwithstanding. IN WITNESS whereof, We have caused these our Letters to be made Patent. Witness ourself at *Westminster*, the 23d Day of *May*, in the seventh Year of our Reign of *England*, *France*, and *Ireland*, and of *Scotland* the ****

PER IPSUM REGEM.

LUKIN.

THIRD VIRGINIA CHARTER—1612.

THE desirability of the Bermudas was first brought to the notice of the Company by Sir Thomas Gates and his companions, who were there shipwrecked on their way to Virginia in 1609, and lived for nine months on the resources of the islands. As the Company's patent limited their possessions to islands within one hundred leagues of the coast, they petitioned for a new charter extending their limits.

More important than the acquisition of Bermuda was the improvement in the government of the Company providing for weekly meetings. The Company sold its rights to the Bermudas to some of its own members, who obtained a charter in 1614. The Third Virginia Charter was sealed March 12, 1612.

Of this charter, as of the second, the most essential articles only are given

THE THIRD CHARTER OF VIRGINIA—1611-12.

JAMES, by the Grace of God, King of *England*, *Scotland*, *France*, and *Ireland*, Defender of the Faith; To all to whom these Presents shall come, Greeting. WHEREAS at the humble Suit of divers and sundry our loving Subjects, as well Adventurers as Planters of the first Colony in *Virginia*, and for the Propagation of *Christian* Religion, and Reclaiming of People barbarous, to Civility and Humanity, We have, by our Letters-Patents, bearing

Date at *Westminster*, the three-and-twentieth Day of *May*, in the seventh Year of our Reign of *England*, *France*, and *Ireland*, and the two-and-fortieth of *Scotland*, GIVEN and GRANTED unto them that they and all such and so many of our loving Subjects as should from time to time, for ever after, be joined with them as Planters or Adventurers in the said Plantation, and their Successors, for ever, should be one Body politick, incorporated by the Name of *The Treasurer and Company of Adventurers and Planters of the City of London for the first Colony in Virginia;* And whereas also for the greater Good and Benefit of the said Company, and for the better Furtherance, Strengthening, and Establishing of the said Plantation, we did further GIVE, GRANT and CONFIRM, by our Letters-patents unto the said Company and their Successors, for ever, all those Lands, Countries or Territories, situate, lying and being in that Part of *America* called *Virginia*, from the Point of Land called *Cape* or *Point Comfort* all along the Sea Coasts to the Northward two hundred Miles; and from the said Point of *Cape Comfort* all along the Sea Coast to the Southward two hundred Miles; and all that Space and Circuit of Land lying from the Sea Coast of the Precinct aforesaid, up into the Land throughout from Sea to Sea West and North-West; and also all the Islands lying within one hundred Miles along the Coast of both the Seas of the Precinct aforesaid; with divers other Grants, Liberties, Franchises and Prehemінences, Privileges, Profits, Benefits, and Commodities granted in and by our said Letters-patents to the said Treasurer and Company and their Successors for ever. Now forasmuch as we are given to understand, that in those Seas adjoining to the said Coasts of *Virginia*, and without the Compass of those two hundred Miles by Us so granted unto the said Treasurer and Company as aforesaid, and yet not far distant from the said Colony in *Virginia*, there are or may be divers Islands lying desolate and uninhabited, some of which are already made known and discovered by the Industry, Travel, and Expences of the said Company, and others also are supposed to be and remain as yet unknown and undiscovered, all and every of which it may import the said Colony both in Safety and Policy of Trade to populate and plant; in Regard whereof, as well for the preventing of Peril, as for the better Commodity of the said Colony, they have been humble suitors unto Us, that We would be pleased to grant unto them an Enlargement of our said former Letters-patents, as well for a more ample Extent of their Limits and Territories into the Seas adjoining to and upon the Coast of *Virginia*, as also for some other Matters and Articles concerning the better government of the said Company and Colony, in which Point our said former Letters-Patents do not extend so far as Time and Experience hath found to be needful and convenient: We therefore tendering the good and happy Success of the said Plantation, both in Regard of the General Weal of human Society, as in Respect of the Good of our own Estate and Kingdoms, and being willing to give Furtherance unto all good Means that may advance the Benefit of the said Company, and which may secure the Safety of our loving Subjects planted in our said Colony, under the Favour and Protection of God Almighty, and of our Royal Power and Authority, have therefore of our especial Grace, certain Knowledge, and mere Motion, given, granted, and confirmed, and for Us, our Heirs and Successors, we do by these Presents give, grant, and confirm to the said Treasurer and Company of Adventurers and Planters of the city of *London* for the first Colony in *Virginia*, and to their Heirs and Successors for ever, all and singular those Islands whatsoever situate and being in any Part of the Ocean Seas bordering upon the Coast of our said first Colony in *Virginia*, and being within three Hundred Leagues of any of the Parts heretofore granted to the said Treasurer and Company in our said former Letters-Patents as aforesaid, and being within or between the one-and-fortieth and thirtieth Degrees of Northerly Latitude.

* * * * * * * * * *

And we do hereby ordain and grant by these Presents, that the said Treasurer and Company of Adventurers and Planters aforesaid, shall and may, once every week, or oftener, at their Pleasure, hold, and keep a Court and Assembly for the better Order and Government of the said Plantation, and such Things as shall concern the same; And that any five Persons of our Council for the said first Colony in *Virginia*, for the Time being, of which Company the Treasurer, or his Deputy, to be always one, and the Number of fifteen others, at the least, of the Generality of the said Company, assembled together in such Manner, as is and hath been heretofore used and accustomed, shall be said, taken, held, and reputed to be, and shall be a *sufficient Court* of the said Company, for the handling and ordering, and dispatching of all such casual and particular Occurrences, and accidental Matters, of less Consequence and Weight, as shall from Time to Time happen, touching and concerning the said Plantation: And that nevertheless, for the handling, ordering, and disposing of Matters and Affairs of greater Weight and Importance, and such as shall or may, in any Sort, concern the Weal Publick and general Good of the said Company and Plantation, as namely, the Manner of Government from Time to Time to be used, the ordering and Disposing of the Lands and Possessions, and the settling and establishing of a Trade there, or such like, there shall be held and kept every Year, upon the last *Wednesday*, save one, of *Hillary* Term, *Easter*, *Trinity*, and *Michaelmas* Terms, for ever, one great, general, and solemn Assembly, which four Assemblies shall be stiled and called, *The four Great and General Courts of the Council and Company of Adventurers for Virginia;* In all and every of which said Great and General Courts, so assembled, our Will and

Pleasure is, and we do, for Us, our Heirs and Successors, for ever, Give and Grant to the said Treasurer and Company, and their Successors for ever, by these Presents, that they, the said Treasurer and Company, or the greater Number of them, so assembled, shall and may have full Power and Authority, from Time to Time, and at all times hereafter, to elect and chuse discreet Persons, to be of our said Council for the said first Colony in *Virginia*, and to nominate and appoint such officers as they shall think fit and requisite, for the Government, managing, ordering, and dispatching of the Affairs of the said Company; And shall likewise have full Power and Authority, to ordain and make such Laws and Ordinances, for the Good and Welfare of the said Plantation, as to them from Time to Time, shall be thought requisite and meet: *So always*, as the same be not contrary to the Laws and Statutes of this our Realm of *England*.

* * * * * * * *

And for the more effectual Advancing of the said Plantation, We do further, for Us, our Heirs, and Successors, of our especial Grace and favour, by Virtue of our Prerogative Royal, and by the Assent and Consent of the Lords and others of our Privy Council, GIVE and GRANT, unto the said Treasurer and Company, full Power and Authority, free Leave, Liberty, and Licence, to set forth, erect, and publish, one or more Lottery or Lotteries, to have Continuance, and to endure and be held, for the Space of our whole Year, next after the opening of the same; And after the End and Expiration of the said Term, the said Lottery or Lotteries to continue and be further kept, during our Will and Pleasure only, and not otherwise. And yet nevertheless, we are contented and pleased, for the Good and Welfare of the said Plantation, that the said Treasurer and Company shall, for the Dispatch and Finishing of the said Lottery or Lotteries, have six Months Warning after the said

Year ended, before our Will and Pleasure shall, for and on that Behalf, be construed, deemed, and adjudged, to be in any wise altered and determined. And our further Will and Pleasure is, that the said Lottery and Lotteries shall and may be opened and held, within our City of *London*, or in any other City or Town, or elsewhere, within this our Realm of *England*, with such Prizes, Articles, Conditions, and Limitations, as to them, the said Treasurer and Company, in their Discretions, shall seem convenient: And it shall and may be lawful, to and for the said Treasurer and Company, to elect and choose Receivers, Surveyors, Auditors, Commissioners, or any other Officers whatsoever, at their Will and Pleasure, for the better marshalling, disposing, guiding, and governing, of the said Lottery and Lotteries; And that it shall likewise be lawful, to and for the said Treasurer and any two of the said Council, to minister to all and every such Person, so elected and chosen for Officers, as aforesaid, one or more Oaths, for their good Behaviour, just and true Dealing, in and about the said Lottery or Lotteries, to the Intent and Purpose, that none of our loving Subjects, putting in their Names, or otherwise adventuring in the said general Lottery or Lotteries, may be, in any wise, defrauded and deceived of their said Monies, or evil and indirectly dealt withal in their said Adventures. And we further GRANT, in Manner and Form aforesaid, that it shall and may be lawful, to and for the said Treasurer and Company, under the Seal of our said Council for the Plantation, to publish, or to cause and procure to be published by Proclamation, or otherwise (the said Proclamation to be made in their Name, by Virtue of these Presents) the said Lottery or Lotteries, in all Cities, Towns, Burroughs, and other Places, within our said Realm of *England;* And we Will and Command all Mayors, Justices of the Peace, Sheriffs, Bailiffs, Constables, and other Officers and loving Subjects, whatsoever, that in no wise, they hinder or delay the Progress and Proceedings of the said Lottery or Lotteries, but be therein, touching the Premises, aiding and assisting, by all honest, good, and lawful Means and Endeavours. And further, our Will and Pleasure is, that in all Questions and Doubts, that shall arise, upon any Difficulty of Construction or Interpretation of any Thing, contained in these, or any other our former Letters-patents, the same shall be taken and interpreted, in most ample and beneficial Manner for the said Treasurer and Company, and their Successors, and every Member thereof. And lastly, we do, by these Presents, RATIFY AND CONFIRM unto the said Treasurer and Company, and their Successors, for ever, all and all Manner of Privileges, Franchises, Liberties, Immunities, Preheminences, Profits, and Commodities, whatsoever, granted unto them in any our former Letters-patents, and not in these Presents revoked, altered, changed, or abridged. ALTHOUGH express Mention of the true Yearly Value or Certainty of the Premises, or any of them, or of any other Gift or Grant, by Us or any our Progenitors or Predecessors, to the aforesaid Treasurer and Company heretofore made in these Presents is not made ; Or any Statute, Act, Ordinance, Provision, Proclamation, or Restraint, to the contrary thereof heretofore made, ordained, or provided, or any other Matter, Cause, or Thing, whatsoever, to the contrary, in any wise, notwithstanding.

IN WITNESS whereof we have caused these our Letters to be made Patents. Witness Ourself, at *Westminster*, the twelfth Day of *March*, in the ninth Year of our Reign of *England*, *France*, and *Ireland*, and of *Scotland* the five and fortieth.

MAYFLOWER COMPACT—1620.

THE need of this compact is thus set forth by one of the Pilgrims: "Some of the strangers among them had let fall from them in the ship that when they came ashore they would use their own liberty, for none had power to command them, the patent they had being for Virginia and not for New England, which belonged to another government, with which the Virginia Company had nothing to do." Bancroft lauds it in the highest terms: "Here was the birth of popular constitutional liberty. The middle ages had been familiar with charters and constitutions; but they had been merely compacts for immunities, partial enfranchisements, patents of nobility, concessions of municipal privileges, or limitations of the sovereign power in favor of feudal institutions. In the cabin of the Mayflower humanity recovered its rights, and instituted government on the basis of 'equal laws,' enacted by all the people for the 'general good.'" (For a different estimate, see *Scott's Development of Constitutional Liberty*, p. 84, and *Crane and Moses' Politics*, p. 103.)

John Quincy Adams regarded it as "perhaps the only instance in human history of the positive original social compact, which speculative philosophers have imagined as the only legitimate source of government." Somewhat similar compacts were drawn up by the settlers of Portsmouth, R. I., 1638, and Newport, 1639, and Exeter, N. H., 1639.

Plymouth obtained a patent for their lands from the New England Company, and though never successful in their numerous applications for a royal charter maintained an independent existence until its incorporation with Massachusetts in 1691.

Consult *Bancroft's Hist. U. S.*, 1st ed. I., 309; Cen. ed. I., 143; last ed. I., 206; *Hildreth's Hist. U. S.*, I., 158; *Palfrey's Hist. New England*, I., 165; *Bryant and Gay's U. S.*, I., 388; *Barry's Hist. Mass.*, First Period, 83; *Webster's Plymouth Oration*, see Works; *Frothingham's Rise of the Republic of the U. S.*, 15; *Doyle's English Colonies*, 158.

THE MAYFLOWER COMPACT.

In the name of God, Amen; We, whose names are underwritten, the loyall subjects of our dread soveraigne King James, by the grace of God, of Great Britaine, France, and Ireland King, defender of the faith, etc., haveing undertaken, for the glorie of God, and advancemente of the Christian faith and honor of our king and countrie, a voyage to plant the first colonie in the Northerne parts of Virginia, doe, by these presents, solemnly and mutually, in the presence of God, and one of another, covenant and combine ourselves together into a civill body politick, for our better ordering and preservation and furtherance of the ends aforesaid; and, by vertue heareof, to enacte, constitute, and frame, such just and equall laws, ordenances, acts, constitutions and offices, from time to time, as shall be thought most meete and convenient for the generall good of the Colonie. Unto which we promise all due submission and obedience. In witnes whereof we have hereunder subscribed our names, at Cap Codd, the 11th of November, in the year of the raigne of our sovereigne lord, King James, of England, France, and Ireland the eighteenth, and of Scotland the fifty-fourth, Anno Domini, 1620.

ORDINANCE FOR VIRGINIA—1621.

SIR GEORGE YEARDLEY, appointed by the Virginia Company Governor of Virginia in 1618, received instructions from the treasurer of the Company "that the planters might have a hand in the governing of themselves." Yeardley, accordingly, summoned the council of state and two burgesses to meet at Jamestown, July 30, 1619. Two years later the Virginia Company passed the following ordinance, giving to the colony the guarantee of a written constitution. The Tory historian, Chalmers, characterizes this ordinance "as no less remarkable for the wisdom of its provisions than for being the principal step in the progress of freedom."

The proceedings of the first assembly are printed in *N. Y. Hist. Soc. Coll., 2d series,* vol. III., p. 331, from a copy found in the Record Office in England.

Consult also *Bancroft's Hist. U. S.,* 1st ed. vol. I., p. 153; Centenary ed. I., 119; last ed. I., 110; *Hildreth's U. S.,* I., 211; *Bryant and Gay's U. S.,* I., 306; *Neil's Va. Co.,* 139; *Chalmers' Political Annals,* 43.

AN ORDINANCE AND CONSTITUTION OF THE TREASURER, COUNCIL, AND COMPANY IN ENGLAND FOR A COUNCIL OF STATE AND GENERAL ASSEMBLY. DATED JULY 21, 1621.

To all People, to whom these Presents shall come, be seen, or heard, The Treasurer, Council, and Company of Adventurers and Planters for the city of London for the first Colony of Virginia, send Greeting. Know ye, that we, the said Treasurer, Council, and Company, taking into our careful Consideration the present State of the said Colony of Virginia, and intending, by the Divine Assistance, to settle a Form of Government there, as may be to the greatest Benefit and Comfort of the People, and whereby all Injustice, Grievances, and Oppression may be prevented and kept off as much as possible from the said Colony, have thought fit to make our Entrance by ordering and establishing such Supreme Councils, as may not only be assisting to the Governor for the Time being, in the Administration of Justice, and the executing of other Duties to this Office belonging; but also by their vigilant Care and Prudence, may provide, as well for a Remedy of all Inconveniences, growing from time to time, as also for the advancing of Increase, Strength, Stability and Prosperity of the said Colony:

We therefore, the said Treasurer, Council, and Company, by Authority directed to us from his Majesty under the Great Seal, upon mature Deliberation, Do hereby order and declare, that, from henceforward, there shall be Two Supreme Councils in Virginia, for the better government of the Colony aforesaid.

One of which Councils to be called the Council of State (and whose office shall chiefly be assisting, with their Care, Advice, and Circumspection, to the said Governor) shall be chosen, nominated, placed, and displaced, from time to time, by us, the said Treasurer, Council, and Company, and our Successors: Which Council of State shall consist for the present, only of these persons, as are here inserted, viz., Sir Francis Wyat, Governor of Virginia, Captain Francis West, Sir George Yeardley, Knight, Sir William Neuce, Knight, Marshal of Virginia, Mr. George Sandys, Treasurer, Mr. George Thorpe, Deputy of the College, Captain Thomas Neuce, Deputy for the Company, Mr. Pawlet, Mr. Leech, Captain Nathaniel Powell, Mr. Christopher Davidson, Secretary, Dr. Pots, Physician to the Company, Mr. Roger Smith, Mr. John Berkeley, Mr. John Rolfe, Mr. Ralph Hamer, Mr. John Pountis, Mr. Michael Lapworth, Mr. Harwood, Mr. Samuel Macock: Which said Counsellors and Council we earnestly pray and desire, and in his Majesty's Name strictly charge and command, that all Factions, Partialities, and sinister respect laid aside, they bend their Care and Endeavours to assist the said Governor; first and principally, in the Advancement of the Honour and Service of God, and the Enlargement of his Kingdom amongst the Heathen People; and next, in erecting of the said Colony in due obedience to his Majesty, and all lawful Authority from his Majesty's Directions; and lastly, in maintaining the said People in Justice and Christian Conversation amongst themselves, and in Strength and Ability to withstand their Enemies. And this Council, to be always, or for the most Part, residing about or near the Governor.

The other, more generally to be called by the Governor, once Yearly, and no oftener, but for very extraordinary and important Occasions, shall consist, for the present, of the said Council of State, and of two Burgesses out of every Town, Hundred, or other particular Plantation, to be respectively chosen by the Inhabitants: Which Council shall be called the General Assembly, wherein (as also in the said Council of State) all Matters shall be decided, determined, and ordered, by the greater

Part of the Voices then present; reserving to the Governor always a Negative Voice. And this General Assembly shall have free Power to treat, consult and conclude, as well of all emergent Occasions concerning the Public Weal of the said Colony and every Part thereof, as also to make, ordain, and enact such general Laws and Orders, for the Behoof of the said Colony, and the good Government thereof, as shall from time to time appear necessary or requisite:

Whereas in all other Things, we require the said General Assembly, as also the said Council of State, to imitate and follow the Policy of the Form of Government, Laws, Customs, and Manner of Trial and other Administration of Justice, used in the Realm of England, as near as may be, even as ourselves, by his Majesty's Letters-patent, are required:

Provided, that no Law or Ordinance, made in the said General Assembly, shall be or continue in Force or Validity, unless the same shall be solemnly ratified and confirmed, in a General Quarter Court of the said Company here in England, and so ratified, be returned to them under our Seal: It being our Intent to afford the like Measure also unto the said Colony that after the Government of the said Colony shall once have been well framed and settled accordingly, which is to be done by Us, as by Authority derived from his Majesty, and the same shall have been so by Us declared, no Orders of Court afterwards shall bind the said Colony, unless they be ratified in like Manner in the General Assemblies.

In Witness whereof we have hereunto set our Common Seal, the 24th of July, 1621, and in the Year of the Reign of our Sovereign Lord, James, King of England, etc., the . . . . and of Scotland the . . . .

MASSACHUSETTS BAY CHARTER—1629.

THE interest awakened by the little colony planted at Cape Ann in 1625 by Rev. John White, of Dorchester, England, led to the formation of the company known as "The Governor and Company of the Massachusetts Bay in New England." They first obtained a patent for lands from the Council for New England (Mar. 14, 1628) and then, in order to exercise power of government, a charter from the king Mar. 4, 1629. The same year they transferred the government and charter to New England. As to the legality of this step historians and jurists have been divided. From the first there was a constant struggle on the part of the colonists to preserve the charter and to resist any infringement of it. The contest ended in the forfeiture of the charter in 1684, and the consolidation of the northern colonies under Sir Edmund Andros.

After the accession of William and Mary, Massachusetts solicited the restoration of the charter, but instead, in 1691, through the agency of Increase Mather, a new charter was issued. But the old liberty was lost, for the king reserved to himself the appointment of the governor, lieutenant-governor, and secretary. This, together with the supplementary charter of 1726, remained the fundamental law of Massachusetts till the State constitution of 1780, which is still in force.

Consult *Palfrey's Hist. N. E.*, I., 290; *Winsor's Memorial Hist. Boston*, I., 87; *Barry's Hist. Mass., First Period*, 158; *Bancroft's U. S.*, 1st ed. I., 242; Cen. ed. I., 265; last ed. I., 224; *Bryant and Gay's U. S.*, I., 518; *Chalmers' Political Annals*, 135.

THE CHARTER OF MASSACHUSETTS BAY—1629.

CHARLES, BY THE GRACE OF GOD, Kinge of England, Scotland, Fraunce, and Ireland, Defendor of the Fayth, etc. TO ALL to whome theis Presents shall come Greeting. WHEREAS, our most Deare and Royall Father, Kinge James, of blessed Memory, by his Highnes Letters-patents bearing Date at Westminster the third Day of November, in the eighteenth Yeare of his Raigne, HATH given and graunted vnto the Councell established at Plymouth, in the County of Devon, for the planting, ruling, ordering, and governing of Newe England in America, and to their Successors and Assignes for ever, all that Parte of America, lyeing and being in Bredth, from Forty Degrees of Northerly Latitude from the Equinoctiall Lyne, to forty eight Degrees of the saide Northerly Latitude inclusively, and in Length, of and within all the Breadth aforesaid, throughout the Maine Landes from Sea to Sea; together also with all the Firme Landes, Soyles, Groundes, Havens, Portes, Rivers, Waters, Fishing, Mynes, and Myneralls, as well Royall Mynes of Gould and Silver, as other Mynes and Mineralls, precious Stones, Quarries, and all and singular other Comodities, Jurisdiccons, Royalties, Priviledges, Franchesies, and Prehemynences, both within the said Tract of Land vpon the Mayne, and also within the Islandes and Seas adjoining: PROVIDED alwayes, That the saide Islandes, or any the Premisses by the said Letters-patents intended and meant to be graunted, were not then actuallie possessed or inhabited, by any other Christian Prince or State, nor within the Boundes, Lymitts, or Territories of the Southerne Colony, then before graunted by our saide Deare Father, to be planted by divers of his loveing Subjects in the South Partes. TO HAVE and to houlde, possess, and enjoy all and singular the aforesaid Continent, Landes, Territories, Islandes, Hereditaments, and Precincts, Seas, Waters, Fishings, with all, and all Manner their Co͠modities, Royalties, Liberties, Prehemynences, and Proffitts that should from thenceforth arise from thence, with all and singuler their Appurtenances, and every Parte and Parcell thereof, vnto the saide Councell and their Successors and Assignes for ever, to the sole and proper Vse, Benefitt, and Behoofe of them the saide Councell, and their Successors and Assignes for ever: To be houlden of our saide most Deare and Royall Father, his Heires and Successors, as of his Mannor of East Greenewich in the County of Kent, in free and comon Soccage, and not in Capite nor by Knight's Service: YEILDINGE and paying therefore to the saide late Kinge, his Heires and Successors, the fifte Parte of the Oare of Gould and Silver, which should from tyme to tyme, and at all Tymes then after happen to be found, gotten, had, and obteyned in, att, or within any of the saide Landes, Lymitts, Territories, and Precincts, or in or within any Parte or Parcell thereof, for or in Respect of all and all Manner of Duties, Demaunds and Services whatsoever, to be don, made, or paide to our saide Dear Father the late Kinge his Heires and Successors, as in and by the saide Letters-patents (amongst sundrie other Clauses, Powers, Priviledges, and Grauntes therein conteyned, more at large appeareth: AND WHEREAS, the saide Councell established at Plymouth, in the County of Devon, for the plantinge, ruling, ordering, and governing of Newe England in America, have by their Deede, indented vnder their Co͠mon Seale, bearing Date the nyneteenth Day of March last past, in the third Yeare of our Raigne, given, graunted, bargained, soulde, enfeoffed, aliened, and confirmed to Sir Henry Rosewell, Sir John Young, Knightes, Thomas Southcott, John Humphrey, John Endecott, and Symon Whetcombe, their Heires and Assignes, and their Associats for ever, all that Parte of Newe England in America aforesaid, which lyes and extendes betweene a greate River there comonlie called Monomack alias Merriemack, and a certen other River there, called Charles River, being in the Bottome of a certayne Bay there, comonlie called Massachusetts, alias Mattachusetts, alias Massatusetts Bay, and also all and singuler those Landes and Hereditaments whatsoever, lyeing within the Space of three English Myles on the South Parte of the said Charles River, or of any, or everie Parte thereof; and also, all and singuler the Landes and Hereditaments whatsoever, lyeing and being within the Space of three English Myles to the Southwarde of the Southermost Parte of the saide Bay called Massachusetts, alias Mattachusetts, alias Massatusets Bay; and also, all those Landes and Hereditaments whatsoever, which lye, and be within the space of three English Myles to the Northward of the said River Monomack, alias Merrymack, or to the Northward of any and every Parte thereof, and all Landes and Hereditaments whatsoever, lyeing within the Lymitts aforesaide, North and South in Latitude and bredth, and in Length and Longitude, of and within all the Bredth aforesaide, throughout the Mayne Landes there, from the Atlantick and Westerne Sea and Ocean on the East Parte, to the South Sea on the West Parte; and all Landes and Groundes, Place and Places, Soyles, Woodes and Wood Groundes, Havens, Portes, Rivers, Waters, Fishings, and Hereditaments whatsoever, lyeing within the saide Boundes and Lymytts, and everie Parte and Parcell thereof; and also, all Islandes lyeing in America aforesaide, in the saide Seas or either of them on the Westerne or Eastern Coastes or Partes of the said Tractes of Lande, by the saide Indenture mencõed to be given, graunted, bargained, sould, enfeoffed, aliened, and confirmed, or any of them; and also, all Mynes and Myneralls, as well Royall Mynes of Gould and Silver, as other Mynes and Myneralls whatsoeuer, in the saide Lands and Premisses, or any Parte thereof; and all Jurisdiccons, Rights, Royalties, Liberties, Freedomes, Ymmunities, Priviledges, Franchises, Preheminences, and Comodities whatsoever, which they, the said Councell established at Plymouth, in the County of Devon, for the planting, ruling, ordering, and governing of Newe England in America, then had, or might vse, exercise, or enjoy, in or within the saide Landes and Premisses by the saide Indenture mencõed to be given, graunted, bargained, sould, enfeoffed, and confirmed, or in, or within any Parte or Parcell thereof: TO HAVE and to hould, the saide Parte of Newe England in America, which lyes and extendes and is abutted as aforesaide, and every Parte and Parcell thereof; and all the saide Islandes, Rivers, Portes, Havens, Waters, Fishings, Mynes, and Myneralls, Jurisdiccons, Franchises, Royalties, Liberties, Priviledges, Comodities, Hereditaments, and Premisses whatsoever, with the Appurtenances vnto the saide Sir Henry Rosewell, Sir John Younge, Thomas Southcott, John Humfrey, John Endecott, and Simon Whetcombe, their Heires and Assignes, and their Associatts, to the onlie proper and absolute vse and Behoofe of the said Sir Henry Rosewell, Sir John Younge, Thomas Southcott, John Humfrey, John Endecott, and Simon Whettcombe, their Heires and Assignes, and their Associatts forevermore; TO BE HOULDEN of Vs, our Heires and Successors, as of our Mannor of Eastgreenwich, in the County of Kent, in free and comon Soccage, and not in Capite, nor by Knightes Service; YEILDING and payeing therefore vnto Vs, our Heires and Successors, the fifte Part of the

Oare of Goulde and Silver, which from Tyme to Tyme, and at all Tymes hereafter, happen to be founde, gotten, had, and obteyned in any of the saide Landes, within the saide Lymitts, or in or within any Parte thereof, for, and in Satisfaccon of all manner Duties, Demaundes, and Services whatsoever to be donn, made, or paid to Vs, our Heires or Successors, as in and by the said recited Indenture more at large maie appeare. NOWE Knowe Yee, that Wee, at the humble Suite and Peticon of the saide Sir Henry Rosewell, Sir John Younge, Thomas Southcott, John Humfrey, John Endecott, and Simon Whetcombe, and of others whome they have associated vnto them, HAVE, for divers good Causes and consideracons, vs moveing, graunted and confirmed, and by theis Presents of our especiall Grace, certen Knowledge, and mere Mocon, doe graunt and confirme vnto the saide Sir Henry Rosewell, Sir John Younge, Thomas Southcott, John Humfrey, John Endecott, and Simon Whetcombe, and to their Associatts hereafter named; (videlicet) Sir Richard Saltonstall, Knight, Isaack Johnson, Samuel Aldersey, John Ven, Mathew Cradock, George Harwood, Increase Nowell, Richard Perry, Richard Bellingham, Nathaniell Wright, Samuel Vassall, Theophilus Eaton, Thomas Goffe, Thomas Adams, John Browne, Samuell Browne, Thomas Hutchins, William Vassall, William Pinchion, and George Foxcrofte, their Heires and Assignes, all the saide Parte of Newe England in America, lyeing and extending betweene the Boundes and Lymytts in the said recited Indenture expressed, and all Landes and Groundes, Place and Places, Soyles, Woods and Wood Groundes, Havens, Portes, Rivers, Waters, Mynes, Mineralls, Jurisdiccons, Rightes, Royalties, Liberties, Freedomes, Immunities, Priviledges, Franchises, Preheminences, Hereditaments, and Comodities whatsoever, to them the saide Sir Henry Rosewell, Sir John Younge, Thomas Southcott,

John Humfrey, John Endecott, and Simon Whetcombe, theire Heires and Assignes, and to their Associatts, by the saide recited Indenture, given, graunted, bargayned, solde, enfeoffed, aliened, and confirmed, or mencõed, or intended thereby to be given, graunted, bargayned, sold, enfeoffed, aliened, and confirmed: To HAVE, and to hould, the saide Parte of Newe England in America, and other the Premisses hereby mencõed to be graunted and confirmed, and every Parte and Parcell thereof with the Appurtennces, to the saide Sir Henry Rosewell, Sir John Younge, Sir Richard Saltonstall, Thomas Southcott, John Humfrey, John Endecott, Simon Whetcombe, Isaack Johnson, Richard Pery, Richard Bellingham, Nathaniell Wright, Samuell Vassall, Theophilus Eaton, Thomas Goffe, Thomas Adams, John Browne, Samuel Browne, Thomas Hutchins, Samuel Aldersey, John Ven, Mathewe Cradock, George Harwood, Increase Nowell, William Vassall, William Pinchion, and George Foxcrofte, their Heires and Assignes forever, to their onlie proper and absolute Vse and Behoofe for evermore; To be holden of Vs, our Heires and Successors, as of our Mannor of Eastgreenewich aforesaid, in free and com̃on Socage, and not in Capite, nor by Knights Service; AND ALSO YEILDING and paying therefore to Vs, our Heires and Successors, the fifte parte onlie of all Oare of Gould and Silver, which from tyme to tyme, and att all tymes hereafter shalbe there gotten, had, or obteyned, for all Services, Exaccons and Demaundes whatsoever, according to the Tenure and Reservacon in the said recited Indenture expressed. AND FURTHER, knowe yee, that of our more especiall Grace, certen Knowledg, and meere mocõn, Wee have given and graunted, and by theis Presents, doe for Vs, our Heires and Successors, give and graunte vnto the saide Sir Henry Rosewell, Sir John Younge, Sir Richard Saltonstall, Thomas Southcott, John Humfrey, John Endecott, Symon Whetcombe, Isaack Johnson, Samuell Aldersey, John Ven, Mathewe

Cradock, George Harwood, Increase Nowell, Richard Pery, Richard Bellingham, Nathaniel Wright, Samuell Vassall, Theophilus Eaton, Thomas Goffe, Thomas Adams, John Browne, Samuell Browne, Thomas Hutchins, William Vassall, William Pinchion, George Foxcrofte, their Heires and Assignes, all that Parte of Newe England in America, which lyes and extendes betweene a great River there, com̃onlie called Monomack River, alias Merrimack River, and a certen other River there, called Charles River, being in the Bottome of a certen Bay there, comonlie called Massachusetts, alias Mattachusetts, alias Massatusetts Bay; and also all and singuler those Landes and Hereditaments whatsoever, lying within the Space of Three Englishe Myles on the South Parte of the said River, called Charles River, or of any or every Parte thereof; and also all and singuler the Landes and Hereditaments whatsoever, lying and being within the Space of Three Englishe Miles to the southward of the southermost Parte of the said Baye, called Massachusetts, alias Mattachusetts, alias Massatusets Bay: And also all those Landes and Hereditaments whatsoever, which lye and be within the Space of Three English Myles to the Northward of the saide River, called Monomack, alias Merrymack, or to the Norward of any and every Parte thereof, and all Landes and Hereditaments whatsoever, lyeing within the Lymitts aforesaide, North and South, in Latitude and Bredth, and in Length and Longitude, of and within all the Bredth aforesaide, throughout the mayne Landes there, from the Atlantick and Westerne Sea and Ocean on the East Parte, to the South Sea on the West Parte; and all Landes and Groundes, Place and Places, Soyles, Woodes, and Wood Groundes, Havens, Portes, Rivers, Waters, and Hereditaments whatsoever, lyeing within the said Boundes and Lymytts, and every Parte and Parcell thereof; and also all Islandes in America aforesaide, in the saide Seas, or either of them, on the Westerne or Easterne Coastes, or Partes of the saide Tracts of Landes hereby mencoed to be given and graunted, or any of them; and all Mynes and Mynerals whatsoever, in the said Landes and Premisses, or any parte thereof, and free Libertie of fishing in or within any the Rivers or Waters within the Boundes and Lymytts aforesaid, and the Seas therevnto adjoining; and all Fishes, Royal Fishes, Whales, Balan, Sturgions, and other Fishes of what Kinde or Nature soever, that shall at any time hereafter be taken in or within the saide Seas or Waters, or any of them, by the said Sir Henry Rosewell, Sir John Younge, Sir Richard Saltonstall, Thomas Southcott, John Humfrey, John Endecott, Simon Whetcombe, Isaack Johnson, Samuell Aldersey, John Ven, Mathewe Cradock, George Harwood, Increase Noell, Richard Pery, Richard Bellingham, Nathaniell Wright, Samuell Vassell, Theophilus Eaton, Thomas Goffe, Thomas Adams, John Browne, Samuell Browne, Thomas Hutchins, William Vassall, William Pinchion, and George Foxcrofte, their Heires and Assignes, or by any other person or persons whatsoever there inhabiting, by them, or any of them, to be appointed to fishe therein. PROVIDED alwayes, That yf the said Landes, Islandes, or any other the Premisses herein before mencōned, and by theis presents, intended and meant to be graunted, were at the tyme of the graunting of the saide former Letters patents, dated the Third Day of November, in the Eighteenth Yeare of our said deare Fathers Raigne aforesaide, actuallie possessed or inhabited by any other Christian Prince or State, or were within the Boundes, Lymytts or Territories of that Southerne Colony, then before graunted by our said late Father, to be planted by divers of his loveing Subiects in the south partes of America, That then this present Graunt shall not extend to any such partes or parcells thereof, soe formerly inhabited, or lyeing within the Boundes of the Southerne Plantacōn as aforesaide, but as to those partes or parcells soe possessed or inhabited by such Christian Prince or State, or being within the Bounders aforesaide shal be vtterlie voyd, theis presents or any Thinge therein conteyned to the contrarie notwithstanding. TO HAVE and hould, possesse and enioy the saide partes of New England in America, which lye, extend, and are abutted as aforesaide, and every parte and parcell thereof; and all the Islandes, Rivers, Portes, Havens, Waters, Fishings, Fishes, Mynes, Myneralls, Jurisdiccõns, Franchises, Royalties, Liberties, Priviledges, Cōmodities, and Premisses whatsoever, with the Appurtenances, vnto the said Sir Henry Rosewell, Sir John Younge, Sir Richard Saltonstall, Thomas Southcott, John Humfrey, John Endecott, Simon Whetcombe, Isaack Johnson, Samuell Aldersey, John Ven, Mathewe Cradock, George Harwood, Increase Nowell, Richard Perry, Richard Bellingham, Nathaniell Wright, Samuell Vassall, Theophilus Eaton, Thomas Goffe, Thomas Adams, John Browne, Samuell Browne, Thomas Hutchins, William Vassall, William Pinchion, and George Foxcroft, their Heires and Assignes forever, to the onlie proper and absolute Vse and Behoufe of the said Sir Henry Rosewell, Sir John Younge, Sir Richard Saltonstall, Thomas Southcott, John Humfrey, John Endecott, Simon Whetcombe, Isaac Johnson, Samuell Aldersey, John Ven, Mathewe Cradocke, George Harwood, Increase Nowell, Richard Pery, Richard Bellingham, Nathaniell Wright, Samuell Vassall, Theophilus Eaton, Thomas Goffe, Thomas Adams, John Browne, Samuell Browne, Thomas Hutchins, William Vassall, William Pinchion, and George Foxcroft, their Heires and Assignes forevermore: TO BE HOLDEN of Vs, our Heires and Successors, as of our Manor of Eastgreenwich in our Countie of Kent, within our Realme of England, in free and comon Soccage, and not in Capite, nor by Knights Service; and also yeilding and paying therefore, to Vs, our Heires and Successors, the fifte Parte onlie of all Oare of Gould and Silver, which from tyme to tyme, and at all tymes hereafter, shal be there gotten, had, or obteyned, for all Services, Exaccons, and Demaundes whatsoever; PROVIDED alwaies, and our expresse Will and Meaninge is, that onlie one fifte Parte of the Gould and Silver Oare above mencõed, in the whole, and noe more be reserved or payeable vnto Vs, our Heires and Successors, by Collour or Vertue of theis Presents, the double Reservacõns or recitalls aforesaid or any Thing herein conteyned notwithstanding. AND FORASMUCH, as the good and prosperous Successe of the Plantacon of the saide Partes of Newe-England aforesaide intended by the said Sir Henry Rosewell, Sir John Younge, Sir Richard Saltonstall, Thomas Southcott, John Humfrey, John Endecott, Simon Whetcombe, Isaack Johnson, Samuell Aldersey, John Ven, Mathew Cradock, George Harwood, Increase Noell, Richard Pery, Richard Bellingham, Nathaniell Wright, Samuell Vassall, Theophilus Eaton, Thomas Goffe, Thomas Adams, John Browne, Samuell Browne, Thomas Hutchins, William Vassall, William Pinchion, and George Foxcrofte, to be speedily sett vpon, cannot but cheifly depend, next vnder the Blessing of Almightie God, and the support of our Royall Authoritie vpon the good Government of the same, To the Ende that the Affaires and Buyssinesses which from tyme to tyme shall happen and arise concerning the saide Landes, and the Plantation of the same maie be the better mannaged and ordered, WEE HAVE FURTHER hereby of our especial Grace, certain Knowledge and mere Mocõn, Given, graunted and confirmed, and for Vs, our Heires and Successors, doe give, graunt, and confirme vnto our said trustie and welbeloved subiects Sir Henry Rosewell, Sir John Younge, Sir Richard Saltonstall, Thomas Southcott, John Humfrey, John Endicott, Simon Whetcombe, Isaack Johnson, Samuell Aldersey, John Ven, Mathewe Cradock, George Harwood, Increase Nowell, Richard Pery, Richard Bellingham, Nathaniell Wright, Samuell Vassall, Theophilus Eaton, Thomas Goffe, Thomas

Adams, John Browne, Samuell Browne, Thomas Hutchins, William Vassall, William Pinchion, and George Foxcrofte: AND for Vs, our Heires and Successors, Wee will and ordeyne, That the saide Sir Henry Rosewell, Sir John Young, Sir Richard Saltonstall, Thomas Southcott, John Humfrey, John Endicott, Symon Whetcombe, Isaack Johnson, Samuell Aldersey, John Ven, Mathewe Cradock, George Harwood, Increase Noell, Richard Pery, Richard Bellingham, Nathaniell Wright, Samuell Vassall, Theophilus Eaton, Thomas Goffe, Thomas Adams, John Browne, Samuell Browne, Thomas Hutchins, William Vassall, William Pinchion, and George Foxcrofte, and all such others as shall hereafter be admitted and made free of the Company and Society hereafter mencõed, shall from tyme to tyme, and att all tymes forever hereafter be, by Vertue of theis presents, one Body corporate and politique in Fact and Name, by the Name of the Governor and Company of the Mattachusetts Bay in Newe-England, and them by the Name of the Governour and Company of the Mattachusetts Bay in Newe-England, one Bodie politique and corporate, in Deede, Fact, and Name; Wee doe for vs, our Heires and Successors, make, ordeyne, constitute, and confirme by theis Presents, and that by that name they shall have perpetuall Succession, and that by the same Name they and their Successors shall and maie be capeable and enabled aswell to implead, and to be impleaded, and to prosecute, demaund, and aunswere, and be aunswered vnto, in all and singuler Suites, Causes, Quarrells, and Accons, of what kinde or nature soever. And also to have, take, possesse, acquire, and purchase any Landes, Tenements, or Hereditaments, or any Goodes or Chattells, and the same to lease, graunte, demise, alien, bargaine, sell, and dispose of, as other our liege People of this our Realme of England, or any other corporacon or Body politique of the same may lawfully doe. AND FURTHER, That the said Governour and Companye, and their Successors, maie have forever one comon Seale, to be vsed in all Causes and Occasions of the said Company, and the same Seale may alter, chaunge, breake, and newe make, from tyme to tyme, at their pleasures. And our Will and Pleasure is, and Wee doe hereby for Vs, our Heires and Successors, ordeyne and graunte, That from henceforth for ever, there shalbe one Governor, one Deputy Governor, and eighteene Assistants of the same Company, to be from tyme to tyme constituted, elected and chosen out of the Freemen of the saide Company, for the tyme being, in such Manner and Forme as hereafter in theis Presents is expressed, which said Officers shall applie themselves to take Care for the best disposeing and ordering of the generall buysines and Affaires of, for, and concerning the said Landes and Premisses hereby mencõed, to be graunted, and the Plantacion thereof, and the Government of the People there. AND FOR the better Execucon of our Royall Pleasure and Graunte in this Behalf, WEE doe, by theis presents, for Vs, our Heires and Successors, nominate, ordeyne, make, & constitute, our welbeloved the saide Mathewe Cradocke, to be the first and present Governor of the said Company, and the saide Thomas Goffe, to be Deputy Governor of the saide Company, and the saide Sir Richard Saltonstall, Isaack Johnson, Samuell Aldersey, John Ven, John Humfrey, John Endecott, Simon Whetcombe, Increase Noell, Richard Pery, Nathaniell Wright, Samuell Vassall, Theophilus Eaton, Thomas Adams, Thomas Hutchins, John Browne, George Foxcrofte, William Vassall, and William Pinchion, to be the present Assistants of the saide Company, to continue in the saide several Offices respectivelie for such tyme, and in such manner, as in and by theis Presents is hereafter declared and appointed. AND FURTHER, Wee will, and by theis Presents, for Vs, our Heires and Successors, doe ordeyne and graunte, That the Governor of the saide Company for the tyme being, or in his Absence by Occasion of Sicknes or otherwise, the Deputie Governor for the tyme being, shall have Authoritie from tyme to tyme vpon all Occasions, to give order for the assembling of the saide Company, and calling them together to consult and advise of the Bussinesses and Affaires of the saide Company, and that the said Governor, Deputie Governor, and Assistants of the saide Company, for the tyme being, shall or maie once every Moneth, or oftener at their Pleasures, assemble and houlde and keepe a Courte or Assemblie of themselves, for the better ordering and directing of their Affaires, and that any seaven or more persons of the Assistants, togither with the Governor, or Deputie Governor soe assembled, shalbe saide, taken, held, and reputed to be, and shalbe a full and sufficient Courte or Assemblie of the said Company, for the handling, ordering, and dispatching of all such Buysinesses and Occurrents as shall from tyme to tyme happen, touching or concerning the said Company or Plantacon; and that there shall or maie be held and kept by the Governor, or Deputie Governor of the said Company, and seaven or more of the said Assistants for the tyme being, vpon every last Wednesday in Hillary, Easter, Trinity, and Michas Termes respectivelie forever, one greate generall and solempe assemblie, which foure generall assemblies shalbe stiled and called the foure greate and generall Courts of the saide Company; IN all and every, or any of which saide greate and generall Courts soe assembled, WEE DOE for Vs, our Heires and Successors, give and graunte to the said Governor and Company, and their Successors, That the Governor, or in his absence, the Deputie Governor of the saide Company for the tyme being, and such of the Assistants and Freemen of the saide Company as shalbe present, or the greater nomber of them so assembled, whereof the Governor or Deputie Governor and six of the Assistants at the least to be seaven, shall have full Power and authoritie to choose, nominate, and appointe, such and soe many others as they shall thinke fitt, and that shall be willing to accept the same, to be free of the said Company and Body, and them into the same to admitt; and to elect and constitute such Officers as they shall thinke fitt and requisite, for the ordering, mannaging, and dispatching of the Affaires of the saide Govenor and Company, and their Successors; And to make Lawes and Ordiñnces for the Good and Welfare of the saide Company, and for the Government and ordering of the saide Landes and Plantac̃on, and the People inhabiting and to inhabite the same, as to them from tyme to tyme shalbe thought meete, soe as such Lawes and Ordinances be not contrarie or repugnant to the Lawes and Statuts of this our Realme of England. AND, our Will nd Pleasure is, and Wee doe hereby for Vs, our Heires and Successors, establish and ordeyne, That yearely once in the yeare, for ever hereafter, namely, the last Wednesday in Easter Tearme, yearely, the Governor, Deputy-Governor, and Assistants of the saide Company and all other officers of the saide Company shalbe in the Generall Court or Assembly to be held for that Day or Tyme, newly chosen for the Yeare ensueing by such greater parte of the saide Company, for the Tyme being, then and there present, as is aforesaide. AND, yf it shall happen the present governor, Deputy Governor, and assistants, by theis presents appointed, or such as shall hereafter be newly chosen into their Roomes, or any of them, or any other of the officers to be appointed for the said Company, to dye, or to be removed from his or their severall Offices or Places before the saide generall Day of Elecc̃on (whome Wee doe hereby declare for any Misdemeanor or Defect to be removeable by the Governor, Deputie Governor, Assistants, and Company, or such greater Parte of them in any of the publique Courts to be assembled as is aforesaid) That then, and in every such Case, it shall and maie be lawfull, to and for the Governor, Deputie Governor, Assistants, and Company aforesaide, or such greater Parte of them soe to be assembled as is aforesaide, in any of their Assemblies, to proceade to a new Eleccon of one or more others of their Company in the Roome or Place, Roomes or Places of such Officer or Officers soe dyeing or removed according to their Discrecons, And, ym̃ediately vpon and after such Elecc̃on and Elecc̃ons made of such Governor, Deputie Governor, Assistant or Assistants, or any other officer of the saide Company, in Manner and Forme aforesaid, the Authoritie, Office, and Power, before given to the former Governor, Deputie Governor, or other Officer and Officers soe removed, in whose Steade and Place newe shalbe soe chosen, shall as to him and them, and everie of them, cease and determine. PROVIDED alsoe, and our Will and Pleasure is, That aswell such as are by theis Presents appointed to be the present Governor, Deputie Governor, and Assistants of the said Company, as those that shall succeed them, and all other Officers to be appointed and chosen as aforesaid, shall, before they vndertake the Execucon of their saide Offices and Places respectivelie, take their Corporal Oathes for the due and faithfull Performance of their Duties in their severall Offices and Places, before such Person or Persons as are by theis Presents herevnder appointed to take and receive the same; That is to saie, the saide Mathewe Cradock, whoe is hereby nominated and appointed the present Governor of the saide Company, shall take the saide Oathes before one or more of the Masters of our Courte of Chauncery for the Tyme being, vnto which Master or Masters of the Chauncery, Wee doe by theis Presents give full Power and Authoritie to take and administer the said Oathe to the said Governor accordinglie: And after the saide Governor shalbe soe sworne, then the said Deputy Governor and Assistants, before by theis Presents nominated and appointed, shall take the said severall Oathes to their Offices and Places respectivelie belonging, before the said Mathew Cradock, the present Governor, soe formerlie sworne as aforesaide. And every such Person as shallbe at the Tyme of the annuall Eleccon, or otherwise, vpon Death or Removeall, be appointed to be the newe Governor of the said Company, shall take the Oathes to that Place belonging, before the Deputy Governor, or two of the Assistants of the said Company at the least, for the Tyme being: And the newe elected Deputie Governor and Assistants, and all other officers to be hereafter chosen as aforesaide from Tyme to Tyme, to take the Oathes to their places respectivelie belonging, before the Governor of the said Company for the Tyme being, vnto which said Governor, Deputie Governor, and assistants, Wee doe by theis Presents give full Power and Authoritie to give and administer the said Oathes respectively, according to our true Meaning herein before declared, without any Comission or further Warrant to be had and obteyned of of Vs, our Heires or Successors, in that Behalf. AND, Wee doe further, of our especial Grace, certen Knowledge, and meere mocon, for Vs, our Heires and Successors, give and graunte to the said Governor and Company, and their Successors for ever by theis Presents, That it shalbe lawfull and free for them and their Assignes, at all and every Tyme and Tymes hereafter, out of any our Realmes or Domynions whatsoever, to take, leade, carry, and transport, for in and into their Voyages, and for and towardes the said Plantacon in Newe England, all such and soe many of our loving Subjects, or any other strangers that will become our loving Subjects, and live under our Allegiance, as shall willinglie accompany them in the same Voyages and Plantacon; and also Shipping, Armour, Weapons, Ordinance, Municon, Powder, Shott, Corne, Victualls, and all Manner of Clothing, Implements, Furniture, Beastes, Cattle, Horses, Mares, Marchandizes, and all other Thinges necessarie for the saide Plantacon, and for their Vse and Defence, and for Trade with the People there, and in passing and returning to and fro, any Lawe or Statute to the contrarie hereof in any wise notwithstanding; and without payeing or yeilding any Custome or Subsidie, either inward or outward, to Vs, our Heires or Successors, for the same, by the Space of seaven Yeares from the Day of the Date of theis Presents. PROVIDED, that none of the saide Persons be such as shalbe hereafter by especiall Name restrayned by Vs, our Heires or Successors. AND, for their further Encouragement, of our especiall Grace and Favor, Wee doe by theis Presents, for Vs, our Heires and Successors, yeild and graunt to the saide Governor and Company, and their Successors, and every of them, their Factors and Assignes, That they and every of them shalbe free and quitt from all Taxes, Subsidies, and Customes, in Newe England, for the like Space of seaven Yeares, and from all Taxes and Imposicons for the Space of twenty and one Yeares, vpon all Goodes and Merchandizes at any Tyme or Tymes hereafter, either vpon Importac̄on thither, or Exportac̄on from thence into our Realme of England, or into any other our Domynions by the said Governor and Company, and their Successors, their Deputies, Factors, and Assignes, or any of them; EXCEPT onlie the five Pounds per Centum due for Custome vpon all such Goodes and Merchandizes as after the saide seaven Yeares shalbe expired, shalbe brought or imported into our Realme of England, or any other of our Dominions, according to the auncient Trade of Merchants, which five Poundes per Centum onlie being paide, it shall be thenceforth lawfull and free for the said Adventurers, the same Goodes and Merchandizes to export and carry out of our said Domynions into forraine Partes, without any Custome, Tax, or other Dutie to be paid to Vs, our Heires or Successors, or to any other Officers or Ministers of Vs, our Heires and Successors. PROVIDED, that the said Goodes and Merchandizes be shipped out within thirteene Monethes, after their first Landing within any Parte of the saide

Domynions. And, Wee doe for Vs, our Heires and Successors, give and graunte vnto the saide Governor and Company, and their Successors, That whensoever, or soe often as any Custome or Subsedie shall growe due or payeable vnto Vs, our Heires, or Successors, according to the Lymittacon and Appointment aforesaide, by Reason of any Goodes, Wares, or Merchandizes to be shipped out, or any Retorne to be made of any Goodes, Wares, or Merchandize vnto or from the said Partes of Newe England hereby mencõed to be graunted as aforesaide, or any the Landes or Territories aforesaide, That then, and soe often, and in such Case, the Farmors, Customers, and Officers of our Customes of England and Ireland, and everie of them for the Tyme being, vpon Request made to them by the saide Governor and Company, or their Successors, Factors, or Assignes, and vpon convenient Security to be given in that Behalf, shall give and allowe vnto the said Governor and Company, and their Successors, and to all and everie Person and Persons free of that Company, as aforesaide, six Monethes Tyme for the Payement of the one halfe of all such Custome and Subsidy as shalbe due and payeable unto Vs, our Heires and Successors, for the same; for which theis our Letters patents, or the Duplicate, or the inrollem[t] thereof, shalbe vnto our saide Officers a sufficient Warrant and Discharge. Nevertheles, our Will and Pleasure is, That yf any of the saide Goodes, Wares, and Merchandize, which be, or shalbe at any Tyme hereafter landed or exported out of any of our Realmes aforesaide, and shalbe shipped with a Purpose not to be carried to the Partes of Newe England aforesaide, but to some other place, That then such Payment, Dutie, Custome, Imposicõn, or Forfeyture shalbe paid, or belonge to Vs, our Heires and Successors, for the said Goodes, Wares, and Merchandize, soe fraudulently sought to be transported, as yf this our Graunte had not been made nor graunted. And, Wee doe further will, and by theis Presents, for Vs, our Heires and Successors, firmlie enioine and com̃aunde, as well the Treasorer, Chauncellor and Barons of the Exchequer, of Vs, our Heires and Successors, as also all and singuler the Customers, Farmors, and Collectors of the Customes, Subsidies, and Imposts, and other the Officers and Ministers of Vs, our Heires, and Successors whatsoever, for the Tyme Being, That they and every of them, vpon the shewing forth vnto them of theis Letters patents, or the Duplicate or exemplificacōn of the same, without any other Writt or Warrant whatsoever from Vs, our Heires or Successors, to be obteyned or sued forth, doe and shall make full, whole, entire, and due Allowance, and cleare Discharge vnto the saide Governor and Company, and their Successors, of all Customes, Subsidies, Inposicōns, Taxes and Duties whatsoever, that shall or maie be claymed by Vs, our Heires and Successors, of or from the said Governor and Company, and their Successors, for or by Reason of the said Goodes, Chattels, Wares, Merchandizes, and Premises to be exported out of our saide Domynions, or any of them, into any parte of the saide Landes or Premises hereby mencōed, to be given, graunted, and confirmed, or for, or by Reason of any of the saide Goodes, Chattells, Wares, or Merchandizes, to be imported from the said Landes and Premises hereby mencoed, to be given, graunted, and confirmed into any of our saide Dominions, or any Parte thereof as aforesaide, excepting onlie the saide five Poundes per Centum hereby reserved and payeable after the Expiracōn of the saide Terme of seaven Yeares as aforesaid, and not before: And theis our Letters-patents, or the Inrollment, Duplicate, or Exemplificacōn of the same shalbe for ever hereafter, from time to tyme, as well to the Treasorer, Chauncellor and Barons of the Exchequer of Vs, our Heires and Successors, as to all and singuler the Customers, Farmors, and Collectors of the Customes, Subsidies, and Imposts of Vs, our Heires and Successors, and all Searchers, and other the Officers and Ministers whatsoever of Vs, our Heires and Successors, for the Time being, a sufficient Warrant and Discharge in this Behalf. AND, further our Will and Pleasure is, and Wee doe hereby for Vs, our Heires and Successors, ordeyne and declare, and graunte to the saide Governor and Company, and their Successors, That all and every the Subiects of Vs, our Heires or Successors, which shall goe to and inhabite within the saide Landes and Premisses hereby mencōed to be graunted, and every of their Children which shall happen to be borne there, or on the Seas in goeing thither, or retorning from thence, shall have and enjoy all liberties and Immunities of free and naturall Subiects within any of the Domynions of Vs, our Heires or Successors, to all Intents, Construccons, and Purposes whatsoever, as yf they and everie of them were borne within the Realme of England. And that the Governor and Deputie Governor of the said Company for the Tyme being, or either of them, and any two or more of such of the saide Assistants as shalbe therevnto appointed by the saide Governor and Company at any of their Courts or Assemblies to be held as aforesaide, shall and maie at all Tymes, and from tyme to tyme hereafter, have full Power and Authoritie to minister and give the Oathe and Oathes of Supremacie and Allegiance, or either of them, to all and everie Person and Persons, which shall at any Tyme or Tymes hereafter goe or passe to the Landes and Premisses hereby mencoed to be graunted to inhabite in the same. AND, Wee doe of our further Grace, certen Knowledg and meere Mocōn, give and graunte to the saide Governor and Company, and their Successors, That it shall and maie be lawfull, to and for the Governor or Deputie Governor, and such of the Assistants and Freemen of the said Company for the Tyme being as shalbe assembled in any of their generall Courts aforesaide, or in any other Courtes to be specially sumoned and assembled for that Purpose, or the greater Parte of them (whereof the Governor or Deputie Governor, and six of the Assistants to be alwaies seaven) from tyme to tyme, to make, ordeine, and establishe all Manner of wholesome and reasonable Orders, Lawes, Statutes, and Ordiñnces, Direccōns, and Instruccōns, not contrarie to the Lawes of this our Realme of England, aswell for setling of the Formes and Ceremonies of Governm^t and Magistracy, fitt and necessary for the said Plantacōn, and the Inhabitants there, and for nameing and stiling of all sorts of Officers, both superior and inferior, which they shall finde needefull for that Governement and Plantacon, and the distinguishing and setting forth of the severall duties, Powers, and Lymytts of every such Office and Place, and the Formes of such Oathes warrantable by the Lawes and Statutes of this our Realme of England, as shalbe respectivelie ministred vnto them for the Execucōn of the said severall Offices and Places; as also, for the disposing and ordering of the Eleccōns of such of the said Officers as shalbe annuall, and of such others as shalbe to succeede in Case of Death or Removeall, and ministring the said Oathes to the newe elected Officers, and for Imposicons of lawfull Fynes, Mulcts, Imprisonment, or other lawfull Correccōn, according to the Course of other Corporacōns in this our Realme of England, and for the directing, ruling, and disposeing of all other Matters and Thinges, whereby our said People, Inhabitants there, may be soe religiously, peaceablie, and civilly governed, as their good Life and orderlie Conversacon, maie wynn and incite the Natives of Country, to the Knowledg and Obedience of the onlie true God and Sauior of Mankinde, and the Christian Fayth, which in our Royall Intencon, and the Adventurers free Profession, is the principall Ende of this Plantacion. WILLING, comaunding, and requiring, and by theis Presents for Vs, our Heires, and Successors, ordeyning and appointing, that all such Orders, Lawes, Statuts and Ordiñnces, Instruccōns and Direccōns, as shalbe soe made by the Governor, or Deputie Governor of the said Company, and such of the Assistants and Freemen as aforesaide, and published in Writing, vnder their comon Seale, shalbe carefullie and dulie observed, kept, performed, and putt in Execucon, according to the true Intent and Meaning of the same; and theis our Letters-patents, or the Duplicate or exemplificacon thereof, shalbe to all and everie such Officers, superior and inferior, from Tyme to Tyme, for the putting of the same Orders, Lawes, Statutes, and Ordinnces, Instruccons, and Direccons, in due Execucon against Vs, our Heires and Successors, a sufficient Warrant and Discharge. AND WEE DOE further, for Vs, our Heires and Successors, give and graunt to the said Governor and Company, and their Successors by theis Presents, that all and everie such Chiefe Comaunders, Captaines, Governors, and other Officers and Ministers, as by the said Orders, Lawes, Statuts, Ordinnces, Instruccons, or Direccons of the said Governor and Company for the Tyme being, shalbe from Tyme to Tyme hereafter ymploied either in the Government of the saide Inhabitants and Plantacon, or in the Waye by Sea thither, or from thence, according to the Natures and Lymitts of their Offices and Places respectively, shall from Tyme to Tyme hereafter for ever, within the Precincts and Partes of Newe England hereby mencoed to be graunted and confirmed, or in the Waie by Sea thither, or from thence, have full and Absolute Power and Authoritie to correct, punishe, pardon, governe, and rule all such the Subiects of Vs, our Heires and Successors, as shall from Tyme to Tyme adventure themselves in any Voyadge, thither or from thence, or that shall at any Tyme hereafter, inhabite within the Precincts and Partes of Newe England aforasaid, according to the Orders, Lawes, Ordinnces, Instruccons, and Direccons aforesaid, not being repugnant to the Lawes and Statutes of our Realme of England as aforesaid. AND WEE DOE further, for Vs, our Heires and Successors, give and graunte to the said Governor and Company, and their Successors, by theis Presents, that it shall and maie be lawfull, to and for the Chiefe Comaunders, Governors, and Officers of the said Company for the Time being, who shalbe resident in the said Parte of Newe England in America, by theis Presents graunted, and others there inhabiting by their Appointment and Direccōn, from Tyme to Tyme, and at all Tymes hereafter for their speciall Defence and Safety, to incounter, expulse, repell, and resist by Force of Armes, aswell by Sea as by Lande, and by all fitting Waies and Meanes whatsoever, all such Person and Persons, as shall at any Tyme hereafter, attempt or enterprise the Destruccōn, Invasion, Detriment, or Annoyaunce to the said Plantation or Inhabitants, and to take and surprise by all Waies and Meanes whatsoever, all and every such Person and Persons, with their Shippes, Armour, Municōn, and other Goodes, as shall in hostile manner invade or attempt the defeating of the said Plantacon, or the Hurt of the said Company and Inhabitants: NEVERTHELES, our Will and Pleasure is, and Wee doe hereby declare to all Christian Kinges, Princes and States, that yf any Person or Persons which shall hereafter be of the said Company or Plantacōn, or any other by Lycense or Appointment of the said Governor and Company for the Tyme being, shall at any Tyme or Tymes hereafter, robb or spoyle, by Sea or by Land, or doe any Hurt, Violence, or vnlawful Hostilitie to any of the Subiects of Vs, our Heires or Successors, or any of the Subiects of any Prince or State, being then in League and Amytie with Vs, our Heires and Successors, and that upon such iniury don and vpon iust Complaint of such Prince or State or their Subjects, WEE, our Heires and Successors shall make open Proclamacōn within any of the Partes within our Realme of England, comodious for that purpose, that the Person or Persons haveing comitted any such Roberie or Spoyle, shall within the Terme lymytted by such a Proclamacon, make full Restitucōn or Satisfaccōn of all such Iniureis don, soe as the said Princes or others soe complayning, maie hould themselves fullie satisfied and contented; and that yf the said Person or Persons, haveing comitted such Robbery or Spoile, shall not make, or cause to be made Satisfaccon accordinglie, within such Tyme soe to be lymytted, that then it shalbe lawfull for Vs, our Heires and Successors, to putt the said Person or Persons out of our Allegiance and Proteccon, and that it shalbe lawfull and free for all Princes to prosecute with Hostilitie, the said Offendors, and every of them, their and every of their Procurers, Ayders, Abettors, and Comforters in that Behalf: PROVIDED also, and our expresse Will and Pleasure is, And Wee doe by theis Presents for Vs, our Heires and Successors ordeyne and appoint That theis Presents shall not in any manner envre, or be taken to abridge, barr, or hinder any of our loving subiects whatsoever, to vse and exercise the Trade of Fishing vpon that Coast of New England in America, by theis Presents mencoed to be graunted. But that they, and every, or any of them, shall have full and free Power and Liberty to continue and vse their said Trade of Fishing vpon the said Coast, in any the Seas therevnto adioyning, or any Armes of the Seas or Saltwater Rivers where they have byn wont to fishe, and to build and sett vp vpon the Landes by theis Presents graunted, such Wharfes, Stages, and Workehouses as shalbe necessarie for the salting, drying, keeping, and packing vp of their Fish, to be taken or gotten vpon that Coast; and to cutt down, and take such Trees and other Materialls there groweing, or being, or shalbe needefull for that Purpose, and for all other necessarie Easements, Helpes, and Advantage concerning their said Trade of Fishing there, in such Manner and Forme as they have byn heretofore at any tyme accustomed to doe, without making any willfull Waste or Spoyle, any Thing in theis Presents conteyned to the contrarie notwithstanding. AND WEE DOE further, for Vs, our Heires and Successors, ordeyne and graunte to the said Governor and Company, and their Successors by theis Presents that theis our Letters-patents shalbe firme, good, effectuall, and availeable in all Things, and to all Intents and Construccons of Lawe, according to our true Meaning herein before declared, and shalbe construed, reputed, and adiudged in all Cases most favourablie on the Behalf, and for the Benefitt and Behoofe of the saide Governor and Company and their Successors: ALTHOUGH expresse mencon of the true yearely Value or certenty of the Premisses or any of them, or of any other Guiftes or Grauntes, by Vs, or any of our Progenitors or Predecessors to the foresaid Governor or Company before this tyme made, in theis Presents is not made; or any Statute, Acte, Ordinnce, Provision, Proclamacon, or Restrainte to the contrarie thereof, heretofore had, made, published, ordeyned, or provided, or any other Matter, Cause, or Thinge whatsoever to the contrarie thereof in any wise notwithstanding.

IN WITNES whereof, Wee have caused theis our Letters to be made Patents.

WITNES ourself, at Westminster, the fourth day of March, in the fourth Yeare of our Raigne.

Per Breve de Privato Sigillo,

WOLSELEY.

CHARTER OF MARYLAND—1632.

Lord Baltimore's first attempt at colonization was at Avalon, Newfoundland. Discouraged by the severity of the climate he visited Virginia, and obtaining from Charles II. a promise of lands there, abandoned Newfoundland. Dying shortly after, the promised patent was issued in 1632 to his son and successor, who made the first settlement at St. Mary's. The Palatinate of Durham served as a model for Lord Baltimore's Avalon patent, and this in turn helped mould the Maryland charter. "The Maryland charter is full of interest as being the first proprietary constitution that bore any actual fruit. It conferred on the grantee probably the most extensive political privileges ever enjoyed by an English subject since the great houses had bowed before the successive oppression of Yorkist and Tudor rule." (Doyle.) With the exception of the reservation of allegiance, and the provision that the laws "be consonant to reason and be not repugnant nor contrary to the laws and statutes of the kingdom of England," Lord Baltimore was an independent monarch. Maryland continued under this charter till 1776, when a convention meeting at Annapolis (Aug. 14—Nov. 11) formulated a constitution for the state. A second constitution was adopted in 1851, a third in 1864, and a fourth in 1867.

Consult *Doyle's English Colonies*, I., 281; *Bancroft's U. S.*, 1st ed. I., 241; cen. ed. I., 181; last ed. I., 157; *Hildreth's U. S.*, I., 206; *Bryant and Gay's U. S.*, I., 487; *Neil's English Colonization*, *Browne's Maryland*, 18; *Bozman's Maryland*; *Chalmers' Political Annals*, 200.

CHARTER OF MARYLAND.

[Translated from the Latin original.]

CHARLES, by the Grace of God, King of England, Scotland, France, and Ireland, Defender of the Faith, etc. To all to whom these presents shall come, greeting: Whereas our right trusty and well-beloved subject Caecilius Calvert, Baron of Baltimore, in our kingdom of Ireland, son and heir of Sir George Calvert, knight, late Baron of Baltimore, in the same kingdom of Ireland, pursuing his father's intentions, being incited with a laudable and pious zeal for the propagation of the Christian faith, and the enlargement of our empire and dominion, hath humbly besought leave of us, by his industry and charge, to transport an ample colony of the English nation into a certain country hereafter described in the parts of America not yet cultivated and planted, though in some parts thereof inhabited by a certain barbarous people, having no knowledge of the Almighty God; and hath humbly besought our royal majesty to give, grant and confirm the said country, with certain privileges and jurisdictions, requisite for the said government and State of his colony and country, aforesaid, to him and his heirs forever.

Know ye, therefore, that we, favoring the pious and noble purpose of the said Barons of Baltimore, of our especial grace, certain knowledge, and mere motion, have given, granted, and confirmed, and by this our present charter, for us, our heirs and successors, do give, grant, and confirm, unto the said Caecilius, now Baron of Baltimore, his heirs and assigns, all that part of a peninsula lying in the parts of America between the ocean on the east, and the bay of Chesapeak on the west, and divided from the other part thereof by a right line drawn from the promontory or cape of land called Watkins' Point (situate in the aforesaid bay, near the river of Wighco) on the west, unto the main ocean on the east; and between that bound on the south unto that part of Delaware Bay on the north, which lieth under the fortieth degree of northerly latitude from the equinoctial where New England ends; and all that tract of land between the bounds aforesaid; that is to say, passing from the aforesaid unto the aforesaid bay called Delaware Bay, in a right line by the degree aforesaid, unto the true meridian of the first fountain of the river Potomac, and from thence tending towards the south unto the further bank of the aforesaid river, and following the west and south side thereof into a certain place called Cinquack situate near the mouth of the said river, where it falls into the bay of Chesapeak, and from thence by a straight line unto the aforesaid promontory and place called Watkins' Point (so that all that tract of land divided by the line aforesaid, drawn between the main ocean and Watkins' Point, unto the Promontory called Cape Charles, and all its appurtenances, do remain entirely excepted to us, our heirs and successors forever).

We do also grant and confirm to the said Lord Baltimore, his heirs and assigns, all islands and islets within the limits aforesaid, and all and singular the islands and islets which are or shall in the ocean, within ten leagues from the eastern shore of the said country towards the east, with all and singular ports, harbors, bays, rivers, and inlets belonging unto the country and islands aforesaid, and all the soil, lands, fields, woods, mountains, fens, lakes, rivers, bays, and inlets, situate or being within the limits and bounds aforesaid. With the fishing of all sorts of fish, whales, sturgeons, and all other royal fishes in the sea, bays, inlets, and rivers, within the premises, and all the fish therein taken.

And moreover all veins, mines, and quarries, as well discovered as not discovered, of gold, silver, gems, and precious stones, and all other whatsoever, be it of stones, metals, or of any other thing or matter whatsoever, found, or to be found within the country, isles and limits aforesaid.

And, futhermore, the patronages and advowsons of all churches, which (as Christian religion shall increase within the country, isles, islets, and limits aforesaid) shall happen hereafter to be erected; together with license and power to build and found churches, chapels, and oratories, in convenient and fit places within the premises, and to cause them to be dedicated and consecrated according to the ecclesiastical laws of our kingdom of England; together with all and singular the like, and as ample rights, jurisdictions, privileges, prerogatives, royalties, liberties, immunities, royal rights and franchises, of what kind soever, temporal, as well by sea as by land, within the country, isles, islets, and limits aforesaid, to have, exercise, use and enjoy the same, as amply as any bishop of Durham, within the bishopric or county palatine of Durham, in our kingdom of England, hath at any time heretofore had, held, used, or enjoyed, or of right, ought or might have had, held, used, or enjoyed.

And him the said now Lord Baltimore, his heirs and assigns, we do by these presents, for us, our heirs, and successors, make, create, and constitute the true and absolute lords and proprietaries of the said country aforesaid, and of all other the premises (except before excepted), saving always the faith and allegiance and sovereign dominion due unto us, our heirs and success-

5

ors. To have, hold, possess, and enjoy the said country, isles, inlets, and other the premises, unto the said now Lord Baltimore, his heirs and assigns, to the sole and proper use and behoof of him the said now Lord Baltimore, his heirs and assigns forever.

To be holden of us, our heirs and successors, Kings of England, as of our castles of Windsor, in our county of Berks, in free and common soccage, by fealty only, for all services, and not in capite, or by knight's service, yielding and paying therefor to us, our heirs and successors, two Indian arrows of those parts, to be delivered at our said castle of Windsor, every year the Tuesday in Easter week, and also the fifth part of all gold and silver ore, within the limits aforesaid, which shall from time to time, happen to be found.

Now, that the said country, thus by us granted and described, may be eminent above all other parts of the said territory, dignified with large title, Know ye, that we, of our further grace, certain knowledge, and mere motion, have thought fit to erect the same country and islands into a province, as out of the fullness of our royal power and prerogative, we do, for us, our heirs and successors, erect and incorporate them into a province, and do call it Maryland, and so from henceforth we will have it called.

And forasmuch as we have hereby made and ordained the aforesaid now Lord Baltimore, the true Lord and proprietary of all the province aforesaid, Know ye, therefore, that we, reposing special trust and confidence in the fidelity, wisdom, justice, and provident circumspection of the said now Lord Baltimore, for us, our heirs and successors, do grant free, full, and absolute power, by virtue of these presents, to him and his heirs, for the good and happy government of the said country, to ordain, make, enact, and under his and their seals to publish any laws whatsoever, appertaining either unto the public state of the said province, or unto the private utility of particular persons, according to their best discretions, by and with the advice, assent, and approbation of the freemen of the said province, or the greater part of them, or of their delegates or deputies, whom, for the enacting of the said laws, when and as often as need shall require, we will that the said now Lord Baltimore, and his heirs, shall assemble in such sort and form as to him and them shall seem best, and the said laws duly to execute upon all people within the said province and limits thereof, for the time being, or that shall be constituted under the government and power of him or them, either sailing towards Maryland, or returning from thence towards England, or any other of ours or foreign dominions, by imposition of penalties, imprisonment or any other punishment: yea, if it shall be needful, and that the quality of the offence require it, by taking away members or life, either by him the said now Lord Baltimore, and his heirs, or by his and their deputies, lieutenants, judges, justices, magistrates, officers, and ministers, to be ordained or appointed, according to the tenor and true intentions of these presents, and likewise to appoint and establish any judges, justices, magistrates, and officers, whatsoever, at sea and land, for what cause soever, and with what power soever, and in such form as to the said now Lord Baltimore, or his heirs, shall seem most convenient; also to remit, release, pardon, and abolish, whether before judgment or after, all crimes and offences whatsoever, against the said laws, and to do all and every other thing or things, which unto the complete establishment of justice unto courts, prætories, and tribunals, forms of judicature, and manners of proceedings, do belong, although in these presents express mention be not made thereof; and by judges by them delegated to award process, hold pleas, and determine, in said courts and tribunals, all actions, suits, and causes whatsoever, as well criminal as civil, personal, real, mixt, and prætorial, which laws, so as aforesaid, to be published, our pleasure is, and so we do enjoin, require, and command, shall be most absolute and available in law; and that all the liege people and subjects of us, our heirs and successors, do observe and keep the same inviolably, in those parts, so far as they concern them, under the pains therein expressed, or to be expressed; provided nevertheless, That the said laws be consonant to reason, and be not repugnant or contrary, but as near as conveniently may be, agreeable to the laws, statute, and rights of this our kingdom of England.

And forasmuch as in the government of so great a province, sudden accidents often happen, whereunto it will be necessary to apply a remedy, before the freeholders of the said province, or their delegates, or deputies, can be assembled to the making of laws, neither will it be convenient that instantly upon every such emergent occasion so great a multitude should be called together; therefore, for the better government of the said province, we will and ordain, and by these presents for us, our heirs and successors, and grant unto the said Lord Baltimore, and his heirs, by themselves, or by their magistrates, and officers, in that behalf duly to be ordained, as aforesaid, to make and constitute fit and wholesome ordinances, from time to time, within the said province, to be kept and observed, as well for the preservation of the peace, as for the better government of the people there inhabiting, and publicly to notify the same to all persons whom the same doth or may in any way concern; which ordinances, our pleasure is, shall be observed inviolably within the said province, under the pains therein to be expressed; so as the said ordinances be consonant to reason, and be not repugnant nor contrary to the laws and statutes of the kingdom of England; and so as the said ordinances be not extended in any sort, to bend, charge, or take away the right or interest of any person or persons, or of their life, members, freehold, goods, or chattels.

Furthermore, that this new colony may the more happily increase by the multitude of people resulting thither, and may likewise be the more strongly defended from the incursions of savages, or other enemies, pirates and robbers, therefore we, for us, our heirs and successors, do give and grant, by these presents, power, license, and liberty, unto all the liege people and subjects, both present and future, for us, our heirs and successors (excepting those who shall be expressly forbidden), to transport themselves, and families into the said province, with convenient shipping, and fitting provisions and there to settle themselves, dwell and inhabit; and to build and fortify castles, forts, and other places of strength for the public, and their own private defence, at the appointment of the said now Lord Baltimore, and his heirs, the statute of fugitives, or any other whatsoever, the contrary of the premises in any wise notwithstanding.

And we will also, and of our more especial grace, for us, our heirs and successors, we do strictly enjoin, constitute, ordain, and command, That the said province shall be of our allegiance, and that all and singular, subjects and liege people of us, our heirs and successors, transported or to be transported into the said province, and the children of them, and of such as shall descend from them, there already born, or hereafter to be born, be, and shall be denizens and lieges of us, our heirs and successors, of our kingdoms of England and Ireland, and be in all things held, treated, reputed, and esteemed, as the liege faithful people of us, our heirs and successors, born within the kingdom of England; and likewise, any lands, tenements, revenues, services and other hereditaments whatsoever, within our kingdom of England, and other our dominions, may inherit, or otherwise purchase, receive, take, hold, have, buy and possess, and then may occupy and enjoy, give, sell, alien and bequeathe as likewise all liberties, franchises and privileges, of this our kingdom of England, freely, quietly and peaceably have and possess, occupy and enjoy, as our liege people, born, or to be born, within our said kingdom of England, without the let, molestation, vexation, trouble or grievance of us, our heirs and successors; any Statute, act, ordinance or provision to the contrary thereof notwithstanding.

And furthermore, that our subject may be the rather encouraged to undertake this expedition with ready and cheerful minds, know ye, that we of our especial grace, certain knowledge, and mere motion, do give and grant, by virtue of these Presents, as well unto the said now Lord Baltimore, and his heirs, as to all others who shall, from time to time, repair unto the said country with a purpose to inhabit there, or to trade with the natives of the said province, full license to lade and trade in any ports whatsoever, of us, our heirs and successors, and into the said province of Maryland, by them, their servants or assigns, to transport all and singular their goods, wares, and merchandises, as likewise all sorts of grain whatsoever, and all other things whatsoever necessary for food and clothing, not prohibited by the laws and statute of our kingdoms and dominions to be carried out of the said kingdoms, any statute, act, ordinance, or other thing whatsoever to the contrary notwithstanding, without any lett or molestation of us, our heirs and successors; or of any of the heirs of us, our heirs and successors, saving always to us, our heirs and successors, the legal impositions, customs, and other duties and payments for the said weighers of merchandise, any statute, act, ordinance, or other thing whatsoever to the contrary notwithstanding.

And because in so remote a country, and situate near so many barbarous nations, the incursions as well of the savages themselves, as of other enemies, pirates, and robbers, may probably be feared, therefore we have given, and for us, our heirs and successors, do give power by these Presents, unto the said now Lord Baltimore, his heirs and assigns, by themselves or their captains, or other their officers to levy, muster, and train all sorts of men, of what condition or wheresoever born, in the said province of Maryland, for the time being, and to make war, and pursue the enemies, robbers, aforesaid, as well by sea as by land, yea, even without the limits of the said province, and (by God's assistance) to vanquish and take them; and being taken, to put them to death, by the law of war, or to save them, at their pleasure; and to all and every other thing which unto the charge and office of a captain-general of an army belongeth, or hath accustomed to belong, as fully and freely as any captain-general of an army hath ever had the same.

Also, our will and pleasure is, and by this our charter, we do give unto the said now Lord Baltimore, his heirs and assigns, full power, liberty and authority, in case of rebellion, tumult or sedition, if any should happen (which God forbid) either upon the land, within the province aforesaid, or upon the main sea, in making a voyage thither, or returning from thence by themselves, or their captains, deputies, or other officers, to be authorized under their seals for that purpose (to whom we also, for us, our heirs and successors, do give and grant by these presents, full power and authority), to exercise martial law against mutinous and seditious persons of those parts, such as shall refuse to submit themselves to his or their government, or shall refuse to serve in the wars, or shall fly to the enemy, or forsake their ensigns, or be loiterers, or stragglers, or otherwise however offending against the law, custom, and discipline military, as freely and in as ample manner and form as a captain-general of any army, by virtue of his office, might, or hath accustomed to use the same.

Furthermore, that the way to honors and dignities may not seem to be altogether precluded and shut up to men well-born, and such as shall prepare themselves unto this present plantation, and shall desire to deserve well of us and our kingdoms, both in peace and war, in so far distant and remote a country, Therefore we, for us, our heirs and successors, do give free and absolute power unto the said now Lord Baltimore, his heirs and assigns, to confer favors, rewards and honors, upon such inhabitants, within the province aforesaid, as shall deserve the same, to invest them with titles and dignities soever as he shall think fit (so as they be not such as are now used in England), as like to erect and incorporate towns into boroughs, and boroughs into cities, with convenient privileges and immunities, according to the merit of the inhabitants, and fitness of the places, and to do all and every other thing or things touching the premises, which to him and them shall seem meet and requisite; albeit they be such as of their own nature might otherwise require a more special commandment and warrant than in these presents is expressed.

We will also, and by these presents for us, our heirs and successors, do give and grant license, by this our charter, unto the said now Lord Baltimore, his heirs and assigns, and to all the inhabitants and dwellers in the said province aforesaid, both present and to come, to import, unlade, by themselves or their servants, factors or assigns, all merchandises and goods whatsoever, that shall arise of the fruits and commodities of the said province, either by sea or land, into any of the ports of us, our heirs and successors, in our kingdoms of England or Ireland, or otherwise to dispose of the said goods, in the said ports, and if need be, within one year next after unlading the same, to lade the same merchandise and goods again into the same or other ships, and export the same into any other countries either of our dominion or foreign (being in amity with us, heirs and successors). Provided always that they pay such customs, impositions, subsidies, and duties, for the same, to us, our heirs and successors, as the rest of our subjects of our kingdom of England, for the time being, shall be bound to pay; beyond which, we will not that the inhabitants of the aforesaid province of Maryland shall be any charged.

And furthermore, of our ample and special grace, certain knowledge, and mere motion, we do, for us, our heirs and successors, grant unto the said now Lord Baltimore, his heirs and assigns, full and absolute power and authority to make, erect, and constitute, within the said province of Maryland, the isles and islets aforesaid, such and so many seaports, harbors, creeks, and other places, for discharging and unlading of goods and merchandises out of ships, boats and other vessels, and lading them in such and so many places, and with such rights, jurisdictions, and liberties, and privileges unto the said ports belonging, as to him or them shall seem most expedient; and that all and singular the ships, boats and other vessels, which shall come for merchandise and trade into the said province, or out of the same shall depart, shall be laden or unladen only at such ports as shall be so erected and constituted by the said now Lord Baltimore, his heirs and assigns, any use, custom, or other things to the contrary notwithstanding; saving always unto us, our heirs and successors, and to all the subjects (of our kingdoms of England and Ireland) of us, our heirs and successors, free liberty of fishing for sea fish, as well in the sea, bays, inlets, and navigable rivers, as in the harbors, bays, and creeks of the province aforesaid, and the privileges of salting and drying their fish on the shore of the said province, and for the same cause, to cut and take underwood and twigs there growing, and to build cottages and sheds necessary in this behalf, as they heretofore have or might reasonably have used; which liberties and privileges, nevertheless, the subjects aforesaid of us, our heirs and successors, shall enjoy without any notable damage or injury to be done to the said now Lord Baltimore, his heirs and assigns, or to the dwellers and inhabitants of the said province, in the ports, creeks, and shores aforesaid, and especially in the woods and copses growing within the said province. And if any shall do any such damage or injury, he shall incur the heavy displeasure of us, our heirs and successors, the punishment of the laws, and shall moreover make satisfaction.

We do furthermore will, appoint, and ordain, and by these presents, for us, our heirs and successors, we do grant unto the said now Lord Baltimore, his heirs and assigns, that he, the said Lord Baltimore, his heirs and assigns, may from time to time, forever, have and enjoy the customs and subsidies in the ports, harbors, and other creeks and places aforesaid, within the province aforesaid, payable or due for merchandises or wares thereto laded or unladed : the said customs and subsidies to be reasonably assessed (upon any occasion) by themselves and the people there as aforesaid, to whom we give power, by these presents, for us, our heirs and successors, upon just cause and in a due proportion, to assess and impose the same.

And further, of special grace, certain knowledge, and mere motion, we have given and granted, and by these presents, for us, our heirs and successors, do give and grant, unto the said now Lord Baltimore, his heirs and assigns, full and absolute power, license, and authority, that he, the said now Lord Baltimore, his heirs and assigns, from time to time hereafter, for ever, at his and their will and pleasure, may assign, alien, grant, demise, or enfeoffe of the premises, so many and such parts and parcels to him or them that shall be willing to purchase the same, as they shall think fit; to have and to hold to them the said person or persons willing to take or purchase the same, their heirs and assigns, in fee simple, or in fee tail, or for the term of life or lives, or years, to be held of the said now Lord Baltimore, his heirs and assigns, by such services, customs, and rents, as shall seem fit to the said now Lord Baltimore, his heirs and assigns, and not immediately of us, our heirs and successors: And to the same person or persons, and to all and every of them, we do give and grant, by these presents, for us, our heirs and successors, license, authority and power, that such person or persons may take the premises, or any parcel thereof, of the said now Lord Baltimore, his heirs or assigns (in what estate of inheritance soever, in fee simple, or in fee tail, or otherwise, as to them and the now Lord Baltimore, his heirs and assigns, shall seem expedient); the statute made in the parliament of Edward, son of King Henry, late King of England, our predecessor, commonly called the statute *Quia emptores tenarum*, lately published in our kingdom of England, or any other statute, act, ordinance, use, law, or custom, or any other thing cause or matter thereupon heretofore had, done, published, ordained or provided to the contrary, in any wise notwithstanding.

And by these presents, we give and grant license unto the said now Lord Baltimore and his heirs, to erect any parcels of land within the province aforesaid into manors, in every the said manors to have and hold a court of Baron, with all things whatsoever which to a court Baron do belong, and to have and hold view of frank-pledge (for the conservation of the peace, and the better government of those parts), by themselves, or their stewards, or by the lords, for the time being, of other manors to be deputed, when they shall be erected, and in the same to use all things belonging to view of frank-pledge.

And further, our pleasure is, and by these presents, for us, our heirs and successors, we do covenant and grant to and with the said now Lord Baltimore, and his heirs and assigns, that we, our heirs and successors, shall at no time hereafter set or make, or cause to set any imposition, custom, or other taxation, rate, or contribution whatsoever, in and upon the dwellers and inhabitants of the aforesaid province, for their lands, tenements, goods, or chattels within the said province, or in or upon any goods or merchandise within the said province, or to be laden or unladen within the ports or harbors of the said province. And our pleasure is, and for us, our heirs and successors, we charge and command, that this our declaration shall henceforward, from time to time, be received and allowed in all our courts, and before all the judges of us, our heirs and successors, for a sufficient and lawful discharge, payment and acquittance; commanding all and singular our officers and ministers of us, our heirs and successors, and enjoining them, upon pain of our high displeasure, that they do not presume, at any time, to attempt anything to the contrary of the premises, or that they do in any sort withstand the same; but that they be at all times aiding and assisting, as fitting, unto the said now Lord Baltimore, and his heirs, and to the inhabitants and merchants of Maryland aforesaid, their servants, ministers, factors and assigns, in the full use and fruition of the benefit of this our charter.

And further, our pleasure is, and by these presents, for us, our heirs and successors, we do grant unto the said now Lord Baltimore, and his heirs and assigns, and to the tenants and inhabitants of the said province of Maryland, both present and to come, and to every of them, that the said province, tenants, and inhabitants of the said colony or country, shall not from henceforth be held or reputed as a member, or as a part of Virginia, or of any other colony whatsoever, now transported or hereafter to be transported, nor shall be depending on, or subject to their government in anything, from whom we do separate that and them. And our pleasure is, by these presents, that they be separated, and that they be subject immediately to our crown of England, as depending thereof forever.

And if perchance hereafter it should happen any doubts or questions should arise concerning the true sense and understanding of any word, clause or sentence contained in this our present charter, we will, ordain and command, that at all times, and in all things, such interpretations be made thereof and allowed, in any of our courts whatsoever, as shall be adjudged most advantageous and favorable unto the said now Lord Baltimore, his heirs and assigns; provided always, that no interpretation be admitted thereof, by which God's holy and truly Christian religion, or the allegiance due unto us, our heirs and successors, may suffer any prejudice or diminution; although express mention be not made in these presents of the true yearly value of certainty of the premises, or of any part thereof, or of other gifts and grants made by us, our progenitors or predecessors, unto the said now Lord Baltimore, or any statute, act, ordinance, provision, proclamation, or restraint heretofore had, made, published, ordained, or provided, or any other thing, cause, or matter whatsoever to the contrary thereof in any wise notwithstanding. In witness, etc., witness Ourself at Westminster, the twenty-eighth day of June, A.D., 1632, in the eighth year of our reign.

By Writ of Privy Seal.

FUNDAMENTAL ORDERS OF CONNECTICUT—1639.

THE towns in the Connecticut Valley, founded by the emigrants from Massachusetts, were governed for a time by persons acting under a commission from the Massachusetts General Court; but in 1639 the towns of Windsor, Hartford and Wethersfield associated themselves under the following constitution, the "first in the series of written American constitutions framed by the people for the people." "Equal laws were the basis of their commonwealth; and therefore its foundations were lasting." (Bancroft.) This, with such slight changes in its practical provision as the increase of population demanded, was the fundamental law of Connecticut for nearly two centuries.

Consult *Bancroft's Hist. U. S.*, 1st ed., I., 402; cen. ed., I., 318; last ed., I., 270; *Palfrey's Hist., N. E.*, I., 535; *Hildreth's U. S.*, I., 261; *Bryant and Gay's U. S.*, II., 23.

FUNDAMENTAL ORDERS OF CONNECTICUT—1638–'39.

FORASMUCH as it hath pleased the Allmighty God by the wise disposition of his diuyne pruidence so to Order and dispose of things that we the Inhabitants and Residents of Windsor, Harteford and Wethersfield are now cohabiting and dwelling in and vppon the River of Conectecotte and the Lands thereunto adioyneing; And well knowing where a people are gathered togather the word of God requires that to mayntayne the peace and vnion of such a people there should be an orderly and decent Gouerment established according to God, to order and dispose of the affayres of the people at all seasons as occation shall require; doe therefore assotiate and conioyne our selues to be as one Publike State or Commonwelth; and doe, for our selues and our Successors and such as shall be adioyned to vs att any tyme hereafter, enter into Combination and Confederation togather, to mayntayne and presearue the liberty and purity of the gospell of our Lord Jesus which we now professe, as also the disciplyne of the Churches, which according to the truth of the said gospell is now practised amongst vs; As also in our Ciuell Affaires to be guided and gouerned according to such Lawes, Rules, Orders and decrees as shall be made, ordered & decreed, as followeth:—

1. It is Ordered, sentenced and decreed, that there shall be yerely two generall Assemblies or Courts, the first on the second thursday in Aprill, the other the second thursday in September, following; the first shall be called the Courte of Election, wherein shall be yerely Chosen from tyme to tyme soe many Magestrats and other publike Officers as shall be found requisitte: Whereof one to be chosen Gouernour for the yeare ensueing and vntill another be chosen, and noe other Magestrate to be chosen for more then one yeare; pruided allwayes there be sixe chosen besids the Gouernour; which being chosen and sworne according to an Oath recorded for that purpose shall haue power to administer iustice according to the Lawes here established, and for want thereof according to the rule of the word of God; which choise shall be made by all that are admitted freemen and haue taken the Oath of Fidellity, and doe cohabitte within this Jurisdiction, (hauing beene admitted Inhabitants by the maior part of the Towne wherein they liue,) or the mayor parte of such as shall be then present.

2. It is Ordered, sentenced and decreed, that the Election of the aforesaid Magestrats shall be on this manner: euery person present and quallified for choyse shall bring in (to the persons deputed to receaue them) one single paper with the name of him written in yt whom he desires to haue Gouernour, and he that hath the greatest number of papers shall be Gouernor for that yeare. And the rest of the Magestrats or publike Officers to be chosen in this manner: The Secretary for the tyme being shall first read the names of all that are to be put to choise and then shall seuerally nominate them distinctly, and euery one that would haue the person nominated to be chosen shall bring in one single paper written vppon, and he that would not haue him chosen shall bring in a blanke: and euery one that hath more written papers then blanks shall be a Magistrat for that yeare; which papers shall be receaued and told by one or more that shall be then chosen by the court and sworne to be faythfull therein; but in case there should not be sixe chosen as aforesaid, besids the Gouernor, out of those which are nominated, then he or they which haue the most written papers shall be a Magestrate or Magestrats for the ensueing yeare, to make vp the foresaid number.

3. It is Ordered, sentenced and decreed, that the Secretary shall not nominate any person, nor shall any person be chosen newly into the Magestracy which was not propownded in some Generall Courte before, to be nominated the next Election; and to that end yt shall be lawfull for ech of the Townes aforesaid by their deputyes to nominate any two whom they conceaue fitte to be put to election; and the Courte may ad so many more as they iudge requisitt.

4. It is Ordered, sentenced and decreed that noe person be chosen Gouernor aboue once in two yeares, and that the Gouernor be always a member of some approved congregation, and formerly of the Magestracy within this Jurisdiction; and all the Magestrats Freemen of this

Commonwelth: and that no Magestrate or other publike officer shall execute any parte of his or their Office before they are seuerally sworne, which shall be done in the face of the Courte if they be present, and in case of absence by some deputed for that purpose.

5. It is Ordered, sentenced and decreed, that to the aforesaid Courte of Election the severall Townes shall send their deputyes, and when the Elections are ended they may proceed in any publike searuice as at other Courts. Also the other Generall Courte in September shall be for makeing of lawes, and any other publike occation, which conserns the good of the Commonwelth.

6. It is Ordered, sentenced and decreed, that the Gouernor shall, ether by himselfe or by the secretary, send out summons to the Constables of eur Towne for the cauleing of these two standing Courts, on month at lest before their seuerall tymes: And also if the Gouernor and the gretest parte of the Magestrats see cause vppon any spetiall occation to call a generall Courte, they may giue order to the secretary soe to doe within fowerteene dayes warneing; and if vrgent necessity so require, vppon a shorter notice, giueing sufficient grownds for yt to the deputyes when they meete, or els be questioned for the same; And if the Gouernor and Mayor parte of Magestrats shall ether neglect or refuse to call the two Generall standing Courts or ether of them, as also at other tymes when the occations of the Commonwelth require, the Freemen thereof, or the Mayor parte of them, shall petition to them soe to doe: if then yt be ether denyed or neglected the said Freemen or the Mayor parte of them shall haue power to giue order to the Constables of the seuerall Townes to doe the same, and so may meete togather, and chuse to themselues a Moderator, and may proceed to do any Acte of power, which any other Generall Courte may.

7. It is Ordered, sentenced and decreed that after there are warrants giuen out for any of the said Generall

Courts, the Constable or Constables of ech Towne shall forthwith give notice distinctly to the inhabitants of the same, in some Publike Assembly or by goeing or sending from howse to howse, that at a place and tyme by him or them lymited and sett, they meet and assemble them selues togather to elect and chuse certen deputyes to be att the Generall Courte then following to agitate the afayres of the commonwelth; which said Deputyes shall be chosen by all that are admitted Inhabitants in the seuerall Townes and haue taken the oath of fidellity; prouided that non be chosen a Deputy for any Generall Courte which is not a Freeman of this Commonwelth.

The foresaid deputyes shall be chosen in manner following: euery person that is present and quallified as before expressed, shall bring the names of such, written in seuerall papers, as they desire to haue chosen for that Imployment, and these 3 or 4, more or lesse, being the number agreed on to be chosen for that tyme, that haue greatest number of papers written for them shall be deputyes for that Courte; whose names shall be endorsed on the backe side of the warrant and returned into the Courte, with the Constable or Constables hand vnto the same.

8. It is Ordered, sentenced and decreed, that Wyndsor, Hartford and Wethersfield shall haue power, ech Towne, to send fower of their freemen as deputyes to euery Generall Courte; and whatsoeuer other Townes shall be hereafter added to this Jurisdiction, they shall send so many deputyes as the Courte shall judge meete, a resonable proportion to the number of Freemen that are in the said Townes being to be attended therein; which deputyes shall have the power of the whole Towne to giue their voats and allowance to all such lawes and orders as may be for the publike good, and unto which the said Townes are to be bownd.

9. It is ordered and decreed, that the deputyes thus chosen shall haue power and liberty to appoynt a tyme

and a place of meeting togather before any Generall Courte to aduise and consult of all such things as may concerne the good of the publike, as also to examine their owne Elections, whether according to the order, and if they or the gretest parte of them find any election to be illegall they may seclud such for present from their meeting, and returne the same and their resons to the Courte; and if yt proue true, the Courte may fyne the party or partyes so intruding and the Towne, if they see cause, and giue out a warrant to goe to a newe election in a legall way, either in parte or in whole. Also the said deputyes shall haue power to fyne any that shall be disorderly at their meetings, or for not coming in due tyme or place according to appoyntment; and they may returne the said fynes into the Courte if yt be refused to be paid, and the tresurer to take notice of yt, and to estreete or levy the same as he doth other fynes.

10. It is Ordered, sentenced and decreed, that euery Generall Courte, except such as through neglecte of the Gouernor and the greatest parte of Magestrats the Freemen themselves doe call, shall consist of the Gouernor, or some one chosen to moderate the Court, and 4 other Magestrats at lest, with the mayor parte of the deputyes of the seuerall Townes legally chosen; and in case the Freemen or mayor parte of them through neglect or refusall of the Gouernor and mayor parte of the magestrats, shall call a Courte, yt shall consist of the mayor parte of Freemen that are present or their deputyes, with a moderator chosen by them. In which said Generall Courts shall consist the supreme power of the commonwelth, and they only shall haue power to make laws or repeale them, to graunt leuyes, to admitt of Freemen, dispose of lands vndisposed of, to seuerall Townes or persons, and also shall haue power to call ether Courte or Magestrate or any other person whatsoeuer into question for any misdemeanour, and may for just causes displace or deale otherwise according to the nature of the

offence; and also may deale in any other matter that concerns the good of this common welth, excepte election of Magestrats, which shall be done by the whole boddy of Freemen.

In which Courte the Gouernour or Moderator shall haue power to order the Courte to giue liberty of speech, and silence vnceasonable and disorderly speakeings, to put all things to voate, and in case the vote be equall to haue the casting voice. But non of these Courts shall be adiorned or dissolued without the consent of the maior parte of the Court.

11. It is ordered, sentenced and decreed, that when any Generall Courte vppon the occations of the commonwelth haue agreed vppon any summe or sommes of mony to be leuyed vppon the seuerall Townes within this Jurisdiction, that a Committee be chosen to sett out and appoynt with shall be the proportion of euery Towne to pay of the said leuy, provided the Committees be made vp of an equall number out of each Towne.

14th January, 1638, the 11 Orders abouesaid are voted.

THE NEW ENGLAND CONFEDERATION.

NEED of protection against the Dutch and Indians led to the formation of this league. The first suggestion came from Connecticut as early as 1637 but the scheme did not assume definite shape until 1643. The articles of confederation were signed by commissioners from Massachusetts Bay, Connecticut and New Haven, May 19, 1643, while Plymouth gave her assent later, after submitting the articles to the approval of the people. The league under the official designation of "The United Colonies of New England" embraced the four colonies of Massachusetts Bay, Plymouth, Connecticut and New Haven, with a population of 24,000 in 39 towns. (Frothingham.) Rhode Island was refused admission. "A great principle was at the bottom of the confederation; but, noble as were the aims of those who handled it, they had not yet attained to sufficient breadth of view to apply it even to the whole of New England." (Frothingham.)

The incorporation of New Haven with Connecticut by the royal charter of 1662 destroyed the balance of power in the confederation and "of the brave confederacy of the Four Colonies only the shadow of a great name was left." (Palfrey.) The last meeting was held at Hartford Sept. 5, 1684. It has been suggested at the idea of this union was derived from the confederacy of the Low Countries.

According to the Tory historian Chalmers, this confederation "offers the first example of collition in colonial story and showed to party leaders in after times the advantages of concert."

Two copies of the acts of the commissioners of the United Colonies are extant, the Connecticut copy, quite complete, now at Hartford, and the Plymouth, slightly incomplete, now at Massachusetts State House. These proceedings have been printed from the Plymouth copy with additions from the Connecticut copy, constituting vols. 9 and 10 of Records of the Plymouth Colony, and the Plymouth copy is also printed in vol. 2 of Hazard's Historical Collections.

A list of the various commissioners may be found in Palfrey's Hist. of N. E., and a full list of meetings is given in Frothingham's Rise, 63, note.

Consult *Palfrey's Hist. New England*, I., 623; et seq. *Bancroft's Hist. U. S.*, 1st ed. I., 420; cen. ed. I., 340; last ed. I., 289; *Hildreth's Hist. U. S.*, I, 285; *Barry's Hist. Mass.*, 1st period, 318; *J. S. Adam's Historical Address*, Mass. Hist. Soc. Coll. 3d series, vol. ix. *Frothingham's Republic U. S.*, 39; *Bryant and Gay's Hist. U. S.*, II., 49; *Chalmers' Political Annals*, 177.

ARTICLES OF CONFEDERATION.

Betweene the plantations vnder the Gouernment of the Massachusetts, the Plantacons vnder the Gouernment of New Plymouth, the Plantacons vnder the Gouern ment of Connectacutt, and the Gouernment of New Haven with the Plantacons in combinacon therewith.

WHEREAS wee all came into these parts of America with one and the same end and ayme, namely, to advaunce the kingdome of our Lord Jesus Christ, and to enjoy the liberties of the Gospell in puritie with peace. And whereas in our settleinge (by a wise Providence of God) we are further dispersed vpon the Sea Coasts and Riuers then was at first intended, so that we cannot according to our desire, with convenience communicate in one Gouernment and Jurisdiccon. And whereas we live encompassed with people of seuerall Nations and strang languages which heareafter may proue injurious to vs or our posteritie. And forasmuch as the Natives have formerly committed sondry insolences and outrages vpon seueral Plantacons of the English and have of late combined themselues against vs. And seing by reason of those sad Distraccons in England, which they have heard of, and by which they know we are hindred from that humble way of seekinge advise or reapeing those comfortable fruits of protection which at other tymes we might well expecte. Wee therefore doe conceiue it our bounden Dutye without delay to enter into a present consotiation amongst our selues for mutual help and strength in all our future concernements: That as in Nation and Religion, so in other Respects we bee and continue one according to the tenor and true meaninge of the ensuing Articles: Wherefore it is fully agreed and concluded by and betweene the parties or Jurisdiccons aboue named, and they joyntly and seuerally doe by these presents agreed and concluded that they all bee, and henceforth bee called by the Name of the United Colonies of New-England.

II. The said United Colonies, for themselues and their posterities, do joyntly and seuerally, hereby enter into a firme and perpetuall league of friendship and amytie, for offence and defence, mutuall advise and succour, vpon all just occations, both for preserueing and propagateing the truth and liberties of the Gospel, and for their owne mutuall safety and wellfare.

III. It is futher agreed That the Plantacons which at present are or hereafter shalbe settled within the limmetts of the Massachusetts, shalbe forever vnder the Massachusetts, and shall have peculiar Jurisdiccon among themselues in all cases as an entire Body, and that Plymouth, Conneckt acutt, and New Haven shall eich of them haue like peculier Jurisdiccon and Gouernment within their limmetts and in referrence to the Plantacons which already are settled or shall hereafter be erected or shall settle within their limmetts respectiuely; prouided that no other Jurisdiccon shall hereafter be taken in as a distinct head or member of this Confederacon, nor shall any other Plantacon or Jurisdiccon in present being and not already in combynacon or vnder the Jurisdiccon of any of these Confederats be received by any of them, nor shall any two of the Confederats joyne in one Jurisdiccon without consent of the rest, which consent to be interpreted as is expressed in the sixth Article ensuinge.

IV. It is by these Confederats agreed that the charge of all just warrs, whether offensiue or defensiue, upon what part or member of this Confederaccon soever they fall, shall both in men and provisions, and all other Disbursements, be borne by all the parts of this Confederacon, in different proporcons according to their different abilitie, in manner following, namely, that the Commissioners for eich Jurisdiccon from tyme to tyme, as there shalbe occation, bring a true account and number of all the males in every Plantacon, or any way belonging to, or under their seuerall Jurisdiccons, of what quality or condicion soeuer they bee, from sixteene yeares old to threescore, being Inhabitants there. And That according to the different numbers which from tyme to tyme shalbe found in eich Jurisdiccon, upon a true and just account, the service of men and all charges of the warr be borne by the Poll: Eich Jurisdiccon, or Plantacon, being left to their owne just course and custome of rating themselues and people according to their different estates, with due respects to their qualites and exemptions among themselues, though the Confederacon take no notice of any such priviledg: And that according to their differrent charge of eich Jurisdiccon and Plantacon, the whole advantage of the warr (if it please God to bless their Endeavours) whether it be in lands, goods or persons, shall be proportionably deuided among the said Confederats.

V. It is further agreed That if any of these Jurisdiccons, or any Plantacons vnder it, or in any combynacon with them be envaded by any enemie whomsoeuer, vpon notice and request of any three majestrats of that Jurisdiccon so invaded, the rest of the Confederates, without any further meeting or expostulacon, shall forthwith send ayde to the Confederate in danger, but in different proporcons; namely, the Massachusetts an hundred men sufficiently armed and provided for such a service and jorney, and eich of the rest fourty-fiue so armed and provided, or any lesse number, if lesse be required, according to this proporcon. But if such Confederate in danger may be supplyed by their next Confederate, not exceeding the number hereby agreed, they may craue help there, and seeke no further for the present. The charge to be borne as in this Article is exprest: And, at the returne, to be victualled and supplyed with poder and shott for their journey (if there be neede) by that Jurisdiccon which employed or sent for them: But none of the Jurisdiccons to exceed these numbers till by a meeting of the Commissioners for this Confederacon a greater ayd appeare necessary. And this proporcon to continue, till upon knowledge of greater numbers in eich Jurisdiccon which shalbe brought to the next meeting some other proporcon be ordered. But in any such case of sending men for present ayd whether before or after such order or alteracon, it is agreed that at the meeting of the Commissioners for this Confederacon, the cause of such warr or invasion be duly considered: And if it appeare that the fault lay in the parties so invaded, that then that Jurisdiccon or Plantacon make just Satisfaccon, both to the Invaders whom they have injured, and beare all the charges of the warr themselves without requireing any allowance from the rest of the Confederats towards the same. And further, that if any Jurisdiccon see any danger of any Invasion approaching, and there be tyme for a meeting, that in such case three majestrats of that Jurisdiccon may summon a meeting at such convenyent place as themselues shall think meete, to consider and provide against the threatned danger, Provided when they are met they may remoue to what place they please, Onely whilst any of these foure Confederats have but three majestrats in their Jurisdiccon, their request or summons from any two of them shalbe accounted of equall force with the three mentoned in both the clauses of this Article, till there be an increase of majestrats there.

VI. It is also agreed that for the mannaging and concluding of all affairs proper and concerneing the whole Confederacon, two Commissioners shalbe chosen by and out of eich of these foure Jurisdiccons, namely, two for the Mattachusetts, two for Plymouth, two for Connectacutt and two for New Haven; being all in Church fellowship with us, which shall bring full power from their seuerall generall Courts respectively to heare, examine, weigh and determine all affaires of our warr or peace, leagues, ayds, charges and numbers of men for warr, divission of spoyles and whatsoever is gotten by conquest, receiueing of more Confederats for plantacons into combinacon with any of the Confederates, and all thinges of like nature which are the proper concomitants or consequence of such a confederacon, for amytie, offence and defence, not intermeddleing with the gouernment of any of the Jurisdiccons which by the third Article is preserued entirely to themselves. But if these eight Commissioners, when they meete, shall not all agree, yet it is concluded that any six of the eight agreeing shall have power to settle and determine the business in question: But if six do not agree, that then such proposicons with their reasons, so farr as they have beene debated, be sent and referred to the foure generall Courts, vizt. the Mattachusetts, Plymouth, Connectacutt, and New Haven: And if at all the said Generall Courts the businesse so referred be concluded, then to bee prosecuted by the Confederates and all their members. It is further agreed that these eight Commissioners shall meete once every yeare, besides extraordinary meetings (according to the fift Article) to consider, treate and conclude of all affaires belonging to this Confederacon, which meeting shall ever be the first Thursday in September. And that the next meeting after the date of these presents, which shalbe accounted the second meeting, shalbe at Bostone in the Massachusetts, the third at Hartford, the fourth at New Haven, the fift at Plymouth, the sixt and seaventh at Bostone. And then Hartford, New Haven and Plymouth, and so in course successiuely, if in the meane tyme some middle place be not found out and agreed on which may be commodious for all the jurisdiccons.

VII. It is further agreed that at eich meeting of these eight Commissioners, whether ordinary or extraordinary, they, or six of them agreeing, as before, may choose their President out of themselues, whose office and worke shalbe to take care and direct for order and a comely carrying on of all proceedings in the present meeting. But he shalbe invested with no such power or respect as by which he shall hinder the propounding or progresse of any businesse, or any way cast the Scales, otherwise then in the precedent Article is agreed.

VIII. It is also agreed that the Commissioners for this Confederacon hereafter at their meetings, whether ordinary or extraordinary, as they may have commission or opertunitie, do endeavoure to frame and establish agreements and orders in generall cases of a civill nature wherein all the plantacons are interested for preserving peace among themselues, and preventing as much as may bee all occations of warr or difference with others, as about the free and speedy passage of Justice in every Jurisdiccon, to all the Confederats equally as their owne, receiving those that remoue from one plantacon to another without due certefycats; how all the Jurisdiccons may carry it towards the Indians, that they neither grow insolent nor be injured without due satisfaccion, lest warr break in vpon the Confederates through such miscarryage. It is also agreed that if any servant runn away from his master into any other of these confederated Jurisdiccons, That in such Case, vpon the Certyficate of one Majistrate in the Jurisdiccon out of which the said servant fled, or upon other due proofe, the said servant shalbe deliuered either to his Master or any other that pursues and brings such Certificate or proofe. And that vpon the escape of any prisoner whatsoever or fugitiue for any criminal cause, whether breaking prison or getting from the officer or otherwise escaping, upon the certificate of two Majistrats of the Jurisdiccon out of which the escape is made that he was a prisoner or such an offender at the tyme of the escape. The Majestrates or some of them of that Jurisdiccon where for the present the said prisoner or fugitive abideth shall forthwith graunt such a warrant as the case will beare for the apprehending of any such person, and the delivery of him into the hands of the officer or other person that pursues him. And if there be help required for the safe returneing of any such offender, then it shalbe graunted to him that craves the same, he paying the charges thereof.

IX. And for that the justest warrs may be of dangerous consequence, espetially to the smaler plantacons in these vnited Colonies, It is agreed that neither the Massachusetts, Plymouth, Connectacutt nor New-Haven, nor any of the members of any of them shall at any tyme hereafter begin, undertake, or engage themselues or this Confederacon, or any part thereof in any warr whatsoever (sudden exegents with the necessary consequents thereof excepted) which are also to be moderated as much as the case will permit) without the consent and agreement of the forenamed eight Commissioners, or at least six of them, as in the sixt Article is provided: And that no charge be required of any of the Confederats in case of a defensiue warr till the said Commissioners haue mett and approued the justice of the warr, and have agreed vpon the sum of money to be levyed, which sum is then to be payd by the severall Confederates in proporcon according to the fourth Article.

X. That in extraordinary occations when meetings are summoned by three Majistrats of any Jurisdiccon, or two as in the fift Article, If any of the Commissioners come not, due warneing being given or sent, It is agreed that foure of the Commissioners shall have power to direct a warr which cannot be delayed and to send for due proporcons of men out of eich Jurisdiccon, as well as six might doe if all mett; but not less than six shall determine the justice of the warr or allow the demanude of bills of charges or cause any levies to be made for the same.

XI. It is further agreed that if any of the Confederates shall hereafter break any of these present Articles, or be any other wayes injurious to any one of thother Jurisdiccons, such breach of Agreement, or injurie, shalbe duly considered and ordered by the Commissioners for thother Jurisdiccons, that both peace and this present Confederacon may be entirely preserued without violation.

XII. Lastly, this perpetuall Confederacon and the several Articles and Agreements thereof being read and seriously considered, both by the Generall Court for the Massachusetts, and by the Commissioners for Plymouth, Connectacutt and New Haven, were fully allowed and confirmed by three of the forenamed Confederates, namely, the Massachusetts, Connectacutt and New-Haven, Onely the Commissioners for Plymouth, having no Commission to conclude, desired respite till they might advise with their Generall Court, wherevpon it was agreed and concluded by the said court of the Massachusetts, and the Commissioners for the other two Confederates, That if Plymouth Consent, then the whole treaty as it stands in these present articles is and shall continue firme and stable without alteracon: But if Plymouth come not in, yet the other three Confederates doe by these presents confirme the whole Confederacon and all the Articles thereof, onely, in September next, when the second meeting of the Commissioners is to be at Bostone, new consideracon may be taken of the sixt Article, which concernes number of Commissioners for meeting and concluding the affaires of this Confederacon to the satisfaccon of the court of the Massachusetts, and the Commissioners for thother two Confederates, but the rest to stand vnquestioned.

In testymony whereof, the Generall Court of the Massachusetts by their Secretary, and the Commissioners for Connectacutt and New-Haven haue subscribed these presente articles, this xixth of the third month, commonly called May, Anno Domini, 1643.

At a Meeting of the Commissioners for the Confederacon, held at Boston, the Seaventh of September. It appeareing that the Generall Court of New Plymouth, and the severall Towneships thereof have read, considered and approoued these articles of Confederacon, as appeareth by Comission from their Generall Court beareing Date the xxixth of August, 1643, to Mr. Edward Winslowe and Mr. Will Collyer, to ratifye and confirme the same on their behalf, wee therefore, the Comissioners for the Mattachusetts, Conecktacutt and New Haven, doe also for our seuerall Gouernments, subscribe vnto them.

JOHN WINTHROP, GOVERNOR OF MASSACHUSETTS,
THO. DUDLEY, THEOPH. EATON,
GEO. FENWICK, EDWA. HOPKINS,
THOMAS GREGSON.

CHARTER OF CONNECTICUT—1662.

On the accession of Chas. II. Connecticut appointed John Winthrop, one of the first settlers, her agent to solicit from the king a royal charter. His mission was successful and the patent was sealed April 20, 1662. This charter was remarkable for its liberality—"all that Massachusetts had given displeasure by claiming for herself was now expressly allowed to the new colony." (Palfrey.) "It confirmed to the colonists the unqualified power to govern themselves, which they had assumed from the beginning. Nothing was changed in their internal administration, nor in their relation to the crown." "The king, far from reserving a negative on their laws, did not even require that they should be transmitted for his inspection; and no provision was made for the interference of the English government in any event whatever. Connecticut was independent except in name." (Bancroft.)

In commenting on the charters of Connecticut and R. I., the tory historian Chalmers remarks: "Thus was established in R. I. and Ct. a mere democracy, or rule of the people. Every power, as well deliberative as active, was invested in the freemen of the corporation or their delegates; and the supreme executive magistrate of the empire, by an inattention which does little honour to the statesmen of those days, was wholly excluded." During the administration of Sir Edmund Adros the charter government was suspended, but on his overthrow it was re-established and the charter was not abrogated by a state constitution till 1818.

Consult *Palfrey's N. E.* II., 540; *Chalmers' Political Annals*, 293; *Bancroft's U. S.*, 1st ed. II., 54; Cen. ed. I., 421; last ed., I., 358; *Hildreth's U. S.*, I., 456; *Bryant and Gay's U. S.*, II., 255.

CHARTER OF CONNECTICUT—1662.

CHARLES the Second, by the Grace of GOD, KING of *England*, *Scotland*, *France*, and *Ireland*, Defender of the Faith, etc. To all to whom these Presents shall come, GREETING.

Whereas by the several Navigations, Discoveries, and Successful Plantations of divers of Our loving Subjects of this Our Realm of England, *several Lands, Islands, Places, Colonies, and Plantations have been obtained and settled in that Part of the Continent of* America *called* New-England, *and thereby the Trade and Commerce there, hath been of late Years much increased: And whereas We have been informed by the humble Petition of our Trusty and Well beloved* John Winthrop, John Mason, Samuel Wyllys, Henry Clarke, Matthew Allyn, John Tapping, Nathan Gold, Richard Treat, Richard Lord, Henry Wolcott, John Talcott, Daniel Clarke, John Ogden, Thomas Wells, Obadiah Bruen, John Clarke, Anthony Hawkins, John Deming, *and* Matthew Camfield, *being Persons principally interested in Our Colony or Plantation of* Connecticut, *in* New-England, *that the same Colony, or the greatest part thereof, was Purchased and obtained for great and valuable Considerations, and some other Part thereof gained by Conquest, and with much difficulty, and at the only Endeavors, Expence, and Charges of them and their Associates, and those under whom they Claim, Subdued, and Improved, and thereby become a considerable Enlargement and Addition of Our Dominions and Interest there.* Now Know Ye, That in Consideration thereof, and in Regard the said Colony is remote from other the *English* Plantations in the Places aforesaid, and to the End the Affairs and Business which shall from Time to Time happen or arise concerning the same, may be duly Ordered and Managed, we have thought fit, and at the humble Petition of the Persons aforesaid, and are graciously Pleased to create and make them a Body Politick and Corporate, with the Powers and Privileges herein after mentioned; and accordingly Our Will and Pleasure is, and of our especial Grace, certain Knowledge, and meer Motion, We have ordained, constituted and declared, and by these Presents, for Us, Our Heirs and Successors, Do ordain, constitute and declare, that they the said *John Winthrop, John Mason, Samuel Wyllys, Henry Clarke, Matthew Allyn, John Tapping, Nathan Gold, Richard Treat, Richard Lord, Henry Wolcott, John Talcott, Daniel Clarke, John Ogden, Thomas Wells, Obadiah Bruen, John Clarke, Anthony Hawkins, John Deming*, and *Matthew Camfield*, and all such others as now are, or hereafter shall be admitted and made Free of the Company and Society of Our Colony of *Connetticut*, in *America*, shall from Time to Time, and for ever hereafter, be One Body Corporate and Politick, in Fact and Name, by the Name of, *Governor and Company of the* English *Colony of* Connecticut *in* New-England, *in* America; and that by the same Name they and their Successors shall and may have perpetual Succession, and shall and may be Persons able and capable in the Law, to plead and be impleaded, to answer and to be answered unto, to defend and be defended in all and singular Suits, Causes, Quarrels, Matters, actions, and

Things, of what Kind or Nature soever; and also to have, take, possess, acquire, and purchase Lands, Tenements, or Hereditaments, or any Goods, or Chattels, and the same to lease, grant, demise, alien, bargain, sell, and dispose of, as other Our liege People of this Our Realm of *England*, or any other Corporation or Body Politick within the same may lawfully do. And further, That the said Governor and Company, and their Successors, shall and may forever hereafter have a common Seal, to serve and use for all Causes, Matters, Things, and affairs whatsoever, of them and their Successors, and the same Seal, to alter, change, break, and make new from Time to Time, at their Wills and Pleasures, as they shall think fit. And further, We will and ordain, and by these Presents, for us, our Heirs and Successors, do declare and appoint, that for the better ordering and managing of the Affairs and Business of the said Company and their Successors, there shall be One Governor, One Deputy-Governor, and Twelve Assistants, to be from time to Time constituted, elected and chosen out of the Freemen of the said Company for the Time being, in such Manner and Form as hereafter in these Presents is expressed, which said Officers shall apply themselves to take Care for the best disposing and ordering of the general Business and affairs of and concerning the Land and Hereditaments herein after mentioned to be granted, and the Plantation thereof, and the Government of the People thereof: And for the better Execution of Our Royal Pleasure herein, We do, for Us, Our Heirs, and Successors, assign, name, constitute and appoint the aforesaid *John Winthrop* to be the first and present Governor of the said Company, and the said *John Mason*, to be the Deputy-Governor, and the said *Samuel Wyllys*, *Matthew Allyn*, *Nathan Gold*, *Henry Clarke*, *Richard Treat*, *John Ogden*, *John Tapping*, *John Talcott*, *Thomas Wells*, *Henry Wolcott*, *Richard Lord*, and *Daniel Clarke*, to be the Twelve present assistants of the said Company, to continue in the said several Offices respectively, until the second Thursday which shall be in the Month of *October* now next coming. And further We Will, and by these Presents for Us, Our Heirs, and Successors, Do ordain and grant, That the Governor of the said Company for the Time being, or in his Absence by occasion of Sickness, or otherwise by his Leave or Permission, the Deputy-Governor for the Time being, shall and may from Time to Time upon all Occasions, give Order for the assembling of the said Company, and calling them together to consult and advise of the Business and Affairs of the said Company, and that for ever hereafter, twice in every Year, *That is to say*, On every Second Thursday in *October*, and on every Second Thursday in *May*, or oftener in case it shall be requisite; the Assistants, and Freemen of the said Company, or such of them (not exceeding Two Persons from each Place, Town, or City) who shall be from Time to Time thereunto elected or deputed by the major Part of the Freemen of the respective Towns, Cities, and Places for which they shall be elected or deputed, shall have a General Meeting, or Assembly, then and there to consult and advise in and about the Affairs and Business of the said Company: and that the Governor, or in his Absence the Deputy-Governor of the said Company for the Time being, and such of the Assistants and Freemen of the said Company as shall be so elected or deputed, and be present at such Meeting or Assembly, or the greatest Number of them, whereof the Governor or Deputy-Governor, and Six of the Assistants at least, to be Seven, shall be called the General Assembly, and shall have full Power and authority to alter and change their Days and Times of Meeting, or General Assemblies, for electing the Governor, Deputy-Governor, and Assistants of other Officers, or any other Courts, Assemblies or Meetings, and to choose, nominate and appoint such and so many other Persons as they shall think fit, and shall be willing to accept the same, to be Free of the said Company and Body Politick, and them into the same to admit; And to elect and constitute such Officers as they shall think fit and requisite for the ordering, managing and disposing of the Affairs of the said Governor and Company, and their Successors: And we do hereby for Us, Our Heirs and Successors, establish and ordain, That once in the Year for ever hereafter, Namely, the said Second Thursday in *May*, the Governor, Deputy-Governor, and Assistants of the said Company, and other Officers of the said Company, or such of them as the said General Assembly shall think fit, shall be in the said General Court and Assembly to be held from that Day or Time, newly chosen for the Year ensuing, by such greater Part of the said Company for the Time being, then and there present; and if the Governor, Deputy-Governor, and Assistants by these Presents appointed, or such as hereafter be newly chosen into their Rooms, or any of them, or any other the Officers to be appointed for the said Company shall die, or be removed from his or their several Offices or Places before the said general Day of Election, whom We do hereby declare for any Misdemeanor or Default, to be removable by the Governor, Assistants, and Company, or such greater Part of them in any of the said public Courts to be assembled, as is aforesaid, that then and in every such Case, it shall and may be lawful to and for the Governor, Deputy-Governor, and Assistants, and Company aforesaid, or such greater Part of them so to be assembled, as is aforesaid, in any of their Assemblies, to proceed to a new Election of one or more of their Company, in the Room or Place, Rooms or Places of such Governor, Deputy-Governor, Assistant, or other Officer or Officers so dying or removed, according to their Discretions, and immediately upon and after such Election or Elections made of such Governor, Deputy-Governor, Assistant or Assistants, or any other Officer of the said Company, in Manner and Form aforesaid, the Authority, Office and Power before given to the former Governor, Deputy-Governor, or other Officer and Officers so removed, in whose Stead and Place new shall be chosen, shall as to him and them, and every of them respectively, cease and determine. *Provided also*, And Our Will and Pleasure is, That as well such as are by these Presents appointed to be the present Governor, Deputy-Governor, and Assistants of the said Company, as those that shall succeed them, and all other Officers to be appointed and chosen, as aforesaid, shall before they undertake the Execution of their said Offices and Places respectively, take their several and respective corporal Oaths for the due and faithful Performance of their Duties, in their several Offices and Places, before such Person or Persons as are by these Presents hereafter appointed to take and receive the same; *That is to say*, The said *John Winthrop*, who is herein before nominated and appointed the present Governor of the said Company, shall take the said Oath before One or more of the Masters of Our Court of Chancery for the Time being, unto which Master of Chancery, We do by these Presents give full Power and Authority to administer the said Oath to the said *John Winthrop* accordingly: And the said *John Mason*, who is herein before nominated and appointed the present Deputy-Governor of the said Company, shall take the said Oath before the said *John Winthrop*, or any Two of the Assistants of the said Company, unto whom We do by these Presents give full Power and Authority to administer the said Oath to the said *John Mason* accordingly: And the said *Samuel Wyllys*, *Henry Clarke*, *Matthew Allyn*, *John Tapping*, *Nathan Gold*, *Richard Treat*, *Richard Lord*, *Henry Wolcott*, *John Talcott*, *Daniel Clarke*, *John Ogden*, and *Thomas Wells*, who are herein before nominated and appointed the present Assistants of the said Company, shall take the Oath before the said *John Winthrop*, and *John Mason*, or One of them, to whom We do hereby give full Power and Authority to administer the same accordingly.

And Our further Will and Pleasure is, that all and every Governor, or Deputy-Governor to be elected and chosen by Virtue of these Presents, shall take the said Oath before Two or more of the Assistants of the said Company for the Time being, unto whom We do by these Presents give full Power and Authority to give and administer the said Oath accordingly; and the said Assistants, and every of them, and all and every other Officer or Officers to be hereafter chosen from Time to Time, to take the said Oath before the Governor, or Deputy-Governor for the Time being, unto which Governor, or Deputy-Governor, We do by these Presents give full Power and Authority to administer the same accordingly. And further, Of Our more ample Grace, certain Knowledge, and meer Motion, We have given and granted, and by these presents for Us, Our Heirs and Successors, do give and grant unto the said Governor and Company of the *English* Colony of *Connecticut*, in *New England*, in *America*, and to every Inhabitant there, and to every Person and Persons trading thither, and to every such Person and Persons as are or shall be Free of the said Colony, full Power and Authority from Time to Time, and at all Times hereafter, to take, Ship, Transport and carry away for and towards the Plantation and Defence of the said Colony, such of Our loving Subjects and Strangers, as shall or will willingly accompany them in, and to their said Colony and Plantation, except such Person and Persons as are or shall be therein restrained by Us, Our Heirs and Successors; and also to ship and transport all, and all Manner of Goods, Chattels, Merchandises, and other Things whatsoever that are or shall be useful or necessary for the Inhabitants of the said Colony, and may lawfully be transported thither; *Nevertheless*, not to be discharged of Payment to Us, our Heirs and Successors, of the Duties, Customs and Subsidies which are or ought to be paid or payable for the same. And further, Our Will and Pleasure is, and We do for Us, Our

Heirs and Successors, ordain, declare, and grant unto the said Governor and Company, and their Successors, That all and every the Subjects of Us, Our Heirs, or Successors, which shall go to inhabit within the said Colony, and every of their Children, which shall happen to be born there, or on the Seas in going thither, or returning from thence, shall have and enjoy all Liberties and Immunities of free and natural Subjects within any the Dominions of Us, Our Heirs or Successors, to all Intents, Constructions and Purposes whatsoever, as if they and every of them were born within the realm of *England;* And We do authorize and impower the Governor, or in his Absence the Deputy-Governor for the Time being, to appoint Two or more of the said Assistants at any of their Courts or Assemblies to be held as aforesaid, to have Power and Authority to administer the Oath of Supremacy and Obedience to all and every Person and Persons which shall at any Time or Times hereafter go or pass into the said Colony of *Connecticut*, unto which said Assistants so to be appointed as aforesaid, We do by these Presents give full Power and Authority to administer the said Oath accordingly. And We do further of Our especial Grace, certain Knowledge, and meer Motion, give, and grant unto the said Governor and Company of the English Colony of *Connecticut*, in *New England*, in *America*, and their Successors, That it shall and may be lawful to and for the Governor, or Deputy-Governor, and such of the Assistants of the said Company for the Time being as shall be assembled in any of the General Courts aforesaid, or in any Courts to be especially summoned or assembled for that Purpose, or the greater part of them, whereof the Governor, or Deputy-Governor, and Six of the Assistants to be always Seven, to erect and make such Judicatories, for the hearing, and determining of all Actions, Causes, Matters, and Things happening within the said Colony, or Plantation, and which shall be in Dispute, and Depending there, as they shall think Fit, and Convenient, and also from Time to Time to Make, Ordain, and Establish all manner of wholesome, and reasonable Laws, Statutes, Ordinances, Directions, and Instructions, not Contrary to the Laws of this Realm of *England*, as well for settling the Forms, and Ceremonies of Government, and Magistracy, fit and necessary for the said Plantation, and the Inhabitants there, as for Naming, and Stiling all Sorts of Officers, both Superior and Inferior, which they shall find Needful for the Government, and Plantation of the said Colony, and the distinguishing and setting forth of the several Duties, Powers, and Limits of every such Office and Place, and the Forms of such Oaths not being contrary to the Laws and Statutes of this Our Realm of *England*, to be administered for the Execution of the said several Offices and Places as also for the disposing and ordering of the Election of such of the said Officers as are to be annually chosen, and of such others as shall succeed in case of Death or Removal, and administering the said Oath to the newly-elected Officers, and granting necessary Commissions, and for Imposition of lawful Fines, Mulcts, Imprisonment or other Punishment upon Offenders and Delinquents according to the Course of other Corporations within this our Kingdom of *England*, and the same Laws, Fines, Mulcts and Executions, to alter, change, revoke, annul, release, or pardon under their Common Seal, as by the said General Assembly, or the major Part of them shall be thought fit, and for the directing, ruling and disposing of all other Matters and things, whereby Our said People, Inhabitants there, may be so religiously, peaceably and civilly governed, as their good Life and orderly Conversation may win and invite the Natives of the Country to the Knowledge and Obedience of the only true GOD, and the Saviour of Mankind, and the Christian Faith, which in Our Royal Intentions, and the adventurers free Possession, is the only and principal End of this Plantation; willing, commanding and requiring, and by these Presents for Us, Our Heirs and Successors, ordaining and appointing, that all such Laws, Statutes and Ordinances, Instructions, Impositions, and Directions as shall be so made by the Governor, Deputy-Governor, and Assistants as aforesaid, and published in Writing under their Common Seal, shall carefully and duly be observed, kept, performed, and put in Execution, according to the true Intent and Meaning of the same, and these Our Letters Patents or the Duplicate, or Exemplification thereof, shall be to all and every such Officers, Superiors and Inferiors from Time to Time, for the putting of the same Orders, Laws, Statutes, Ordinances, Instructions, and Directions in due Execution, against Us, Our Heirs and Successors, a sufficient Warrant and Discharge. And We do further for Us, Our Heirs and Successors, give and grant into the said Governor and Company, and their Successors, by these Presents, That it shall and may be lawful to, and for the Chief Commanders, Governors and Officers of the said Company for the Time being, who shall be resident in the Parts of *New-England* hereafter mentioned, and others inhabiting there, by their Leave, Admittance, Appointment, or Direction, from Time to Time, and at all Times hereafter, for their special Defence and Safety, to Assemble, Martial-Array, and put in warlike Posture the Inhabitants of the said Colony, and to Commissionate, Impower, and Authorize such Person or Persons as they shall think fit, to lead and conduct the said Inhabitants, and to encounter, expulse, repel and resist by Force of Arms, as well by Sea as by Land, and also to kill, slay, and destroy by all fitting Ways, Enterprises, and Means whatsoever, all and every such Person or Persons as shall at any Time hereafter attempt or enterprize the Destruction, Invasion, Detriment, or Annoyance of the said Inhabitants or Plantation, and to use and exercise the Law Martial in such

Cases only as Occasion shall require; and to take or surprize by all Ways and Means whatsoever, all and every such Person and Persons, with their Ships, Armour, Ammunition and other Goods of such as shall in such hostile Manner invade or attempt the defeating of the said Plantation, or the hurt of the said Company and Inhabitants, and upon just Causes to invade and destroy the Natives, or other Enemies of the said Colony. *Nevertheless*, Our Will and Pleasure is, and We do hereby declare unto all Christian Kings, Princes, and States, that if any Persons which shall hereafter be of the said Company or Plantation, or any other by Appointment of the said Governor and Company for the Time being, shall at any Time or Times hereafter rob or spoil by Sea or by Land, and do any Hurt, Violence or unlawful Hostility to any of the Subjects of Us, Our Heirs or Successors, or any of the Subjects of any Prince or State, being then in League with Us, Our Heirs or Successors, upon Complaint of such Injury done to any such Prince or State, or their Subjects, We, Our Heirs and Successors will make open Proclamation within any Parts of Our Realm of *England* fit for that Purpose, that the Person or Persons committing any such Robbery or Spoil, shall within the Time limited by such Proclamation, make full Restitution or Satisfaction of all such Injuries done or committed, so as the said Prince, or others so complaining may be fully satisfied and contented; and if the said Person or Persons who shall commit any such Robbery or Spoil shall not make Satisfaction accordingly, within such Time so to be limited, that then it shall and may be lawful for Us, Our Heirs and Successors, to put such Person or Persons out of Our Allegiance and Protection; and that it shall and may be lawful and free for all Princes or others to prosecute with Hostility such Offenders, and every of them, their, and every of their Procurors, Aiders, Abettors and Counsellors in that Behalf. *Provided also*, and Our express Will and Pleasure is, and We do by these Presents, for Us, Our Heirs, and Successors, Ordain and Appoint, that these Presents shall not in any Manner hinder any of Our loving Subjects whatsoever to use and exercise the Trade of Fishing upon the Coast of *New-England* in *America*, but they and every or any of them shall have full and free Power and Liberty, to continue, and use the said Trade of Fishing upon the said Coast, in any of the Seas thereunto adjoining, or any Arms of the Seas, or Salt Water Rivers where they have been accustomed to fish, and to build and set up on the waste Land belonging to the said Colony of *Connecticut*, such Wharves, Stages, and Work-Houses as shall be necessary for the salting, drying, and keeping of their Fish to be taken, or gotten upon that Coast, any Thing in these Presents contained to the contrary notwithstanding. And Know Ye further, That We, of Our abundant Grace, certain Knowledge, and mere Motion, have given, granted, and confirmed, and by these Presents for Us, our Heirs and Successors, do give, grant and confirm unto the said Governor and Company, and their Successors, all that Part of Our Dominions in *New-England* in *America*, bounded on the *East* by *Narraganset-River*, commonly called *Narraganset-Bay*, where the said River falleth into the Sea ; and on the *North* by the Line of the *Massachusetts Plantation ;* and on the *South* by the Sea ; and in Longitude as the Line of the *Massachusetts Colony*, running from *East* to *West*, *That is to say*, From the said *Narraganset-Bay* on the *East*, to the *South* Sea on the *West* Part, with the *Islands* thereunto adjoining, together with all firm Lands, Soils, Grounds, Havens, Ports, Rivers, Waters, Fishings, Mines, Minerals, precious Stones, Quarries, and all and singular other Commodities, Jurisdictions, Royalties, Privileges, Franchises, Preheminences, and Hereditaments whatsoever, within the said Tract, Bounds, Lands, and Islands, aforesaid, or to them or any of them belonging. *To have and to hold* the same unto the said Governor and Company, their Successors and Assigns for ever, upon Trust, and for the Use and Benefit of Themselves and their Associates, Freemen of the said Colony, their Heirs and Assigns, to be holden of Us, Our Heirs and Successors. as of Our Manor of *East-Greenwich*, in free and common Soccage, and not in Capite, nor by Knights Service, yielding and paying therefore to Us, Our Heirs and Successors, only the Fifth Part of all the Ore of Gold and Silver which from Time to Time, and at all times hereafter, shall be there gotten, had, or obtained, in Lieu of all Services, Duties, and Demands whatsoever, to be to Us, our Heirs, or Successors therefore, or thereout rendered, made, or paid. *And lastly*, We do for Us, our Heirs and Successors, grant to the said Governor and Company, and their Successors, by these Presents, That these Our Letters Patents, shall be firm, good and effectual in the Law, to all Intents, Constructions, and Purposes whatsoever, according to Our true Intent and Meaning herein before declared, as shall be construed, reputed and adjudged most favourable on the Behalf, and for the best Benefit, and Behoof of the said Governor and Company, and their Successors, although express Mention of the true Yearly Value or Certainty of the Premises, or of any of them, or of any other Gifts or Grants by Us, or by any of Our Progenitors, or Predecessors, heretofore made to the said Governor and Company of the *English* Colony of *Connecticut*, in *New-England*, in *America*, aforesaid, in these Presents is not made, or any Statute, Act, Ordinance, Provision, Proclamation, or Restriction heretofore had, made, enacted, ordained, or provided, or any other Matter, Cause, or Thing whatsoever, to the contrary thereof, in any wise notwithstanding. *In Witness whereof*, We have caused these Our Letters to be made Patents. Witness Ourself at *Westminster*, the Three and Twentieth Day of *April*, in the Fourteenth Year of our Reign.

By Writ of Privy Seal,

HOWARD.

CHARTER OF RHODE ISLAND—1663.

In 1644 Roger Williams obtained from the colonial commissioners of the Long Parliament a patent uniting the three colonies or towns of Providence, Portsmouth and Newport under the style of the "Incorporation of Providence Plantations in Narraganset Bay in New England." Under this charter the three towns and Warwick formed a general government in 1647.

Rhode Island, shut out by her neighbors from the New England Confederacy, was on this account favored the more by the crown, so that when John Winthrop obtained a charter for Connecticut, John Clarke the agent of Rhode Island readily obtained the like for Rhode Island. This charter was marked by the same liberality as the Connecticut Charter, but passes beyond it in guaranteeing religious freedom.

"This charter of government constituting, as it then seemed, a pure democracy, and establishing a political system which few besides the Rhode Islanders themselves believed to be practical, remained in existence till it became the oldest constitutional charter in the world." (Bancroft.)

It was not till 1842 after the so-called Dorr War that this charter gave place to a more popular constitution, which is still in force.

Consult *Palfrey's New England*, II., 562; *Ar-*

nold's Hist. Rhode Island, I., 290; *Greene's Short Hist. Rhode Island*, 40; *Bancroft's Hist. U. S.*, 1st ed. II., 61; cen. ed., I., 427; last ed., I., 363; *Hildreth's Hist. U. S.*, I., 456; *Bryant and Gay's Hist. U. S.*, II., 112.

THE CHARTER OF RHODE ISLAND.

CHARLES the Second, by the Grace of God, King of England, Scotland, France and Ireland, Defender of the Faith, etc., to all to whom these presents shall come, greeting: Whereas, we have been informed, by the humble petition of our trusty and well-beloved subject, John Clarke, on the behalf of Benjamin Arnold, William Brenton, William Codington, Nicholas Easton, William Boulston, John Porter, John Smith, Samuel Gorton, John Weeks, Roger Williams, Thomas Olney, Gregory Dexter, John Coggeshall, Joseph Clarke, Randall Holden, John Greene, John Roome, Samuel Wildbore, William Field, James Barker, Richard Tew, Thomas Harris, and William Dyre, and the rest of the purchasers and free inhabitants of our island, called Rhode Island, and the rest of the colony of Providence Plantations, in the Narragansett Bay, in New England, in America, that they, pursuing, with peaceable and loyal minds, their sober, serious, and religious intentions, of godly edifying themselves, and one another, in the holy Christian faith and worship, as they were persuaded; together with the gaining over and conversion of the poor ignorant Indian natives, in those parts of America, to the sincere profession and obedience of the same faith and worship, did not only by the consent and good encouragement of our royal progenitors, transport themselves out of this kingdom of England into America, but also, since their arrival there, after their first settlement amongst other our subjects in those parts, for the avoiding of discord, and those many evils which were likely to ensue upon some of those our subjects not being able to bear, in these remote parts, their different apprehensions in religious concernments, and in pursuance of the aforesaid ends, did once again leave their desirable stations and habitations, and with excessive labor and travel, hazard and charge, did transplant themselves into the midst of the Indian natives, who, as we are informed, are the most potent princes and people of all that country; where, by the good Providence of God, from whom the Plantations have taken their name, upon their labor and industry, they have not only been preserved to admiration, but have increased and prospered, and are seized and possessed by purchase and consent of the said natives, to their full content of such lands, islands, rivers, harbors and roads, as are very convenient, both for plantations, and also for building of ships, supply of pipestaves, and other merchandize; and which lie very commodious, in many respects, for commerce, and to accommodate our southern plantations, and may much advance the trade of this our realm, and greatly enlarge the territories thereof; they having, by near neighborhood to and friendly society with the great body of the Narragansett Indians, given them encouragement, of their own accord, to subject themselves, their people and lands, unto us; whereby, as is hoped, there may, in time, by the blessing of God upon their endeavors be laid a sure foundation of happiness to all America: And whereas, in their humble address, they have freely declared, that it is much on their hearts (if they may be permitted) to hold forth a lively experiment, that a most flourishing civil State may stand and best be maintained, and that among our English subjects, with a full liberty in religious concernments; and that true piety rightly grounded upon gospel principles, will give the best and greatest security to sovereignty, and will lay in the hearts of men the strongest obligations to true loyalty: Now, know ye, that we, being willing to encourage the hopeful undertaking of our said loyal and loving subjects, and to secure them in the free exercise and enjoyment of all their civil and religious rights, appertaining to them, as our loving subjects ; and to preserve unto them that liberty, in the true Christian faith and worship of God which they have sought with so much travail, and with peaceable minds, and loyal subjection to our royal progenitors and ourselves, to enjoy; and because some of the people and inhabitants of the same colony cannot, in their private opinions, conform to the public exercise of religion, according to the liturgy, forms and ceremonies of the Church of England, or take or subscribe the oaths and articles made and established in that behalf ; and for that the same, by reason of the remote distances of those places, will (as we hope) be no breach of the unity and uniformity established in this nation: Have therefore thought fit, and do hereby publish, grant, ordain and declare, That our royal will and pleasure is, that no person within the said colony, at any time hereafter, shall be any wise molested, punished, disquieted, or called in question, for any differences in opinion in matters of religion, and do not actually disturb the civil peace of our said colony ; but that all and every person and persons may, from time to time, and at all times hereafter, freely and fully have and enjoy his and their own judgments and consciences, in matters of religious concernments, throughout the tract of land hereafter mentioned, they behaving themselves peaceably and quietly, and not using this liberty to licentiousness and profaneness, nor to the civil injury or outward disturbance of others, any law, statute, or clause therein contained, or to be contained, usage or custom of this realm, to the contrary hereof, in any wise, notwithstanding. And that they may be in the better capacity to defend themselves, in their just rights and liberties, against all the enemies of the Christian faith, and others, in all respects, we have further thought fit, and at the humble petition of the persons aforesaid are graciously pleased to declare, That they shall have and enjoy the benefit of our late act of indemnity and free pardon, as the rest of our subjects in other our dominions and territories have; and to create and make them a body politic or corporate, with the powers and privileges hereinafter mentioned. And accordingly our will and pleasure is, and of our especial grace, certain knowledge, and mere motion, we have ordained, constituted and declared, and by these presents, for us, our heirs and successors, do ordain, constitute and declare, That they, the said William Brenton, William Codington, Nicholas Easton, Benedict Arnold, William Boulston, John Porter, Samuel Gorton, John Smith, John Weeks, Roger Williams, Thomas Olney, Gregory Dexter, John Coggeshall, Joseph Clarke, Randall Holden, John Greene, John Roome, William Dyre, Samuel Wildbore, Richard Tew, William Field, Thomas Harris, James Barker, —— Rainsborrow, —— Williams, and John Nickson and all such others as now are, or hereafter shall be, admitted and made free of the company and society of our colony of Providence Plantations, in the Narragansett Bay, in New England, shall be, from time to time, and forever hereafter, a body corporate and politic, in fact and name, by the name of the Governor and Company of the English Colony of Rhode-Island and Providence Plantations, in New England, in America; and that, by the same name, they and their successors shall and may have perpetual succession, and shall and may in all and singular suits, causes, quarrels, matters, actions and things, of what kind or nature soever; and also to have, take, possess, acquire, and be persons able and capable, in the law, to sue and be sued, to plead and be impleaded, to answer, and be answered unto, to defend and to be defended, purchase lands, tenements or hereditaments, or any goods or chattels, and the same to lease, grant, demise, aliene, bargain, sell and dispose of, at their own will and pleasure, as other our liege people of this our realm of England, or any corporation or body politic, within the same, may lawfully do. And further, that they the said Governor and Company, and their successors, shall and may, forever hereafter, have a common seal, to serve and use for all matters, causes, things and affairs, whatsoever, of them, and their successors; and the same seal to alter, change, break, and make new, from time to time, at their will and pleasure, as they shall think fit. And further, we will and ordain, and by these presents, for us, our heirs, and successors, do declare and appoint that, for the better ordering and managing of the affairs and business of the said Company, and their successors, there shall be one Governor, one Deputy-Governor and ten Assistants, to be from time to time, constitued, elected and chosen, out of the freemen of the said Company, for the time being, in such manner and form as is hereafter in these presents expressed, which said officers shall apply themselves to take care for the best disposing and ordering of the general business and affairs of and concerning the lands, and hereditaments hereinafter mentioned to be granted, and the plantation thereof, and the government of the people there. And, for the better execution of our royal pleasure herein, we do, for us, our heirs and successors, assign, name, constitute, and appoint the aforesaid Benedict Arnold to be the first and present Governor of the said Company, and the said William Brenton to be the Deputy-Governor, and the said William Boulston, John Porter, Roger Williams, Thomas Olney, John Smith, John Greene, John Coggeshall, James Barker, William Field, and Joseph Clarke, to be the ten present Assistants of the said Company, to continue in the said several offices, respectively, until the first Wednesday which shall be in the month of May now next coming. And further, we will, and by these presents, for us, our heirs and successors, do ordain and grant that the Governor of the said Company, for the time being, or, in his absence, by occasion of sickness, or otherwise, by his leave and permission, the Deputy-Governor, for the time being, shall and may, from time to time, upon all occasions, give order for the assembling of the said Company, and calling them together, to consult and advise of the business and affairs of the said Company. And that forever hereafter, twice in every year, that is to say, on every first Wednesday in the month of May, and on every last Wednesday in October, or oftener, in case it shall be requisite, the Assistants and such of the freemen of the said Company, not exceeding six persons for Newport, four persons for each of the respective towns of Providence, Portsmouth and Warwick, and two persons for each other place, town or city, who shall be, from time to time, thereunto elected or deputed by the major part of the freemen of the respective towns or places for which they shall be so elected or deputed, shall have a general meeting or assembly, then and there to consult, advise and determine, in and about the affairs and business of the said Company and Plantations. And, further, we do, of our especial grace, certain knowledge, and mere motion, give and grant unto the said Governor and Company of the English colony of Rhode-Island and Providence Plantations, in New England, in America, and their successors, that the Governor, or, in his absence, or, by his permission, the Deputy-Governor of the said Company, for the time being, the Assistants, and such of the freemen of the said Company as shall be so as aforesaid elected or deputed, or so many of them as shall be present at such meeting or assembly, as aforesaid, shall be called the General Assembly; and that they, or the greatest part of them present, whereof the Governor or Deputy-Governor, and six of the Assistants, at least to be seven, shall have, and have hereby given and granted unto them, full power and authority, from time to time, and at all times hereafter, to appoint, alter and change such days, times and places of meeting and General Assembly, as they shall think fit; and to choose, nominate and appoint, such and so many other persons as they shall think fit, and shall be willing to accept the same, to be free of the said Company and body politic, and them into the same to admit; and to elect and constitute such offices and officers, and to grant such needful commissions, as they shall think fit and requisite, for the ordering, managing and dispatching of the affairs of the said Governor and Company, and their successors, and from time to time, to make, ordain, constitute or repeal, such laws, statutes, orders and ordinances, forms and ceremonies of government and magistracy, as to them shall seem meet, for the good and welfare of the said Company, and for the government and ordering of the lands and hereditaments hereinafter mentioned to be granted, and of the people that do, or at any time hereafter shall, inhabit or be within the same; so as such laws, ordinances and constitutions, so made, be not contrary and repugnant unto, but as near as may be, agreeable to the laws of this our realm of England, considering the nature and constitution of the place and people there; and also to appoint, order and direct, erect and settle, such places and courts of jurisdiction, for the hearing and determining of all actions, cases, matters and things, happening within the said colony and plantation, and which shall be in dispute, and depending there, as they shall think fit; and also to distinguish and set forth the several names and titles, duties, powers and limits, of each court, office and officer, superior and inferior; and also to contrive and appoint such forms of oaths and attestations, not repugnant, but as near as may be agreeable, as aforesaid, to the laws and statutes of this our realm, as are convenient and requisite, with respect to the due administration of justice, and due execution and discharge of all offices and places of trust by the persons that shall be therein concerned; and also to regulate and order the way and manner of all elections to offices and places of trust, and to prescribe, limit and distinguish the numbers and bounds of all places, towns or cities, within the limits and bounds hereinafter mentioned, and not herein particularly named, who have, or shall have, the power of electing and sending of freemen to the said General Assembly; and also to order, direct and authorize the imposing of lawful and reasonable fines, mulcts, imprisonments, and executing other punishments, pecuniary and corporal, upon offenders and delinquents, according to the course of other corporations within this our kingdom of England; and again to alter, revoke, annul or pardon, under their common seal, or otherwise, such fines, mulcts, imprisonments, sentences, judgments and condemnations, as shall be thought fit; and to direct rule, order and dispose of, all other matters and things, and particularly that which relates to the making of purchases of the native Indians, as to them shall seem meet; whereby our said people and inhabitants in the said Plantation, may be so religiously, peaceably and civilly governed, as that by their good life and orderly conversation, they may win and invite the native Indians of the country to the knowledge and obedience of the only true God and Saviour of mankind; willing, commanding and requiring, and by these presents, for us, our heirs and successors, ordaining and appointing, that all such laws, statutes, orders and ordinances, instructions, impositions and directions, as shall be so made by the Governor, Deputy-Governor, Assistants and freemen, or such number of them as aforesaid, and published in writing, under their common seal shall be carefully and duly observed, kept, performed and put in execution, according to the true intent and meaning of the same. And these our letters patent, or the duplicate or exemplification thereof, shall be to all and every such officer, superior or inferior, from time to time, for the putting of the same orders, laws, statutes, ordinances, instructions and directions, in due execution, against us, our heirs and successors, a sufficient warrant and discharge. And further, our will and pleasure is, and we do hereby, for us, our heirs and successors, establish and ordain, that, yearly, once in the year, forever hereafter, namely, the aforesaid Wednesday in May, and at the town of Newport, or elsewhere, if urgent occasion do require, the Governor, Deputy-Governor and Assistants of the said Company, and other officers of the said Company, or such of them as the General Assembly shall think fit, shall be, in the said General Court or Assembly to be held from that day or time, newly chosen for the year ensuing, by such greater part of the said Company, for the time being, as shall be then and there present; and if it shall happen that the present Governor, Deputy-Governor and Assistants, by these presents appointed, or any such as shall hereafter be newly chosen into their rooms, or any of them, or any other the officers of the said Company, shall die or be removed from his or their several offices or places, before the said general day of election, (whom we do hereby declare, for any misdemeanor or default, to be removable by the Governor, Assistants and Company, or such greater part of them, in any of the said public courts, to be assembled as aforesaid,) that then, and in every such case, it shall and may be lawful to and for the said Governor, Deputy Governor, Assistants and Company aforesaid, or such greater part of them, so to be assembled as is aforesaid, in any their assemblies, to proceed to a new election of one or more of their Company, in the room or place, rooms or places, of such officer or officers, so dying or removed, according to their discretions; and immediately upon and after such election or elections made of such Governor, Deputy-Governor, Assistant or Assistants, or any other officer of the said Company, in manner and form aforesaid, the authority, office and power, before given to the former Governor, Deputy-Governor, and other officer and officers, so removed, in whose stead and place new shall be chosen, shall, as to him and them, and every of them, respectively, cease and determine: *Provided always*, and our will and pleasure is, that as well such as are by these presents appointed to be the present Governor, Deputy-Governor and Assistants of the said Company, as those that shall succeed them, and all other officers to be appointed and chosen as aforesaid, shall, before the undertaking, the execution of the said offices and places respectively, give their solemn engagement, by oath, or otherwise, for the due and faithful performance of their duties in their several offices and places, before such person or persons as are by these presents hereafter appointed to take and receive the same, that is to say: the said Benedict Arnold, who is hereinbefore nominated and appointed the present Governor of the said Company, shall give the aforesaid engagement before William Brenton, or any two of the said Assistants of the said Company; unto whom we do by these presents give full power and authority to require and receive the same; and the said William Brenton, who is hereby before nominated and appointed the present Deputy-Governor of the said Company, shall give the aforesaid engagement before the said Benedict Arnold, or any two of the Assistants of the said Company; unto whom we do by these presents give full power and authority to require and receive the same; and the said William Boulston, John Porter, Roger Williams, Thomas Olney, John Smith, John Greene, John Coggeshall, James Barker, William Field, and Joseph Clarke, who are herein before nominated and appointed the present Assistants of the said Company, shall give the said engagement to their offices and places respectively belonging, before the said Benedict Arnold and William Brenton, or one of them; to whom respectively we do hereby give full power and authority to require, administer or receive the same: and further, our will and pleasure is, that all and every other future Governor or Deputy-Governor, to be elected and chosen by virtue of these presents, shall give the said engagement before two or more of the said Assistants of the said Company for the time being; unto whom we do by these presents give full power and authority to require, administer or receive the same; and the said Assistants, and every of them, and all and every other officer or officers to be hereafter elected and chosen by virtue of these presents, from time to time, shall give the like engagements, to their offices and places respectively belonging, before the Governor or Deputy-Governor for the time being; unto which said Governor, or Deputy-Governor, we do by these presents give full power and authority to require, administer or receive the same accordingly. And we do likewise, for us, our heirs and successors, give and grant unto the said Governor and Company, and their successors, by these presents, that, for the more peaceable and orderly government of the said Plantations, it shall and may be lawful for the Governor, Deputy-Governor, Assistants and all other officers and ministers of the said Company, in the administration of justice, and exercise of government, in the said Plantations, to use, exercise, and put in execution, such methods, rules, orders and directions, not being contrary or repugnant to the laws and statutes of this our realm, as have been heretofore given, used and accustomed, in such cases respectively, to be put in practice, until at the next or some other General Assembly, special provision shall be made and ordained in the cases aforesaid. And we do further, for us, our heirs and successors, give and grant unto the said Governor and Company, and their successors, by these presents, that it shall and may be lawful to and for the said Governor, or, in his absence, the Deputy-Governor, and major part of the said Assistants, for the time being, at any time when the said General Assembly is not sitting, to nominate, appoint and constitute, such and so many commanders, governors and military officers, as to them shall seem requisite, for the leading, conducting and training up the inhabitants of the said Plantations in martial affairs, and for the defence and safeguard of the said Plantations: and that it shall and may be lawful to and for all and every such commander, governor and military officer, that shall be so as aforesaid, or by the Governor, or in his absence, the Deputy-Governor, and six of the said Assistants, and major part of the freemen of the said Company present at any General Assemblies, nominated, appointed and constituted, according to the tenor of his and their respective commissions and directions to assemble, exercise in arms, martial array, and put in warlike posture, the inhabitants of the said colony, for their special defence and safety; and to lead and conduct the said inhabitants, and to encounter, expulse, expel and resist, by force of arms, as well by sea as by land, and also to kill, slay and destroy, by all fitting ways, enterprizes and means, whatsoever, all and every such person or persons as shall, at any time hereafter, attempt or enterprize the destruction, invasion, detriment, or annoyance of the said inhabitants or Plantations; and to use and exercise the law martial in such cases only as occasion shall necessarily require; and to take or surprise, by all ways and means whatsoever, all and every such person and persons, with their ship or ships, armor, ammunition or other goods of such persons, as shall, in hostile manner, invade or attempt the defeating of the said Plantation, or the hurt of the said Company and inhabitants; and upon just causes, to invade and destroy the native Indians, or other enemies of the said Colony. Nevertheless, our will and pleasure is, and we do hereby declare to the rest of our Colonies in New England, that it shall not be lawful for this our said Colony of Rhode Island and Providence Plantations, in America, in New England, to invade the natives inhabiting within the bounds and limits of their said Colonies, without the knowledge and consent of the said other Colonies. And it is hereby declared, that it shall not be lawful to or for the rest of the Colonies to invade or molest the native Indians or any other inhabitants inhabiting without the bounds and limits hereafter mentioned, (they having subjected themselves unto us, and being by us taken into our special protection,) without the knowledge and consent of the Governor and Company of our Colony of Rhode-Island and Providence Plantations. Also our will and pleasure is, and we do hereby declare unto all Christian Kings, Princes and States, that if any person, which shall hereafter be of the said Company or Plantations, or any other, by appointment of the said Governor and Company for the time being, shall at any time or times hereafter, rob or spoil, by sea or land, or do any hurt or unlawful hostility to any of the subjects of us, our heirs or successors, or any of the subjects of any Prince or State, being then in league with us, our heirs or successors, upon complaint of such injury done to any such Prince or State, or their subjects, we, our heirs and successors, will make open proclamation within any parts of our realm of England, fit for that purpose, that the person or persons committing any such robbery or spoil, shall, within the time limited by such proclamation, make full restitution, or satisfaction of all such injuries, done or committed, so as the said Prince, or others so complaining, may be fully satisfied and contented; and if the said person or persons who shall commit any such robbery or spoil shall not make satisfaction, accordingly, within such time, so to be limited, that then we, our heirs and successors, will put such person or persons out of our allegiance and protection; and that then it shall and may be lawful and free for all Princes or others to prosecute with hostility, such offenders, and every of them, their and every of their procurers, aiders, abettors and counsellors, in that behalf: *Provided also*, and our express will and pleasure is, and we do, by these presents, for us, our heirs and successors, ordain and appoint, that these presents, shall not, in any manner, hinder any of our loving subjects, whatsoever, from using and exercising the trade of fishing upon the coast of New England, in America ; but that they, and every or any of them, shall have full and free power and liberty to continue and use the trade of fishing upon the said coast, in any of the seas thereunto adjoining, or any arms of the seas, or salt water, rivers and creeks, where they have been accustomed to fish : and to build and to set upon the waste land belonging to the said Colony and Plantations, such wharves, stages and work-houses as shall be necessary for the salting, drying and keeping of their fish, to be taken or gotten upon that coast. And further, for the encouragement of the inhabitants of our said Colony of Providence Plantations to set upon the business of taking whales, it shall be lawful for them, or any of them, having struck whale, dubertus, or other great fish, it or them, to pursue unto any part of that coast, and into any bay, river, cove, creek, or shore, belonging thereto, and it or them, upon the said coast, or in the said bay, river, cove, creek, or shore, belonging thereto, to kill and order for the best advantage, without molestation, they making no wilful waste or spoil ; anything in these presents contained, or any other matter or thing, to the contrary, notwithstanding. And further also, we are graciously pleased, and do hereby declare, that if any of the inhabitants of our said Colony do set upon the planting of vineyards (the soil and climate both seeming naturally to concur to the production of wines) or be industrious in the discovery of fishing banks, in or about the said Colony, we will, from time to time, give and allow all due and fitting encouragement therein, as to others, in cases of like nature. And further, of our more ample grace, certain knowledge and mere motion, we have given and granted, and by these presents, for us, our heirs and successors, do give and grant unto the said Governor and Company of the English Colony of Rhode-Island and

Providence Plantations, in the Narragansett Bay, in New England, in America, and to every inhabitant there, and to every person and persons, trading thither, and to every such person or persons as are or shall be free of the said Colony, full power and authority, from time to time, and at all times hereafter, to take, ship, transport and carry away, out of any of our realms and dominions, for and towards the plantation and defence of the said Colony, such and so many of our loving subjects and strangers as shall or will willingly accompany them in and to their said Colony and Plantation ; except such person or persons as are or shall be therein restrained by us, our heirs and successors, or any law or statute of this realm : and also to ship and transport all and all manner of goods, chattels, merchandizes and other things whatsoever, that are or shall be useful or necessary for the said Plantations, and defence thereof, and usually transported, and not prohibited by any law or statute of this our realm ; yielding and paying unto us, our heirs and successors, such the duties, customes and subsidies, as are or ought to be paid or payable for the same. And further, our will and pleasure is, and we do, for us, our heirs and successors, ordain, declare, and grant unto the said Governor and Company, and their successors, that all and every the subjects of us, our heirs and successors, which are already planted and settled within our said Colony of Providence Plantations, or which shall hereafter go to inhabit within the said Colony, and all and every of their children, which have been born there, or which shall happen hereafter to be born there, or on the sea, going thither, or returning from thence, shall have and enjoy all liberties and immunities of free and natural subjects within any the dominions of us, our heirs or successors, to all intents, constructions and purposes, whatsoever, as if they, and every of them, were born within the realm of England. And further, know ye, that we, of our more abundant grace, certain knowledge, and mere motion, have given, granted and confirmed, and by these presents, for us, our heirs and successors, do give, grant and confirm, unto the said Governor and Company, and their successors, all that part of our dominions in New England, in America, containing the Nahantick and Nanhyganset, alias Narragansett Bay, and countries and parts adjacent, bounded on the west, or westerly, to the middle or channel of a river there, commonly called and known by the name of Pawcatuck, alias Pawcawtuck river, and so along the said river, as the greater or middle stream thereof reacheth or lies up into the north country, northward, unto the head thereof, and from thence, by a straight line drawn due north, until it meets with the south line of the Massachusetts Colony; and on the north, or northerly, by the aforesaid south or southerly line of the Massachusetts Colony or Plantation, and extending towards the east, or eastwardly, three English miles to the east and north-east of the most eastern and north-eastern parts of the aforesaid Narragansett Bay, as the said bay lyeth or extendeth itself from the ocean on the south, or southwardly unto the mouth of the river which runneth towards the town of Providence, and from thence along the easterly side or bank of the said river (higher called by the name of Seacunck river) up to the falls called Patuckett falls, being the most westwardly line of Plymouth Colony, and so from the said falls, in a straight line, due north, until it meet with the aforesaid line of the Massachusetts Colony; and bounded on the south by the ocean; and, in particular, the lands belonging to the towns of Providence, Pawtuxet, Warwick, Misquammacok, alias Pawcatuck, and the rest upon the main land in the tract aforesaid, together with Rhode-Island, Block-Island, and all the rest of the islands and banks in the Narragansett Bay, and bordering upon the coast of the tract aforesaid, (Fisher's Island only excepted,) together with all firm lands, soils, grounds, havens, ports, rivers, waters, fishings, mines royal, and all other mines, minerals, precious stones, quarries, woods, wood grounds, rocks, slates, and all and singular other commodities, jurisdictions, royalties, privileges, franchises, preheminancies, and hereditaments, whatsoever, within the said tract, bonds, lands and islands aforesaid, or to them or any of them belonging, or in any wise appertaining; *to have and to hold* the same, unto the said Governor and Company, and their successors, forever, upon trust, for the use and benefit of themselves and their associates freemen of the said Colony, their heirs and assigns, to be holden of us, our heirs and successors, as of the Manor of East-Greenwich, in our county of Kent, in free and common soccage, and not in capite, nor by knight service; yielding and paying therefor, to us, our heirs and successors, only the fifth part of all the ore of gold and silver which, from time to time, and at all times hereafter, shall be there gotten, had or obtained, in lieu and satisfaction of all services, duties, fines, forfeitures, made or to be made, claims and demands whatsoever, to be to us, our heirs or successors, therefor or thereout rendered, made or paid; any grant, or clause in a late grant, to the Governor and Company of Connecticut Colony, in America, to the contrary thereof in any wise notwithstanding; the aforesaid Pawcatuck river having been yielded, after much debate, for the fixed and certain bounds between these our said Colonies, by the agents thereof; who have also agreed, that the said Pawcatuck river shall be also called alias Norrogansett or Narrogansett river; and, to prevent future disputes, that otherwise might arise thereby, forever hereafter shall be construed, deemed and taken to be the Narragansett river in our late grant to Connecticut Colony mentioned as the easterly bounds of that Colony. And further, our will and pleasure is, that in all matters of public controversy which may fall out between our Colony of Providence Plantations, and the rest of our colonies in New England, it shall and may be lawful to and for the Governor and Company of the said Colony of Providence Plantations to make their appeals therein to us, our heirs and successors, for redress in such cases, within this our realm of England: and that it shall be lawful to and for the inhabitants of the said Colony of Providence Plantations, without let or molestation, to pass and repass, with freedom, into and through the rest of the English Colonies, upon their lawful and civil occasions, and to converse, and hold commerce and trade, with such of the inhabitants of our other English Colonies as shall be willing to admit them thereunto, they behaving themselves peaceably among them; any act, clause or sentence, in any of the said Colonies provided, or that shall be provided, to the contrary in anywise notwithstanding. And lastly, we do, for us, our heirs and successors, ordain and grant unto the said Governor and Company, and their successors, by these presents, that these our letters patent shall be firm, good, effectual and available in all things in the law, to all intents, constructions and purposes whatsoever, according to our true intent and meaning hereinbefore declared; and shall be construed, reputed and adjudged in all cases most favorably on the behalf, and for the best benefit and behoof, of the said Governor and Company, and their successors; although express mention of the true yearly value or certainty of the premises, or any of them, or of any other gifts or grants, by us, or by any of our progenitors or predecessors, heretofore made to the said Governor and Company of the English Colony of Rhode-Island and Providence Plantations, in the Narragansett Bay, New England, in America, in these presents is not made, or any statute, act, ordinance, provision, proclamation or restriction, heretofore had, made, enacted, ordained or provided, or any other matter, cause or thing whatsoever, to the contrary thereof in anywise notwithstanding. In witness whereof, we have caused these our letters to be made patent. Witness ourself at Westminster, the eighth day of July, in the fifteenth year of our reign.

By the King:

HOWARD.

CHARTER OF PENNSYLVANIA—1681.

William Penn inheriting from his father, Admiral Richard Penn, a claim of £60,000 against the crown, requested from Charles II., in settlement of the same, a tract of land north of Maryland and west of Jersey for a province. The king consented to this easy mode of settlement, and the patent was sealed March 5, 1681. Penn obtained from the Duke of York the three lower counties on the Delaware, now the State of Delaware. In July, 1681, Penn drew his "Concession" to the province and the next year granted a liberal frame of government followed in 1683 by a second, and in 1696 by a third "Frame." Penn, unwearied in his care for the province, in 1701 granted the "Charter of Privileges," under which Pennsylvania remained till the Revolution. A State constitution was adopted in 1776 by a convention under the presidency of Benjamin Franklin. Another constitution was adopted in 1790, a third in 1838, and a fourth, the present, in 1873. Consult *Bancroft's U. S.*, 1st ed., II., 364; cen. ed., II., 107; last ed., I., 552; *Hildreth*, II., 63; *Bryant and Gay*, II., 487; *Proud's Pennsylvania*, I., 167; *Chalmers' Political Annals*, 635.

CHARTER FOR THE PROVINCE OF PENNSYLVANIA—1681.

CHARLES the Second, by the Grace of God, King of *England*, *Scotland*, *France*, and *Ireland*, Defender of the Faith, etc. To all whom these presents shall come, *Greeting*. WHEREAS Our Trustie and well-beloved Subject WILLIAM PENN, Esquire, Sonne and heire of Sir WILLIAM PENN deceased, out of a commendable Desire to enlarge our *English* Empire, and promote such usefull comodities as may bee of Benefit to us and Our Dominions, as also to reduce the Savage Natives by gentle and just manners to the Love of Civil Societie and Christian Religion, hath humbley besought Leave of Us to transport an ample Colonie unto a certaine Countrey hereinafter described, in the Partes of *America* not yet cultivated and planted; And hath likewise humbley besought Our Royall Majestie to Give, Grant, and Confirme all the said Countrey, with certaine Privileges and Jurisdictions, requisite for the good Government and Safetie of the said Countrey and Colonie, to him and his Heires forever: KNOW YE THEREFORE, That Wee, favouring the Petition and good Purpose of the said *William Penn*, and haveing Regard to the Memorie and Meritts of his late Father in divers Services, and perticulerly to his Conduct, Courage, and Discretion under our Dearest Brother *JAMES* Duke of *York*, in that Signall Battell and Victorie fought and obteyned against the *Dutch* Fleete, command by the Heer *Van Opdam*, in the yeare One thousand six hundred and sixty-five: In consideration thereof, of Our Speciall grace, certaine Knowledge, and meere Motion have Given and Granted, and by this Our present Charter, for Us, Our Heires and Successors, Doe give and Grant unto the said *William Penn*, his Heires and Assignes, all that Tract or Parte of Land in *America*, with all the Islands therein conteyned, as the same is bounded on the East by

Delaware River, from twelve miles distance Northwards of *New Castle* Towne unto the three and fortieth degree of Northerne Latitude, if the said River doeth extende so farre Northwards; But if the said River shall not extend soe farre Northward, then by the said River soe farr as it doth extend; and from the head of the said River, the Easterne Bounds are to bee determined by a Meridian Line, to bee drawne from the head of the said River, unto the said three and fortieth Degree. The said Lands to extend westwards five degrees in longitude, to bee computed from the said Easterne Bounds; and the said Lands to bee bounded on the North by the beginning of the three and fortieth degree of Northern Latitude, and on the South by a Circle drawne at twelve miles distance from *New Castle* Northward and Westward unto the beginning of the fortieth degree of Northern Latitude, and then by a streight Line Westward to the Limitt of Longitude above-mentioned. WEE do also give and grant unto the said *William Penn*, his heires and assignes, the free and undisturbed use and continuance in, and passage into and out of all and singuler Ports, Harbours, Bays, Waters, Rivers, Isles, and Inletts, belonging unto, or leading to and from the Countrey or Islands aforesaid, And all the Soyle, lands, fields, woods, underwoods, mountaines, hills, fenns, Isles, Lakes, Rivers, waters, Rivuletts, Bays, and Inletts, scituate or being within, or belonging unto the Limitts and Bounds aforesaid, togeather with the fishing of all sortes of fish, whales, Sturgeons, and all Royall and other Fishes, in the Sea, Bayes, Inletts, waters, or Rivers within the premisses, and the Fish therein taken; And also all Veines, Mines, and Quarries, as well discovered as not discovered, of Gold, Silver, Gemms, and Pretious Stones, and all other whatsoever, be it Stones, Mettals, or of any other thing or matter whatsoever, found or to bee found within the Countrey, Isles, or Limitts aforesaid; AND him, the said *William Penn*, his heires and assignes, Wee doe by this Our Royall Charter, for Us, Our heires and Successors, make, create, and constitute the true and absolute Proprietarie of the Countrey aforesaid, and of all other the premisses, Saving alwayes to Us, Our heires and Successors, the Faith and Allegiance of the said *William Penn*, his heires and assignes, and of all other Proprietaries, Tenants, and Inhabitants that are or shall be within the Territories and Precincts aforesaid; and Saving also, unto Us, Our heires and Successors, the Sovereignty of the aforesaid Countrey; TO HAVE, hold, possess, and enjoy the said Tract of Land, Countrey, Isles, Inletts, and other the premisses unto the said *William Penn*, his heires and assignes, to the only proper use and behoofe of the said *William Penn*, his heires and assignes for ever, to bee holden of Us, Our heires and Successors, Kings of *England*, as of Our Castle of *Windsor* in Our County of *Berks*, in free and comon Socage, by fealty only for all Services, and not *in Capite* or by Knights Service: Yielding and paying therefore to Us, Our heires and Successors, Two Beaver Skins, to bee delivered at Our said Castle of *Windsor* on the First Day of *January* in every Year; and also the Fifth Part of all Gold and Silver Oare, which shall from Time to Time happen to bee found within the Limitts aforesaid, cleare of all Charges. And of Our further Grace, certaine Knowledge, and meer motion, We have thought fitt to erect, and We doe hereby erect the aforesaid Countrey and Islands into a Province and Seigniorie, and doe call itt PENSILVANIA, and soe from henceforth we will have itt called.

AND forasmuch as Wee have hereby made and ordained the aforesaid *William Penn*, his heires and assignes, the true and absolute Proprietaries of all the Lands and Dominions aforesaid, KNOW YE THEREFORE, That We reposing speciall trust and Confidence in the fidelitie, wisedom, Justice, and provident circumspection of the said *William Penn* for us, our heires and Successors, Doe grant free, full, and absolute power by vertue of these presents to him and his heires, and to his and their Deputies, and Lieutenants, for the good and happy government of the said countrey, to ordeyne, make, and enact, and under his and their Seales to publish any Lawes whatsoever, for the raising of money for the publick use of the said Province, or for any other End, apperteyning either unto the publick state, peace, or safety of the said Countrey, or unto the private utility of perticular persons, according unto their best discretions, by and with the advice, assent, and approbation of the Freemen of the said Countrey, or the greater parte of them, or of their Delegates or Deputies, whom for the Enacting of the said Lawes, when, and as often as need shall require, Wee will that the said *William Penn* and his heires, shall assemble in such sort and forme, as to him and them shall seeme best, and the same Lawes duly to execute, unto and upon all People within the said Countrey and the Limitts thereof.

AND wee doe likewise give and grant unto the said *William Penn*, and his heires, and to his and their Deputies and Lieutenants, such power and authoritie to appoint and establish any Judges and Justices, Magistrates and Officers whatsoever, for what Causes soever, for the probates of wills, and for the granting of Administrations within the precincts aforesaid and with what Power soever, and in such forme as to the said *William Penn* or his heires shall seeme most convenient: Also to remitt, release, pardon, and abolish whether before Judgement or after all Crimes and Offences whatsoever comitted within the said Countrey against the said Lawes, Treason and wilful and malitious Murder onely excepted, and in those Cases to grant Reprieves, until Our pleasure may bee known therein and to doe all and every other thing and things, which unto the compleate Establishment of Justice, unto Courts and Tribunalls, formes of Judicature, and manner of Proceedings doe belong, altho in these presents expresse mention bee not made thereof; And by Judges by them delegated, to award Processe, hold Pleas, and determine in all the said Courts and Tribunalls all Actions, Suits, and Causes whatsoever, as well Criminall as Civill, Personall, reall and mixt; which Lawes, soe as aforesaid to bee published, Our Pleasure is, and soe Wee enjoyne, require, and command, shall bee most absolute and avaylable in law; and that all the Liege People and subjects of Us, Our heires and Successors, doe observe and keepe the same inviolabl in those partes, soe farr as they concerne them, under the paine therein expressed, or to bee expressed. PROVIDED nevertheles, That the said Lawes bee consonant to reason, and bee not repugnant or contrarie, but as neare as conveniently may bee agreeable to the Lawes and Statutes, and rights of this Our Kingdome of *England;* And Saving and reserving to Us, Our heires and Successors, the receiving, heareing, and determining of the appeale and appeales of all or any Person or Persons, of, in, or belonging to the Territories aforesaid, or touching any Judgement to bee there made or given.

AND forasmuch as in the Government of soe great a Countrey, sudden Accidents doe often happen, whereunto itt will bee necessarie to apply remedie before the Freeholders of the said Province, or their Delegates or Deputies, can bee assembled to the making of Lawes; neither will itt bee convenient that instantly upon every such emergent occasion, soe greate a multitude should be called together: Therefore for the better Government of the said Countrey Wee will, and ordaine, and by these presents, for us, our Heires and successors, Doe Grant unto the said *William Penn* and his heires, by themselves or by their Magistrates and Officers, in that behalfe duely to bee ordeyned as aforesaid, to make and constitute fitt and wholsome Ordinances, from time to time, within the said Countrey to bee kept and observed, as well for the preservation of the peace, as for the better government of the People there inhabiting; and publickly to notifie the same to all persons, whome the same doeth or anyway may concerne. Which ordinances, Our Will and Pleasure is, shall bee observed inviolably within the said Province, under Paines therein to be expressed, soe as the said Ordinances bee consonant to reason, and bee not repugnant nor contrary, but soe farre as conveniently may bee agreeable with the Lawes of our Kingdome of *England*, and soe as the said Ordinances be not extended in any Sort to bind, charge, or take away the right or Interest of any person or persons, for or in their Life, members, Freehold, goods, or Chattles. And our further will and pleasure is, that the Lawes for regulateing and governing of Propertie within the said Province, as well for the descent and enjoyment of lands, as likewise for the enjoyment and succession of goods and Chattles, and likewise as to Felonies, shall bee and continue the same, as they shall bee for the time being by the generall course of the Law in our Kingdome of *England*, until the said Lawes shall bee altered by the said *William Penn*, his heires or assignes, and by the Freemen of the said Province, their Delegates or Deputies, or the greater Part of them.

AND to the End the said *William Penn*, or heires, or other the Planters, Owners, or Inhabitants of the said Province, may not att any time hereafter by misconstruction of the powers aforesaid through inadvertencie or designe depart from that Faith and due allegiance, which by the lawes of this our Realme of *England*, they and all our subjects, in our Dominions and Territories, alwayes owe unto us, Our heires and Successors, by colour of any Extent or largenesse of powers hereby given, or pretended to bee given, or by force or colour of any lawes hereafter to bee made in the said Province, by vertue of any such Powers; OUR further will and Pleasure is, that a transcript or Duplicate of all Lawes, which shall bee soe as aforesaid made and published within the said Province, shall within five yeares after the makeing thereof, be transmitted and delivered to the Privy Councell, for the time being, of us, our heires and successors: And if any of the said Lawes, within the space of six moneths after that they shall be soe transmitted and delivered, bee declared by us, Our heires and Successors, in Our or their Privy Councell, inconsistent with the Sovereigntey or lawful Prerogative of us, our heires or Successors, or contrary to the Faith and Allegiance due by the legall government of this Realme, from the said *William Penn*, or his heires, or of the Planters and Inhabitants of the said Province, and that thereupon any of the said Lawes shall bee adjudged and declared to bee void by us, our heires or Successors, under our or their Privy Seale, that then and from thenceforth, such Lawes, concerning which such Judgement and declaration shall bee made, shall become voyd: Otherwise the said Lawes soe transmitted, shall remaine, and stand in full force, according to the true intent and meaneing thereof.

FURTHERMORE, that this new Colony may the more happily increase, by the multitude of People resorting thither; Therefore wee for us, our heirs and Successors, doe give and grant by these presents, power, Licence, and Libertie unto all the Liege People and Subjects, both present and future, of us, our heires, and Successors, excepting those who shall bee Specially forbidden to transport themselves and Families unto the said Countrey, with such convenient Shipping as by the lawes of this our Kingdome of *England* they ought to use, with fitting provisions, paying only the customes therefore due, and there to settle themselves, dwell and inhabitt, and plant, for the publick and their owne private advantage.

AND FURTHERMORE, that our Subjects may bee the rather encouraged to undertake this expedicion with ready and cheerful mindes, KNOW YE, That wee, of Our especiall grace, certaine knowledge, and meere motion, Doe Give and Grant by vertue of these presents, as well unto the said *William Penn*, and his heires, as to all others, who shall from time to time repaire unto the said Countrey, with a purpose to inhabitt there, or trade with the Natives of the said Countrey, full Licence to lade and freight in any ports whatsoever, of us, our heires and Successors, according to the lawes made or to be made within our Kingdome of *England*, and unto the said Countrey, by them, theire Servants or assignes, to transport all and singuler theire wares, goods, and Merchandizes, as likewise all sorts of graine whatsoever, and all other things whatsoever, necessary for food or cloathing, not prohibited by the Lawes and Statutes of our Kingdomes and Dominiones to be carryed out of the said Kingdomes, without any Lett or molestation of us, our heires and Successors, or of any of the Officers of us, our heires and Successors; saveing alwayes to us, our heires and Successors, the legall impositions, customes, and other Duties and payments, for the said Wares and Merchandize, by any Law or Statute due or to be due to us, our heires and Successors.

AND Wee doe further, for us, our heires and Successors, Give and grant unto the said *William Penn*, his heires and assignes, free and absolute power, to Divide the said Countrey and Islands into Townes, Hundreds and Counties, and to erect and incorporate Townes into Borroughs, and Borroughs into Citties, and to make and constitute ffaires and Marketts therein, with all other convenient priviledges and munities, according to the meritt of the inhabitants, and the ffitnes of the places, and to doe all and every other thing and things touching the premisses, which to him or them shall seeme requisite and meet; albeit they be such as of their owne nature might otherwise require a more especiall comandment and Warrant then in these presents is expressed.

WE Will alsoe, and by these presents, for us, our heires and Successors, Wee doe Give and grant Licence by this our Charter, unto the said *William Penn*, his heires and assignes, and to all the inhabitants and dwellers in the Province aforesaid, both present and to come, to import or unlade, by themselves or theire Servants, ffactors or assignes, all merchandizes and goods whatsoever, that shall arise of the fruites and comodities of the said Province, either by Land or Sea, into any of the ports of us, our heires and successors, in our Kingdome of *England*, and not into any other Countrey whatsoever: And wee give him full power to dispose of the said goods in the said ports; and if need bee, within one yeare next after the unladeing of the same, to lade the said Merchandizes and Goods again into the same or other shipps, and to export the same into any other Countreys, either of our Dominions or fforeigne, according to Lawe: Provided alwayes, that they pay such customes and impositions, subsidies and duties for the same, to us, our heires and Successors, as the rest of our Subjects of our Kingdome of *England*, for the time being, shall be bound to pay, and doe observe the Acts of Navigation, and other Lawes in that behalfe made.

AND FURTHERMORE, of our most ample and esspeciall grace, certaine knowledge, and meere motion, Wee doe, for us, our heires and Successors, Grant unto the said *William Penn*, his heires and assignes, full and absolute power and authoritie to make, erect, and constitute within the said Province and the Isles and Islets aforesaid, such and soe many Sea-ports, harbours, Creeks, Havens, Keyes, and other places, for discharge and unladeing of goods and Merchandizes, out of the shipps, Boates, and other Vessells, and ladeing them in such and soe many Places, and with such rights, Jurisdictions, liberties and priviledges unto the said ports belonging, as to him or them shall seeme most expedient; and that all and singuler the shipps, boates, and other Vessells, which shall come for merchandize and trade unto the said Province, or out of the same shall depart, shall be laden or unladen onely at such Ports as shall be erected and constituted by the said *William Penn*, his heires and assignes, any use, custome, or other thing to the contrary notwithstanding. Provided, that the said *William Penn*, and his heires, and the Lieutenants and Governors for the time being, shall admitt and receive in and about all such Ports, Havens, Creeks, and Keyes, all Officers and their Deputies, who shall from time to time be appointed for that Purpose by the ffarmers or Commissioners of our Customes for the time being.

AND Wee doe further appoint and ordaine, and by these presents, for us, our heires and Successors, Wee doe grant unto the said *William Penn*, his heires and assignes, That he, the said *William Penn*, his heires and assignes, may from time to time for ever, have and enjoy the Customes and Subsidies, in the Portes, Harbours, and other Creeks and Places aforesaid, within the Province aforesaid, payable or due for merchandizes and wares there to be laded and unladed, the said Customes and Subsidies to be reasonably assessed upon any occasion, by themselves and the People there as aforesaid to be assembled, to whom wee give power by these presents, for us, our heires and Successors, upon just cause and in dudue p'portion, to assesse and impose the same; Saveing unto us, our heires and Successors, such impositions and Customes, as by Act of Parliament are and shall be appointed.

AND it is Our further Will and pleasure, that the said *William Penn*, his heires and assignes, shall from time to time constitute and appoint an Attorney or Agent, to Reside in or neare our City of *London*, who shall make knowne the place where he shall dwell or may be found, unto the Clerke of our Privy Counsell for the time being, or one of them, and shall be ready to appeare in any of our Courts att *Westminster*, to Answer for any Misdemeanors that shall be comitted, or by any wilfull default or neglect permitted by the said *William Penn*, his heires or assignes, against our Lawes of Trade or Navigation; and after it shall be ascertained in any of our said Courts, what damages Wee or our heires or Successors shall have sustained by such default or neglect, the said *William Penn*, his heirs and assignes shall pay the same within one yeare after such taxation, and demand thereof from such Attorney: or in case there shall be noe such Attorney by the space of one yeare, or such Attorney shall not make payment of such damages within the space of one yeare, and answer such other forfeitures and penalties within the said time, as by the Acts of Parliament in *England* are or shall be provided, according to the true intent and meaneing of these presents; then it shall be lawfull for us, our heires and Successors, to seize and Resume the government of the said Province or Countrey, and the same to retaine untill payment shall be made thereof: But notwithstanding any such Seizure or resumption of the government, nothing concerneing the propriety or ownership of any Lands, tenements, or other hereditaments, or goods or chattels of any of the Adventurers, Planters, or owners, other then the respective Offenders there, shall anyway be affected or molested thereby.

PROVIDED alwayes, and our will and pleasure is, that neither the said *William Penn*, nor his heires, or any other the inhabitants of the said Province, shall at any time hereafter have or maintain any Correspondence with any other king, prince, or State, or with any of theire subjects, who shall then be in Warr against us, our heires or Successors; Nor shall the said *William Penn*, or his heires, or any other the Inhabitants of the said Province, make Warre or doe any act of Hostility against any other king, prince, or State, or any of theire Subjects, who shall then be in league or amity with us, our heires or successors.

AND, because in soe remote a Countrey, and scituate neare many Barbarous Nations, the incursions as well of the Savages themselves, as of other enemies, pirates and robbers, may probably be feared ; Therefore Wee have given, and for us, our heires and Successors, Doe give power by these presents unto the said *William Penn*, his heires and assignes, by themselves or theire Captaines or other their Officers, to levy, muster and traine all sorts of men, of what condition soever or wheresoever borne, in the said Province of *Pensilvania*, for the time being, and to make Warre, and to pursue the enemies and Robbers aforesaid, as well by Sea as by Land, even without the Limitts of the said Province, and by God's assistance to vanquish and take them, and being taken to put them to death by the Law of Warre, or to save them, att theire pleasure, and to doe all and every other Art and Thing which to the Charge and Office of a Captaine-Generall of an Army belongeth or hath accustomed to belong, as fully and ffreely as any Captaine-Generall of an Army hath ever had the same.

AND FURTHERMORE, of Our especiall grace and of our certaine knowledge and meere motion, wee have given and granted, and by these presents, for us, our heires and Successors, do Give and Grant unto the said *William Penn*, his Heires and Assigns, full and absolute power, licence and authoritie, that he, the said *William Penn*, his heires and assignes, from time to time hereafter forever, att his or theire own Will and pleasure may assigne, alien, Grant, demise, or enfeoffe of the Premises soe many and such partes and parcells to him or them that shall be willing to purchase the same, as they shall thinke fitt, To have and to hold to them the said person and persons willing to take or purchase, theire heires and assignes, in ffee-simple or ffee-taile, or for the terme of life, or lives or yeares, to be held of the said *William Penn*, his heires and assignes, as of the said Seigniory of *Windsor*, by such services, customes and rents, as shall seeme ffitt to the said *William Penn*, his heires and assignes, and not imediately of us, our heires and successors. AND to the same person or persons, and to all and every of them, wee doe give and grant by these presents, for us, our heires and successors, licence, authoritie and power, that such person or persons may take the premisses, or any parcell thereof, of the aforesaid *William Penn*, his heires or assignes, and the same hold to themselves, their heires and assignes, in what estate of inheritance soever, in ffee-simple or in ffee-taile, or otherwise, as to him, the said *William Penn*, his heires and assignes, shall seem expedient: The Statute made in the parliament of *EDWARD*, sonne of King *HENRY*, late King of *England*, our predecessor, commonly called *The Statute QUIA EMPTORES TERRARUM*, lately published in our Kingdome of *England* in any wise notwithstanding.

AND by these presents wee give and Grant Licence unto the said *William Penn*, and his heires, likewise to all and every such person and persons to whom the said *William Penn* or his heires shall att any time hereafter grant any estate or inheritance as aforesaid, to erect any parcells of Land within the Province aforesaid into Mannors, by and with the Licence to be first had and obteyned for that purpose, under the hand and Seale of the said *William Penn* or his heires; and in every of the said Mannors to have and to hold a Court-Baron, with all thinges whatsoever which to a Court-Baron do belong, and to have and to hold View of ffrank-pledge for the conservation of the peace and the better government of those partes, by themselves or their Stewards, or by the Lords for the time being of the Mannors to be deputed when they shall be erected, and in the same to use all things belonging to the View of ffrank-pledge. AND Wee doe further grant licence and authoritie, that every such person or persons who shall erect any such Mannor or Mannors, as aforesaid, shall or may grant all or any parte of his said Lands to any person or persons, in ffee-simple, or any other estate of inheritance to be held of the said Mannors respectively, soe as noe further tenures shall be created, but that upon all further and other alienations thereafter to be made, the said lands soe aliened shall be held of the same Lord and his heires, of whom the alienor did then before hold, and by the like rents and Services which were before due and accustomed.

AND FURTHER our pleasure is, and by these presents, for us, our heires and Successors, Wee doe covenant and grant to and with the said *William Penn*, and his heires and assignes, That Wee, our heires and Successors, shall at no time hereafter sett or make, or cause to be sett, any impossition, custome or other taxation, rate or contribution whatsoever, in and upon the dwellers and inhabitants of the aforesaid Province, for their Lands, tenements, goods or chattells within the said Province, or in and upon any goods or merchandize within the said Province, or to be laden or unladen within the ports or harbours of the said Province, unless the same be with the consent of the Proprietary, or chiefe governor, and assembly, or by act of Parliament in *England*.

AND Our Pleasure is, and for us, our heires and Successors, Wee charge and comand, that this our Declaration shall from henceforth be received and allowed from time to time in all our courts, and before all the Judges of us, our heires and Successors, for a sufficient and lawfull discharge, payment and acquittance; commanding all and singular the officers and ministers of us, our heires and Successors, and enjoyneing them upon pain of our high displeasure, that they doe not presume att any time to attempt anything to the contrary of the premisses, or that doe in any sort withstand the same, but that they be att all times aiding and assisting, as is fitting unto the said *William Penn*, and his heires, and to the inhabitants and merchants of the Province aforesaid, their Servants, Ministers, ffactors and Assignes, in the full use and fruition of the benefitt of this our Charter.

AND Our further pleasure is, and wee doe hereby, for us, our heires and Successors, charge and require, that if any of the inhabitants of the said Province, to the number of Twenty, shall at any time hereafter be desirous, and shall by any writeing, or by any person deputed for them, signify such their desire to the Bishop of *London* that any preacher or preachers, to be approved of by the said Bishop, may be sent unto them for their instruction, that then such preacher or preachers shall and may be and reside within the said Province, without any deniall or molestation whatsoever.

AND if perchance it should happen hereafter any doubts or questions should arise, concerneing the true Sense and meaning of any word, clause, or Sentence conteyned in this our present Charter, Wee will ordaine, and comand, that att all times and in all things, such interpretation be made thereof, and allowed in any of our Courts whatsoever, as shall be adjudged most advantageous and favourable unto the said *William Penn*, his heires and assignes: Provided always that no interpretation be admitted thereof by which the allegiance due unto us, our heires and Successors, may suffer any prejudice or diminution; Although express mention be not made in these presents of the true yearly value, or certainty of the premisses, or of any parte thereof, or of other gifts and grants made by us and our progenitors or predecessors unto the said *William Penn:* Any Statute, Act, ordinance, provision, proclamation, or restraint heretofore had, made, published, ordained or provided, or any other thing, cause, or matter whatsoever, to the contrary thereof in any wise notwithstanding.

IN WITNESS whereof wee have caused these our Letters to be made patents: Witness OUR SELFE, at *Westminster*, the *Fourth* day of *March*, in the *Three and Thirtieth* Yeare of Our Reign.

By Writt of Privy Seale,

PIGOTT.

PENN'S PLAN OF UNION—1697.

THIS plan of Union was presented to the Board of Trade in 1697 by Wm. Penn, in opposition to the Board's plan of consolidation. This is the first of the native plans of Union.

Consult *Frothingham's Rise*, 110; *Bancroft's U. S.*, cen, ed. II., 277; last ed., II., 74; *Chalmers' Revolt*, I., 271; *Hildreth's U. S.*, II., 198.

MR. PENN'S PLAN FOR A UNION OF THE COLONIES IN AMERICA.

A BRIEFE and Plaine Scheam how the English Colonies in the North parts of America, viz.: Boston, Connecticut, Road Island, New York, New Jerseys, Pensilvania, Maryland, Virginia, and Carolina may be made more usefull to the Crowne, and one another's peace and safty with an universall concurrence.

1st. That the severall Colonies before mentioned do meet once a year, and oftener if need be, during the war, and at least once in two years in times of peace, by their stated and appointed Deputies, to debate and resolve of such measures as are most adviseable for their better understanding, and the public tranquility and safety.

2d. That in order to it two persons well qualified for sence, sobriety and substance be appointed by each Province, as their Representatives or Deputies, which in the whole make the Congress to consist of twenty persons.

3d. That the King's Commissioner for that purpose

specially appointed shall have the chaire and preside in the said Congresse.

4th. That they shall meet as near as conveniently may be to the most centrall Colony for use of the Deputies.

5th. Since that may in all probability, be New York both because it is near the Center of the Colonies and for that it is a Frontier and in the King's nomination, the Govr. of that Colony may therefore also be the King's High Commissioner during the Session after the manner of Scotland.

6th. That their business shall be to hear and adjust all matters of Complaint or difference between Province and Province. As, 1st, where persons quit their own Province and goe to another, that they may avoid their just debts, tho they be able to pay them, 2nd, where offenders fly Justice, or Justice cannot well be had upon such offenders in the Provinces that entertaine them, 3dly, to prevent or cure injuries in point of Commerce, 4th, to consider of ways and means to support the union and safety of these Provinces against the publick enemies. In which Congresse the Quotas of men and charges will be much easier, and more equally sett, then it is possible for any establishment made here to do; for the Provinces, knowing their own condition and one another's, can debate that matter with more freedome and satisfaction and better adjust and ballance their affairs in all respects for their common safty.

7ly. That in times of war the King's High Commissioner shall be generall or chief Commander of the severall Quotas upon service against a common enemy as he shall be advised, for the good and benefit of the whole.

CHARTER OF GEORGIA—1732.

THE colony originated in the philanthropy of Gen. James Oglethrope who sought to provide in America a refuge for the poor debtors of England. Oglethrope created a general interest in the scheme. The Society for Propagating the Gospel in Foreign Parts lent its aid and donated ten thousand pounds. The charter was issued June 9, 1732, for territory included in the Carolina Charters of 1662–63. In November, 1732, Oglethrope sailed with thirty-five families and began a settlement at Charleston early the next year. The charter expired by limitation in 1752 and the trustees, discouraged by the result thus far, did not seek a renewal of the grant, but allowed the colony to become a royal province. This patent is of interest as showing the final form assumed by the charters.

Consult *Bancroft's U. S.*, 1st ed., III., 491; cen. ed., II., 560; last ed., II., 281; *Hildreth's U. S.*, II., 362; *Bryant and Gay's U. S.*, III., 140; *Chalmers' Revolt*, 180.

CHARTER OF GEORGIA—1732.

GEORGE the second, by the grace of God, of Great Britain, France and Ireland, king, defender of the faith, and so forth. To all to whom these presents shall come, greeting.

Whereas we are credibly informed, that many of our poor subjects are, through misfortunes and want of employment, reduced to great necessity, insomuch as by their labor they are not able to provide a maintenance for themselves and families; and if they had means to defray their charges of passage, and other expences, incident to new settlements, they would be glad to settle in any of our provinces in America where by cultivating the lands, at present waste and desolate, they might not only gain a comfortable subsistence for themselves and families, but also strengthen our colonies and increase the trade, navigation and wealth of these our realms. And whereas our provinces in North America, have been frequently ravaged by Indian enemies; more especially that of South-Carolina, which in the late war, by the neighboring savages, was laid waste by fire and sword, and great numbers of English inhabitants, miserably massacred, and our loving subjects who now inhabit them, by reason of the smallness of their numbers, will in case of a new war, be exposed to the late calamities; inasmuch as their whole southern frontier continueth unsettled, and lieth open to the said savages—And whereas we think it highly becoming our crown and royal dignity, to protect all our loving subjects, be they never so distant from us; to extend our fatherly compassion even to the meanest and most infatuated of our people, and to relieve the wants of our above mentioned poor subjects; and that it will be highly conducive for accomplishing those ends, that a regular colony of the said poor people be settled and established in the southern territories of Carolina. And whereas we have been well assured, that if we will be graciously pleased to erect and settle a corporation, for the receiving, managing and disposing of the contributions of our loving subjects: divers persons would be induced to contribute to the purposes aforesaid—Know ye therefore, that we have, for the considerations aforesaid, and for the better and more orderly carrying on of the said good purposes; of our special grace, certain knowledge and mere motion, willed, ordained, constituted and appointed, and by these presents, for us, our heirs and successors, do will, ordain, constitute, declare and grant, that our right trusty and well beloved John, lord-viscount Purcival, of our kingdom of Ireland, our trusty and well beloved Edward Digby, George Carpenter, James Oglethorpe, George Heathcote, Thomas Tower, Robert Moore, Robert Hucks, Roger Holland, William Sloper, Francis Eyles, John Laroche, James Vernon, William Beletha, esquires, A. M. John Burton, B. D. Richard Bundy, A. M. Arthur Bedford, A. M. Samuel Smith, A. M. Adam Anderson and Thomas Corane, gentleman; and such other persons as shall be elected in the manner herein after mentioned, and their successors to be elected in the manner herein after directed; be, and shall be one body politic and corporate, in deed and in name, by the name of the Trustees for establishing the colony of Georgia in America; and them and their successors by the same name, we do, by these presents, for us, our heirs and successors, really and fully make, ordain, constitute and declare, to be one body politic in deed and in name forever; and that by the same name, they and their successors, shall and may have perpetual succession; and that they and their successors by that name shall and may forever hereafter, be persons able and capable in the law, to purchase, have, take, receive and enjoy, to them and their successors, any manors, messuages, lands, tenements, rents, advowsons, liberties, privileges, jurisdictions, franchises, and other hereditaments whatsoever, lying and being in Great Britain, or any part thereof, of whatsoever nature, kind or quality, or value they be, in fee and in perpetuity, not exceeding the yearly value of one thousand pounds, beyond reprises; also estates for lives, and for years, and all other manner of goods, chattels and things whatsoever they be; for the better settling and supporting, and maintaining the said colony, and other uses aforesaid; and to give, grant, let and demise the said manors, messuages, lands, tenements, hereditaments, goods, chattels and things whatsoever aforesaid, by lease or leases, for term of years, in possession at the time of granting thereof, and not in reversion, not exceeding the term of thirty-one years, from the time of granting thereof; on which in case no fine be taken, shall be reserved the full, and in case a fine be taken, shall be reserved at least a moiety of the value that the same shall reasonably and *bona fide* be worth at the time of such demise; and that they and their successors, by the name aforesaid, shall and may forever hereafter, be persons able, capable in the law, to purchase, have, take, receive, and enjoy, to them and their successors, any lands, territories, possessions, tenements, jurisdictions, franchises and hereditaments whatsoever, lying and being in America, of what quantity, quality or value whatsoever they be, for the better settling and supporting and maintaining the said colony; and that by the name aforesaid they shall and may be able to sue and be sued, plead and be impleaded, answer and be answered unto, defend and be defended, in all courts and places whatsoever, and before whatsoever judges, justices, and other officers, of us, our heirs and successors, in all and singular actions, plaints, pleas, matters, suits and demands, of what kind, nature or quality soever they be; and to act and to do, all matters and things in as ample manner and form as any other our liege subjects of this realm of Great Britain, and that they and their successors forever hereafter, shall and may have a common seal, to serve for the causes and businesses of them and their successors; and that it shall and may be lawful for them and their successors, to change, break, alter and make new the said seal, from time to time, and at their pleasure, and as they shall think best. And we do further grant, for us, our heirs and successors, that the said corporation, and the common council of the said corporation, hereinafter by us appointed, may from time to time, and at all times, meet about their affairs when and where they please, and transact and carry on the business of the said corporation. And for the better execution of the purposes aforesaid, we do, by these presents, for us, our heirs and successors, give and grant to the said corporation, and their successors, that they and their successors forever, may upon the third Thursday in the month of March, yearly, meet at some convenient place to be appointed by the said corporation, or major part of them who shall be present at any meeting of the said corporation, to be had for the appointing of the said place; and that they, or two thirds of such of them, that shall be present at such yearly meeting, and at no other meeting of the said corporation, between the hours of ten in the morning and four in the afternoon of the same day, choose and elect such person or persons to be members of the said corporation, as they shall think beneficial to the good designs of the said corporation. And our further will and pleasure is, that if it shall happen that any person hereinafter by us appointed, as the common council of the said corporation, or any persons to be elected or admitted members of the said common council in the manner hereafter directed, shall die, or shall by writing under his and their hands respectively resign his or their office or offices of common council man or common council men; the said corporation, or the major part of such of them as shall be present, shall and may at such meeting, on the said third Thursday in March yearly, in manner as aforesaid, next after such death or resignation, and at no other meeting of the said corporation, into the room or place of such person or persons so dead or so resigning, elect and choose one or more such person or persons, being members of the said corporation, as to them shall seem meet: and our will is, that all and every the person or persons which shall from time to time hereafter be elected common council men of the said corporation as aforesaid, do and shall, before he or they act as common men of the said corporation, take an oath for the faithful and due execution of their office; which oath the president of the said corporation for the time being, is hereby authorized and required to administer to such person or persons elected as aforesaid. And our will and pleasure is, that the first president of the said corporation is and shall be our trusty and well-beloved, the said Lord John Viscount Percival; and that the said president shall, within thirty days after the passing this charter, cause a summons to be issued to the several members of the said corporation herein particularly named, to meet at such time and place as he shall appoint, to consult about and transact the business of said corporation. And our will and pleasure is, and we, by these presents, for us, our heirs, and successors, grant, ordain, and direct, that the common council of this corporation shall consist of fifteen in number; and we do, by these presents, nominate, constitute, and appoint our right trusty and well-beloved John Lord Viscount Percival, our trusty and beloved Edward Digby, George Carpenter, James Oglethorpe, George Heathcote, Thomas Laroche, James Vernon, William Beletha, esqrs., and Stephen Hales, Master of Arts, to be the common council of the said corporation, to continue in the said office during their good behavior. And whereas it is our royal intention, that the members of the said corporation should be increased by election, as soon as conveniently may be, to a greater number than is hereby nominated; Our further will and pleasure is, and we do hereby, for us, our heirs and successors, ordain and direct, that from the time of such increase of the members of the said corporation, the number of the common council shall be increased to twenty-four; and that the same assembly at which such additional members of the said corporation shall be chosen, there shall likewise be elected in the manner hereinbefore directed for the election of common council men, nine persons to be the said common council men, and to make up the number twenty-four. And our further will and pleasure is, that our trusty and well beloved Edward Digby, esquire, shall be the first chairman of the common council of the said corporation ; and that the said lord-viscount Purcival shall be, and continue, president of the said corporation, and that the said Edward Digby shall be and continue chairman of the common council of the said corporation, respectively, until the meeting which shall be had next and immediately after the first meeting of the said corporation, or of the common council of the said corporation respectively, and no longer; at which said second meeting, and every other subsequent and future meeting of the said corporation or of the common council of the said corporation respectively, in order to preserve an indifferent rotation of the several offices, of president of the corporation, and of chairman of the common council of the said corporation we do direct and ordain that all and every the person and persons, members of the said common council for the time being, and no other, being present at such meetings, shall severally and respectively in their turns, preside at the meetings which shall from time to time be held of the said corporation, or of the common council of the said corporation respectively: and in case any doubt or question shall at any time arise touching or concerning the right of any member of the said common council to preside at any meeting of the said corporation, or at the common council of the said corporation, the same shall respectively be determined by the major part of the said corporation, or of the common council of the said corporation respectively, who shall be present at such meeting. Provided always, that no member of the said common council having served in the offices of president of the said corporation, or of chairman of the common council of the said corporation, shall be capable of being, or of serving as president or chairman at any meeting of the said corporation, or common council of the said corporation next and immediately ensuing that in which he so served as president of the said corporation or chairman of the said common council of the said corporation respectively ; unless it shall so happen that at any such meeting of the said corporation, there shall not be any other member of the said common council present. And our will and pleasure is, that at all and every of the meetings of the said corporation, or of the common council of the said corporation, the president or chairman for the time being, shall have a voice and shall vote, and shall act as a member of the said corporation or of the common council of the said corporation, at such meeting ; and in case of any equality of votes, the said president or chairman for the time being, shall have a casting vote. And our further will and pleasure is, that no president of the said corporation, or chairman of the common council of the said corporation or member of the said common council or corporation, by us by these presents appointed, or hereafter from time to time to be elected and appointed in manner aforesaid, shall have, take, or receive, directly or indirectly, any salary, fee, perquisite, benefit or profit whatsoever, for or by reason of his or their serving the said corporation, or common council of the said corporation, or president, chairman or common council-man, or as being a member of the said corporation. And our will and pleasure is, that the said herein before appointed president, chairman or common council-men, before he and they act respectively as such, shall severally take an oath for the faithful and due execution of their trust, to be administered to the president by the Chief Baron of our Court of Exchequer, for the time being, and by the president of the said corporation to the rest of the common council, who are hereby authorised severally and respectively, to administer the same. And our will and pleasure is, that all and every person and persons, shall have in his or their own name or names, or in the name or names of any person or persons in trust for him or them, or for his or their benefit, any place, office or employment of profit, under the said corporation, shall be incapable of being elected a member of the said corporation; and if any member of the said corporation during such time as he shall continue a member thereof, shall in his own name or in the name of any person or persons, in trust for him or for his benefit, have, hold or exercise, accept, possess or enjoy, any office, place or employment of profit, under the said corporation, or under the common council of the said corporation—such member shall from the time of his having, holding, exercising, accepting, possessing and enjoying such office, place and employment of profit, cease to be a member of the said corporation. And we do for us, our heirs and successors, grant unto the said corporation, that they and their successors or the major part of such of them as shall be present at any meeting of the said corporation, convened and assembled for that purpose by a convenient notice thereof, shall have power from time to time, and at all times hereafter, to authorize and appoint such persons as they shall think fit to take subscriptions, and to gather and collect such moneys as shall be by any person or persons contributed for the purposes aforesaid; and shall and may revoke and make void such authorities and appointments, as often as they shall see cause so to do. And we do hereby for us, our heirs and successors, ordain and direct, that the said corporation every year lay an account in writing before the chancellor, or speaker, or commissioners, for the custody of the great seal of Great-Britain, of us, our heirs and successors; the Chief Justice of the Court of King's Bench, the Master of Rolls, the Chief Justice of the Court of Common Pleas, and the chief Baron of the Exchequer of us, our heirs and successors for the time being, or any two of them; of all moneys and effects by them received or expended, for carrying on the good purposes aforesaid. And we do hereby, for us, our heirs and successors, give and grant unto the said corporation, and their successors, full power and authority to constitute, ordain and make, such and so many by-laws, constitutions, orders and ordinances, as to them, or the greater part of them, at their general meeting for that purpose, shall seem necessary and convenient for the well ordaining and governing of the said corporation; and the said by-laws, constitutions, orders and ordinances, or any of them, to alter and annul, as they or the major part of them then present shall see requisite; and in and by such by-laws, rules, orders and ordinances, to sell, impose and inflict, reasonable pains and penalties upon any offender or offenders, who shall trangress, break or violate the said by-laws, constitutions, orders and ordinances, so made as aforesaid, and to mitigate the same as they or the major part of them then present shall think convenient; which said pains and penalties, shall and may be levied, sued for, taken, retained, and recovered, by the said corporation and their successors, by their officers and servants, from time to time, to be appointed for that purpose, by action of debt, or by any other lawful ways or means, to the use and behoof of the said corporation and their successors, all and singular: which by-laws, constitutions, orders and ordinances, so as aforesaid to be made, we will shall be duly observed and kept, under the pains and penalties therein to be contained, so always, as the said by-laws, constitutions, orders, and ordinances, pains and penalties, from time to time to be made and imposed, be reasonable and not contrary or repugnant to the laws or statutes of this our realm; and that such by-laws, constitutions and ordinances, pains and penalties, from time to time to be made and imposed; and any repeal or alteration thereof, or any of them, may be likewise agreed to be established and confirmed by the said general meeting of the said corporation, to be held and kept next after the same shall be respectively made. And whereas the said corporation intend to settle a colony, and to make an habitation and plantation in that part of our province of South-Carolina, in America, herein after described—Know ye, that we greatly desiring the happy success of the said corporation, for their further encouragement in accomplishing so excellent a work have of our aforesaid grace, certain knowledge and mere motion, given and granted by these presents, for us, our heirs and successors, do give and grant to the said corporation and their successors under the reservation, limitation and declaration, hereafter expressed, seven undivided parts, the whole in eight equal parts to be divided, of all those lands, countrys and territories situate, lying and being in that part of South-Carolina, in America, which lies from the most northern part of a stream or river there, commonly called the Savannah, all along the sea coast to the southward, unto the most southern stream of a certain other great water or river called the Alatamaha, and westterly from the heads of the said rivers respectively, in direct lines to the south seas; and all that share, circuit and precinct of land, within the said boundaries, with the islands on the sea, lying opposite to the eastern coast of the said lands, within twenty leagues of the same, which are not inhabited already, or settled, by any authority derived from the crown of Great-Britain: together with all the soils, grounds, havens, ports, gulfs, and bays, mines, as well royal mines of gold and silver, as other minerals, precious stones, quarries, woods, rivers, waters, fishings, as well royal fishings of whale and sturgeon as other fishings, pearls, commodities, jurisdictions, royalties, franchises, privileges and pre-eminences within the said frontiers and precincts thereof and thereunto, in any sort belonging or appertaining, and which we by our letters patent may or can grant, and in as ample manner and sort as we may or any of our royal progenitors have hitherto granted to any company, body politic or corporate, or to any adventurer or adventurers, undertaker or undertakers, of any discoveries plantations or traffic, of, in, or unto any foreign parts whatsoever; and in as legal and ample manner, as if the same were herein particularly mentioned and expressed; to have, hold, possess and enjoy, the said seven undivided parts, the whole into eight equal parts, to be divided as aforesaid, of all and singular the lands, countries and territories, with all and singular other the premises herein before by these presents granted or mentioned, or intended to be granted to them, the said corporation, and their successors forever, for the better support of the said colony, to be holden of us, our heirs and successors as of our honour of Hampton-court, in our county of Middlesex in free and common soccage, and not in capite, yielding, and paying therefor to us, our heirs and successors yearly forever, the sum of four shillings for every hundred acres of the said lands, which the said corporation shall grant, demise, plant or settle; the said payment not to commence or to be made, until ten years after such grant, demise, planting or settling; and to be answered and paid to us, our heirs and successors, in such manner and in such species of money or notes, as shall be current in payment, by proclamation from time to time, in our said province of South-Carolina. All which lands, countries, territories and premises, hereby granted or mentioned, and intended to be granted, we do by these presents, make, erect and create one independent and separate province, by the name of Georgia, by which name we will, the same henceforth be called. And that all and every person or persons, who shall at any time hereafter inhabit or reside within our said province, shall be, and are hereby declared to be free, and shall not be subject to or be bound to obey any laws, orders, statutes or constitutions, which have been heretofore made, ordered or enacted by, for, or as, the laws, orders, statutes or constitutions of our said province of South-Carolina, (save and except only the in chief of the militia, of our said province of Georgia, to our governor for the time being of South-Carolina, in manner hereafter declared;) but shall be subject to, and bound to obey, such laws, orders, statutes and constitutions as shall from time to time be made, ordered and enacted, for the better government of the said province of Georgia, in the manner hereinafter declared. And we do hereby, for our heirs and successors, ordain, will and establish, that for and during the term of twenty-one years, to commence from the date of these our letters patent, the said corporation assembled for that purpose, shall and may form and prepare, laws, statutes and ordinances, fit and necessary for and concerning the government of the said colony, and not repugnant to the laws and statutes of England; and the same shall and may present under their common seal to us, our heirs and successors, in our or their privy council for our or their approbation or disallowance: and the said laws, statutes and ordinances, being approved of by us, our heirs and successors, in our or their privy council, shall from thence forth be in full force and virtue within our said province of Georgia. And forasmuch as the good and prosperous success of the said colony cannot but chiefly depend, next under the blessing of God, and the support of our royal authority, upon the provident and good direction of the whole enterprise, and that it will be too great a burthen upon all the members of the said corporation to be convened so often as may be requisite, to hold meetings for the settling, supporting, ordering, and maintaining the said colony; therefore we do will, ordain and establish, that the said common council for the time being, of the said corporation being assembled for that purpose, or the major part of them, shall from time to time, and at all times hereafter, have full power and authority to dispose of, extend and apply all the monies and effects belonging to the said corporation, in such manner and ways and by such expenses as they shall think best to conduce to the carrying on and effecting the good purposes herein mentioned and intended; and also shall have full power in the name and on account of the said corporation, and with and under their common seal, to enter under any covenants or contracts, for carrying on and effecting the purposes aforesaid. And our further will and pleasure is, that the said common council for the time being, or the major part of such common council, which shall be present and assembled for that purpose, from time to time, and at all times hereafter, shall and may nominate, constitute and appoint a treasurer or treasurers, secretary or secretaries, and such other officers, ministers and servants of the said corporation as to them or the major part of them as shall be present, shall seem proper or requisite for the good management of their affairs; and at their will and pleasure to displace, remove and put out such treasurer or treasurers, secretary or secretaries, and all such other officers, ministers and servants, as often as they shall think fit so to do; and others in the room, office, place or station of him or them so displaced, removed or put out, to nominate, constitute and appoint; and shall and may determine and appoint, such reasonable salaries, perquisites and other rewards, for their labor, or service of such officers, servants and persons as to the said common council shall seem meet; and all such officers servants and persons shall, before the acting in their respective offices, take an oath to be to them administered by the chairman for the time being of the said common council of the said corporation, who is hereby authorized to administer the same, for the faithful and due execution of their respective offices and places. And our will and pleasure is, that all such person and persons, who shall from time to time be chosen or appointed treasurer, or treasurers, secretary or secretaries of the said corporation, in manner herein after directed, shall during such times as they shall serve in the said offices respectively, be incapable of being a member of the said corporation. And we do further of our special grace, certain knowledge and mere motion, for us, our heirs and successors, grant, by these presents, to the said corporation and their successors, that it shall be lawful for them and their officers or agents, at all times hereafter, to transport and convey out of our realm of Great-Britain, or any other of our dominions, into the said province of Georgia, to be there settled so many of our loving subjects, or any foreigners that are willing to become our subjects, and live under our allegiance, in the said colony, as shall be willing to go to, inhabit, or reside there, with sufficient shipping, armour, weapons, powder, shot, ordnance, munition, victuals, merchandize and wares, as are esteemed by the wild people; clothing, implements, furniture, cattle, horses, mares, and all other things necessary for the said colony, and for the use and defence and trade with the people there, and in passing and returning to and from the same. Also we do, for ourselves and successors, declare, by these presents, that all and every the persons which shall happen to be born within the said province, and every of their children and posterity, shall have and enjoy all liberties, franchises and immunities of free denizens and natural born subjects, within any of our dominions, to all intents and purposes, as if abiding and born within this our kingdom of Great-Britain, or any other dominion.——And for the greater ease and encouragement of our loving subjects and such others as shall come to inhabit in our said colony, we do by these presents, for us, our heirs and successors, grant, establish and ordain, that forever hereafter, there shall be a liberty of conscience allowed in the worship of God, to all persons inhabiting, or which shall inhabit or be resident within our said province, and that all such persons, except papists, shall have a free exercise of religion, so they be contented with the quiet and peaceable enjoyment of the same, not giving offence or scandal to the government. And our further will and pleasure is, and we do hereby for us, our heirs and successors, declare and grant, that it shall and may be lawful for the said common council, or the major part of them assembled for that purpose, in the name of the corporation, and under the common seal, to distribute, convey, assign and set over such particular portions of lands, tenements and hereditaments by these presents granted to the said corporation, unto such our loving subjects, natural born, denizens or others that shall be willing to become our subjects, and live under our allegiance in the said colony, upon such terms, and for such estates, and upon such rents, reservations and conditions as the same may be lawfully granted, and as to the said common council, or the major part of them so present, shall seem fit and proper. Provided always that no grants shall be made of any part of the said lands unto any person, being a member of the said corporation; or to any other person in trust, for the benefit of any member of the said corporation; and that no person having any estate or interest, in law or equity, in any part of the said lands, shall be capable of being a member of the said corporation, during the continuance of such estate or interest. Provided also, that no greater quantity of lands be granted, either entirely or in parcels, to or for the use, or in trust for any one person, than five hundred acres; and that all grants made contrary to the true intent and meaning hereof, shall be absolutely null and void. And we do hereby grant and ordain, that such person or persons, for the time being as shall be thereunto appointed by the said corporation, shall and may at all times, and from time to time hereafter, have full power and authority to administer and give the oaths, appointed by an act of parliament, made in the first year of the reign of our late royal father, to be taken instead of the oaths of allegiance and supremacy; and also the oath of abjuration, to all and every person and persons which shall at any time be inhabiting or residing with our said colony; and in like cases to administer the solemn affirmation to any of the persons commonly called quakers, in such manner as by the laws of our realm of Great-Britain, the same may be administered. And we do, of our further grace, certain knowledge and mere motion, grant, establish and ordain, for us, our heirs and successors, that the said corporation and their successors, shall have full power and authority, for and during the term of twenty-one years, to commence from the date of these our letters patent, to erect and constitute judicatories and courts of record, or other courts, to be held in the name of us, our heirs and successors, for the hearing and determining of all manner of crimes, offences, pleas, processes, plaints, actions, matters, causes and things whatsoever, arising or happening, within the said province of Georgia, or between persons of Georgia; whether the same be criminal or civil, and whether the said crimes be capital or not capital, and whether the said pleas be real, personal or mixed: and for awarding and making out executions thereupon; to which courts and judicatories, we do hereby, for us, our heirs and successors, give and grant full power and authority from time to time, to administer oaths for the discovery of truth in any matter in controversy, or depending before them, or the solemn affirmation, to any of the persons commonly called quakers, in such manner, as by the laws of our realm of Great-Britain, the same may be administered. And our further will and pleasure is, that the said corporation and their successors, do from time to time, and at all times hereafter, register or cause to be registered, all such leases, grants, plantings, conveyances, settlements, and improvements whatsoever, as shall at any time hereafter be made by, or in the name of the said corporation of any lands, tenements or hereditaments within the said province; and shall yearly send and transmit, or cause to be sent or transmitted, authentic accounts of such leases, grants, conveyances, settlements and improvements respectively, unto the auditor of the plantations for the time being, or his deputy, and also to our surveyor for the time being of our said province of South-Carolina; to whom we do hereby grant full power and authority from time to time, as often as need shall require, to inspect and survey, such of the said lands and premises, as shall be demised, granted and settled as aforesaid; which said survey and inspection, we do hereby declare, to be intended to ascertain the quitrents which shall from time to time become due to us, our heirs and successors, according to the reservation herein before mentioned, and for no other purposes whatsoever; hereby for us, our heirs and successors, strictly enjoining and commanding, that neither our or their surveyor, or any person whatsoever, under the pretext and colour of making the said survey or inspection, shall take, demand or receive, any gratuity, fee or reward, of or from, any person or persons, inhabiting in the said colony, or from the said corporation or common council of the same, on the pain of forfeiture of the said office or offices, and incurring our highest displeasure. Provided always, and our further will and pleasure is, that all leases, grants and conveyances to be made by or in the name of the said corporation, of any lands within the said province, or a memorial containing the substance and effect thereof, shall be registered with the auditor of the said plantations, of us, our heirs and successors, within the space of one year, to be computed from the date thereof, otherwise the same shall be void. And our further will and pleasure is, that the rents, issues and all other profits, which shall at any time hereafter come to the said corporation, or the major part of them which shall be present at any meeting for that purpose assembled, shall think will most improve and enlarge the said colony, and best answer the good purposes herein before mentioned, and for defraying all other charges about the same. And our will and pleasure is, that the said corporation and their successors, shall from time to time give in to one of the principal secretaries of state, and to the commissioners of trade and plantations, accounts of the progresses of the said colony. And our will and pleasure is that no act done at any meeting of the said common council of the said corporation, shall be effectual and valid, unless eight members at least of the said common council, including the member who shall serve as chairman at the said meeting, be present, and the major part of them consenting thereunto. And our will and pleasure is, that the common council of the said corporation for the time being, or the major part of them who shall be present, being assembled for that purpose, shall from time to time, for, and during, and unto the full end and expiration of twenty-one years, to commence from the date of these our letters patent, have full power and authority to nominate, make, constitute and commission, ordain and appoint, by such name or names, style or styles, as to them shall seem meet and fitting, all and singular such governors, judges, magistrates, ministers and officers, civil and military, both by sea and land, within the said districts, as shall by them be thought fit and needful to be made or used for the said government of the said colony; save always, and except such offices only as shall by us, our heirs and successors, be from time to time constituted and appointed, for the managing collecting and receiving such revenues, as shall from time to time arise within the said province of Georgia, and become due to us, our heirs and successors. Provided always, and it is our will and pleasure, that every governor of the said province of Georgia, to be appointed by the common council of the said corporation, before he shall enter upon or execute the said office of governor, shall be approved by us, our heirs or successors, and shall take such oaths, and shall qualify himself in such manner, in all respects, as any governor or commander in chief of any of our colonies or plantations in America, are by law required to do; and shall give good and sufficient security for observing the several acts of parliament relating to trade and navigation, and to observe and obey all instructions that shall be sent to him by us, our heirs and successors, or any acting under our or their authority, pursuant to the said acts, or any of them. And we do by these presents for us, our heirs and successors, will, grant and ordain, that the said corporation and their successors, shall have full power for and during and until the full end and term of twenty-one years, to commence from the date of these our letters patent, by any commander or other officer or officers, by them for that purpose from time to time appointed, to train and instruct, exercise and govern a militia, for the special defence and safety of our said colony, to assemble in martial array, the inhabitants of the said colony, and to lead and conduct them, and with them to encounter, expulse, repel, resist and pursue, by force of arms, as well by sea as by land, within or without the limits of our said colony; and also to kill, slay and destroy, and conquer by all fitting ways, enterprizes and means whatsoever, all and every such person or persons as shall at any time hereafter, in any hostile manner, attempt or enterprize the destruction, invasion, detriment or annoyance of our said colony; and to use and exercise the martial law in time of actual war and invasion or rebellion, in such cases, where by law the same may be used or exercised; and also from time to time to erect forts, and fortify any place or places within our said colony, and the same to furnish with all necessary ammunition, provisions and stores of war, for offence and defence, and to commit from time to time the custody or government of the same, to such person or persons as to them shall seem meet: and the said forts and fortifications to demolish at their pleasure; and to take and surprize, by all ways and means, all and every such person or persons, with their ships, arms, ammunition and other goods, as shall in an hostile manner, invade or attempt the invading, conquering or annoying of our said colony. And our will and pleasure is, and we do hereby, for us, our heirs and successors, declare and grant, that the governor and commander in chief of the province of South-Carolina, of us, our heirs and successors, for the time being, shall at all times hereafter have the chief command of the militia of our said province, hereby erected and established; and that such militia shall observe and obey all orders and directions, that shall from time to time be given or sent to them by the said governor or commander in chief; any thing in these presents before contained to the contrary hereof, in any wise notwithstanding. And, of our more special grace, certain knowledge and mere motion, we have given and granted, and by these presents, for us, our heirs and successors, do give and grant, unto the said corporation and their successors, full power and authority to import and export their goods, at and from any port or ports that shall be appointed by us, our heirs and successors, within the said province of Georgia, for that purpose, without being obliged to touch at any other port in South-Carolina. And we do, by these presents, for us, our heirs and successors, will and declare, that from and after the termination of the said term of twenty-one years, such form of government and method of making laws, statutes and ordinances, for the better governing and ordering the said province of Georgia, and the inhabitants thereof, shall be established and observed within the same, as we, our heirs and successors, shall hereafter ordain and appoint, and shall be agreeably to law; and that from and after the determination of the said term of twenty-one years, the governor of our said province of Georgia, and all officers civil and military, within the same, shall from time to time be nominated and constituted, and appointed by us, our heirs and successors. And lastly, we do hereby, for us, our heirs and successors, grant unto the said corporation and their successors, that these our letters patent, or the enrolments or exemplification thereof, shall be in and by all things good, firm, valid, sufficient and effectual in the law, according to the true intent and meaning thereof, and shall be taken, construed and adjudged, in all courts and elsewhere in the most favorable and beneficial sense, and for the best advantage of the said corporation and their successors any omission, imperfection, defect, matter or cause, or thing whatsoever to the contrary, in any wise notwithstanding. In witness, we have caused these our letters to be made patent: witness ourself at Westminster, the ninth day of June, in the fifth year of our reign.

By writ of privy-seal.

COOKS.

FRANKLIN'S PLAN OF UNION—1754.

VIEWING with apprehension the encroachments of France in America, the Lords of Trade in 1753 directed the governors to recommend their respective assemblies to appoint delegates to a congress to meet at time and place to be fixed by the Governor of New York. The congress was to treat with the Six Nations of New York, and secure their alliance in a possible war with France. It was suggested that the colonies form a league for mutual defence. Commissioners from seven colonies met at Albany June 19, 1754. After concluding the treaty with the Six Nations, the following plan of Union, largely drawn by Franklin, was adopted for recommendation to colonial assemblies. The plan was, as Frothingham tersely says, "rejected in America because it had too much of the prerogative, and in England because it was too democratic."

The plan is here given with the interesting comments of Franklin, which are distinguished by italics.

Consult *Bancroft's U. S.*, 1st ed., IV., 123; cen. ed., III., 80; last ed., IV., 387; *Hildreth's U. S.*, II., 443; *Frothingham's Rise*, 136; *Bryant and Gay's U. S.*, III., 261; *Greene's Historical View*, 69; *Chalmers' Revolt*, II., 271.

FRANKLIN'S PLAN OF UNION—1754.

PLAN of a proposed Union of the several Colonies of Massachusetts-Bay, New Hampshire, Connecticut, Rhode Island, New-York, New-Jersey, Pennsylvania, Maryland, Virginia, North Carolina, and South Carolina for their mutual Defence and Security, and for the extending the British Settlements in North America.

That humble application be made for an act of Parliament of Great Britain, by virtue of which one general government may be formed in America, including all the said Colonies, within and under which government each Colony may retain its present constitution, except in the particulars wherein a change may be directed by the said act, as hereafter follows.

PRESIDENT-GENERAL AND GRAND COUNCIL.

That the said general government be administered by a President-General, to be appointed and supported by the crown; and a Grand Council to be chosen by the representatives of the people of the several Colonies met in their respective assemblies.

It was thought that it would be best the President-General should be supported as well as appointed by the crown, that so all disputes between him and the Grand-Council concerning his salary might be prevented; as such disputes have been frequently of mischievous consequence in particular Colonies, especially in time of public danger. The quitrents of crown lands in America might in a short time be sufficient for this purpose. The choice of members for the Grand-Council is placed in the House of Representatives of each government, in order to give the people a share in this new general government, as the crown has its share by the appointment of the President-General.

But it being proposed by the gentlemen of the Council of New York, and some other counsellors among the commis-

sioners, to alter the plan in this particular, and to give the governors and councils of the several Provinces a share in the choice of the Grand-Council, or at least a power of approving and confirming, or of disallowing, the choice made by the House of Representatives, it was said,—" That the government or constitution, proposed to be formed by the plan, consists of two branches: a President-General appointed by the crown, and a Council chosen by the people, or by the people's representatives, which is the same thing.

" That, by a subsequent article, the council chosen by the people can effect nothing without the consent of the President-General appointed by the crown; the crown possesses, therefore, full one half of the power of this constitution.

" That in the British constitution, the crown is supposed to possess but one third, the Lords having their share.

" That the constitution seemed rather more favorable for the crown.

" That it is essential to English liberty that the subject should not be taxed but by his own consent, or the consent of his elected representatives.

" That taxes to be laid and levied by this proposed constitution will be proposed and agreed to by the representatives of the people, if the plan in this particular be preserved.

" But if the proposed alteration should take place, it seemed as if matters may be so managed, as that the crown shall finally have the appointment, not only of the President-General, but of a majority of the Grand-Council; for seven out of eleven governors and councils are appointed by the crown.

" And so the people in all the Colonies would in effect be taxed by their governors.

" It was therefore apprehended, that such alterations of the plan would give great dissatisfaction, and that the Colonies could not be easy under such a power in governors, and such an infringement of what they take to be English liberty.

"Besides, the giving a share in the choice of the Grand Council would not be equal with respect to all the Colonies, as their constitutions differ. In some, both governor and council are appointed by the crown. In others, they are both appointed by the proprietors. In some, the people have a share in the choice of the council; in others, both government and council are wholly chosen by the people. But the House of Representatives is everywhere chosen by the people; and, therefore, placing the right of choosing the Grand Council in the representatives is equal with respect to all.

"That the Grand Council is intended to represent all the several Houses of Representatives of the Colonies, as a House of Representatives doth the several towns or counties of a Colony. Could all the people of a Colony be consulted and unite in public measures, a House of Representatives would be needless, and could all the Assemblies consult and unite in general measures, the Grand Council would be unnecessary.

"That a House of Commons or the House of Representatives, and the Grand Council are alike in their nature and intention. And, as it would seem improper that the King or House of Lords should have a power of disallowing or appointing Members of the House of Commons; so, likewise, that a governor and council appointed by the crown should have a power of disallowing or appointing members of the Grand Council, who, in this constitution, are to be the representatives of the people.

"If the governor and councils therefore were to have a share in the choice of any that are to conduct this general government, it should seem more proper that they should choose the President-General. But this being an office of great trust and importance to the nation, it was thought better to be filled by the immediate appointment of the crown.

"The power proposed to be given by the plan to the Grand Council is only a concentration of the powers of the several assemblies in certain points for the general welfare; as the

power of the President-General is of the several governors in the same point.

"*And as the choice therefore of the Grand Council, by the representatives of the people, neither gives the people any new powers, nor diminishes the power of the crown, it was thought and hoped the crown would not disapprove of it.*"

Upon the whole, the commissioners were of opinion, that the choice was most properly placed in the representatives of the people.

ELECTION OF MEMBERS.

That within months after the passing such act, the House of Representatives that happens to be sitting within that time, or that shall be especially for that purpose convened, may and shall choose members for the Grand Council, in the following proportion, that is to say,

Massachusetts Bay	7
New Hampshire	2
Connecticut	5
Rhode Island	2
New York	4
New Jersey	3
Pennsylvania	6
Maryland	4
Virginia	7
North Carolina	4
South Carolina	4
	48

It was thought, that if the least Colony was allowed two, and the others in proportion, the number would be very great, and the expense heavy; and that less than two would not be convenient, as, a single person being by any accident prevented appearing at the meeting, the Colony he ought appear for would not be represented. That, as the choice was not immediately popular, they would be generally men of good abilities for business, and men of reputation for integrity, and that forty-eight such men might be a number sufficient. But, though it was thought reasonable that each Colony should have a share in the representative body in some degree according to the proportion it contributed to the general treasury, yet the proportion of wealth or power of the Colonies is not to be judged by the proportion here fixed: because it was at first agreed, that the greatest Colony should not have more than seven members, nor the least less than two; and the setting these proportions between these two extremes was not nicely attended to, as it would find itself, after the first election, from the sum brought into the treasury by a subsequent article.

PLACE OF FIRST MEETING.

—Who shall meet for the first time at the city of Philadelphia in Pennsylvania, being called by the President-General as soon as conveniently may be after his appointment.

Philadelphia was named as being nearer the centre of the Colonies, where the commissioners would be well and cheaply accommodated. The high roads, through the whole extent, are for the most part very good, in which forty or fifty miles a day may very well be, and frequently are, travelled. Great part of the way may likewise be gone by water. In summer time, the passages are frequently performed in a week from Charleston to Philadelphia and New York, and from Rhode Island to New York through the Sound, in two or three days, and from New York to Philadelphia, by water and land, in two days, by stage boats, and street carriages that set out every other day. The journey from Charleston to Philadelphia may likewise be facilitated by boats running up Chesapeake Bay three hundred miles. But if the whole journey be performed on horseback, the most distant members, viz., the two from New Hampshire and from South Carolina, may probably render themselves at Philadelphia in fifteen or twenty days; the majority may be there in much less time.

NEW ELECTION.

That there shall be a new election of the members of the Grand Council every three years; and, on the death or resignation of any member, his place should be supplied by a new choice at the next sitting of the Assembly of the Colony he represented.

Some Colonies have annual assemblies, some continue during a governor's pleasure; three years was thought a reasonable medium as affording a new member time to improve himself in the business, and to act after such improvement, and yet giving opportunities, frequently enough, to change him if he has misbehaved.

PROPORTION OF MEMBERS AFTER THE FIRST THREE YEARS.

That after the first three years, when the proportion of money arising out of each Colony to the general treasury can be known, the number of members to be chosen for each Colony shall, from time to time, in all ensuing elections, be regulated by that proportion, yet so as that the number to be chosen by any one Province be not more than seven, nor less than two.

By a subsequent article, it is proposed that the General Council shall lay and levy such general duties as to them may appear most equal and least burdensome, etc. Suppose, for instance, they lay a small duty or excise on some commodity imported into or made in the Colonies, and pretty generally and equally used in all of them, as rum, perhaps, or wine; the yearly produce of this duty or excise, if fairly collected, would be in some Colonies greater, in others less, as the Colonies are greater or smaller. When the collector's accounts are brought in, the proportions will appear; and from them it is proposed to regulate the proportion of the representatives to be chosen at the next general election, within the limits, however, of seven and two. These numbers may therefore vary in the course of years, as the Colonies may in the growth and increase of people. And thus the quota of tax from each Colony would naturally vary with its circumstances, thereby preventing all disputes and dissatisfaction about the just proportions due from each, which might otherwise produce penicious consequences, and destroy the harmony and good agreement that ought to subsist between the several parts of the Union.

MEETINGS OF THE GRAND COUNCIL AND CALL.

That the Grand Council shall meet once in every year, and oftener if occasion require, at such time and place as they shall adjourn to at the last preceding meeting, or as they shall be called to meet at by the President-General on any emergency; he having first obtained in writing the consent of seven of the members to such call, and sent due and timely notice to the whole.

It was thought, in establishing and governing new Colonies or settlements, or regulating Indian trade, Indian treaties, etc., there would, every year, sufficient business arise to require at least one meeting, and at such meeting many things might be suggested for the benefit of all the Colonies. This annual meeting may either be at a time and place certain, to be fixed by the President-General and Grand Council at their first meeting; or left at liberty, to be at such time and place as they shall adjourn to, or be called to meet at, by the President-General.

In time of war, it seems convenient that the meeting should be in that colony which is nearest the seat of action.

The power of calling them on any emergency seemed necessary to be vested in the President-General; but, that such power might not be wantonly used to harass the members, and oblige them to make frequent long journeys to little purpose, the consent of seven at least to such call was supposed a convenient guard.

CONTINUANCE.

That the Grand Council have power to choose their speaker; and shall neither be dissolved, prorogued, nor continued sitting longer than six weeks at one time, without their own consent or the special command of the crown.

The speaker should be presented for approbation; it being convenient, to prevent misunderstandings and disgusts, that the mouth of the Council should be a person agreeable, if possible, to the Council and President-General.

Governors have sometimes wantonly exercised the power of proroguing or continuing the sessions of assemblies, merely to harass the members and compel a compliance; and sometimes dissolve them on slight disgusts. This it was feared might be done by the President-General, if not provided against; and the inconvenience and hardship would be greater in the general government than in particular Colonies, in proportion to the distance the members must be from home during sittings, and the long journeys some of them must necessarily take.

MEMBERS' ALLOWANCE.

That the members of the Grand Council shall be allowed for their service ten shillings per diem, during their session and journey to and from the place of meeting; twenty miles to be reckoned a day's journey.

It was thought proper to allow some wages, lest the expense might deter some suitable persons from the service; and not to allow too great wages, lest unsuitable persons should be tempted to cabal for the employment, for the sake of gain. Twenty miles were set down as a day's journey, to allow for accidental hindrances on the road, and the greater expenses of travelling than residing at the place of meeting.

ASSENT OF PRESIDENT-GENERAL AND HIS DUTY.

That the assent of the President-General be requisite to all acts of the Grand Council, and that it be his office and duty to cause them to be carried into execution.

The assent of the President-General to all acts of the Grand Council was made necessary in order to give the crown its due share of influence in this government, and connect it with that of Great Britain. The President-General, besides one half of the legislative power, hath in his hands the whole executive power.

POWER OF PRESIDENT-GENERAL AND GRAND COUNCIL, TREATIES OF PEACE AND WAR.

That the President-General, with the advice of the Grand Council, hold or direct all Indian treaties, in which the general interest of the Colonies may be concerned, and make peace or declare war with Indian nations.

The power of making peace or war with Indian nations is at present supposed to be in every Colony, and is expressly granted to some by charter, so that no new power is hereby intended to be granted to the Colonies. But as, in consequence of this power, one Colony might make peace with a nation that another was justly engaged in war with; or make war on slight occasion without the concurrence or approbation of neighboring Colonies, greatly endangered by it; or make particular treaties of neutrality in case of a general war, to their own private advantage in trade, by supplying the common enemy, of all which there have been instances, it was thought better to have all treaties of a general nature under a general direction, that so the good of the whole may be consulted and provided for.

INDIAN TRADE.

That they make such laws as they judge necessary for regulating all Indian trade.

Many quarrels and wars have arisen between the colonies and Indian nations, through the bad conduct of traders, who cheat the Indians after making them drunk, etc., to the great expense of the colonies, both in blood and treasure. Particular colonies are so interested in the trade, as not to be willing to admit such a regulation as might be best for the whole; and therefore it was thought best under a general direction.

INDIAN PURCHASES.

That they make all purchases from Indians, for the crown, of lands not now within the bounds of particular colonies, or that shall not be within their bounds when some of them are reduced to more convenient dimensions.

Purchases from the Indians, made by private persons, have been attended with many inconveniences. They have frequently interfered and occasioned uncertainty of titles, many disputes and expensive lawsuits, and hindered the settlement of the land so disputed. Then the Indians have been cheated by such private purchases, and discontent and wars have been the consequence. These would be prevented by public fair purchases.

Several of the Colony charters in America extend their bounds to the South Sea, which may perhaps be three or four thousand miles in length to one or two hundred miles in breadth. It is supposed they must in time be reduced to dimensions more convenient for the common purposes of government.

Very little of the land in these grants is yet purchased of the Indians.

It is much cheaper to purchase of them, than to take and maintain the possession by force; for they are generally very reasonable in their demands for land; and the expense of guarding a large frontier against their incursions is vastly great; because all must be guarded, and always guarded, as we know not where or when to expect them.

NEW SETTLEMENTS.

That they make new settlements on such purchases by granting lands in the King's name, reserving a quit-rent to the crown for the use of the general treasury.

It is supposed better that there should be one purchaser than many; and that the crown should be that purchaser, or the Union in the name of the crown. By this means the bargains may be more easily made, the price not enhanced by numerous bidders, future disputes about private Indian purchases, and monopolies of vast tracts to particular persons (which are prejudicial to the settlement and peopling of the country), prevented; and, the land being again granted in small tracts to the settlers, the quit-rents reserved may in time become a fund for support of government, for defence of the country, ease of taxes, etc.

Strong forts on the Lakes, the Ohio, etc., may, at the same time they secure our present frontiers, serve to defend new colonies settled under their protection; and such colonies would also mutually defend and support such forts, and better secure the friendship of the far Indians.

A particular colony has scarce strength enough to exert itself by new settlements, at so great a distance from the old; but the joint force of the Union might suddenly establish a new colony or two in those parts, or extend an old colony to particular passes, greatly to the security of our present frontiers, increase of trade and people, breaking off the French communication between Canada and Louisiana, and speedy settlement of the intermediate lands.

The power of settling new colonies is therefore thought a valuable part of the plan, and what cannot so well be executed by two unions as by one.

LAWS TO GOVERN THEM.

That they make laws for regulating and governing such new settlements, till the crown shall think fit to form them into particular governments.

The making of laws suitable for the new colonies, it was thought, would be properly vested in the president-general and grand council; under whose protection they must at first necessarily be, and who would be well acquainted with their circumstances, as having settled them. When they are become sufficiently populous, they may by the crown be formed into complete and distinct governments.

The appointment of a sub-president by the crown, to take place in case of the death or absence of the president-general, would perhaps be an improvement of the plan; and if all the governors of particular provinces were to be formed into a standing council of state, for the advice and assistance of the president-general, it might be another considerable improvement.

RAISE SOLDIERS, AND EQUIP VESSELS, ETC.

That they raise and pay soldiers and build forts for the defence of any of the colonies, and equip vessels of force to guard the coasts and protect the trade on the ocean, lakes, or great rivers; but they shall not impress men in any colony, without the consent of the legislature.

It was thought, that quotas of men, to be raised and paid by the several colonies, and joined for any public service, could not always be got together with the necessary expedition. For instance, suppose one thousand men should be wanted in New Hampshire on any emergency. To fetch them by fifties and hundreds out of every colony, as far as South Carolina, would be inconvenient, the transportation chargeable, and the occasion perhaps passed before they could be assembled; and therefore it would be best to raise them (by offering bounty money and pay) near the place where they would be wanted, to be discharged again when the service should be over.

Particular colonies are at present backward to build forts at their own expense, which they say will be equally useful to their neighboring colonies, who refuse to join, on a presumption that such forts will be built and kept up, though they contribute nothing. This unjust conduct weakens the whole; but, the forts being for the good of the whole, it was thought best they should be built and maintained by the whole, out of the common treasury.

In the time of war, small vessels of force are sometimes necessary in the colonies to scour the coasts of small privateers. These being provided by the Union will be an advantage in turn to the colonies which are situated on the sea, and whose frontiers on the land-side, being covered by other colonies, reap but little immediate benefit from the advanced forts.

POWER TO MAKE LAWS, LAY DUTIES, ETC.

That for these purposes they have power to make laws and lay and levy such general duties, imposts or taxes, as to them shall appear most equal and just (considering the ability and other circumstances of the inhabitants in the several colonies), and such as may be collected with the least inconvenience to the people; rather discouraging luxury, than loading industry with unnecessary burdens.

The laws which the president-general and grand council are empowered to make are such only as shall be necessary for the government of the settlements; the raising, regulating, and paying soldiers for the general service; the regulating of Indian trade; and laying and collecting the general duties and taxes. They should also have a power to restrain the exportation of provisions to the enemy from any of the colonies, on particular occasions, in time of war. But it is not intended that they may interfere with the constitution or government of the particular colonies, who are to be left to their own laws, and to lay, levy and apply their own taxes as before.

GENERAL TREASURER AND PARTICULAR TREASURER.

That they may appoint a General Treasurer, and Particular Treasurer in government when necessary; and, from time to time, may order the sums in the treasuries of each government into the general treasury, or draw on them for special payments, as they find most convenient.

The treasurers here meant are only for the general funds and not for the particular funds of each colony, which remain in the hands of their own treasurers at their own disposal.

MONEY, HOW TO ISSUE.

Yet no money to issue but by joint orders of the President-General and Grand Council, except where sums have been appointed to particular purposes, and the President-General is previously empowered by an act to draw such sums.

To prevent misapplication of the money, or even application that might be dissatisfactory to the crown or the people, it was thought necessary to join the president-general and grand council in all issues of money

ACCOUNTS.

That the general accounts shall be yearly settled and reported to the several Assemblies.

By communicating the accounts yearly to each Assembly, they will be satisfied of the prudent and honest conduct of their representatives in the grand council.

QUORUM.

That a quorum of the Grand Council, empowered to act with the President-General, do consist of twenty-five members; among whom there shall be one or more from a majority of the Colonies.

The quorum seems large, but it was thought it would not be satisfactory to the colonies in general, to have matters of importance to the whole transacted by a smaller number, or even by this number of twenty-five, unless there were among them one at least from a majority of the colonies, because otherwise, the whole quorum being made up of members from three or four colonies at one end of the union, something might be done that would not be equal with respect to the rest, and thence dissatisfaction and discords might rise to the prejudice of the whole.

LAWS TO BE TRANSMITTED.

That the laws made by them for the purposes aforesaid shall not be repugnant, but, as near as may be, agreeable to the laws of England, and shall be transmitted to the King in Council for approbation, as soon as may be after their passing; and if not disapproved within three years after presentation, to remain in force.

This was thought necessary for the satisfaction of the crown, to preserve the connection of the parts of the British empire with the whole, of the members with the head, and to induce greater care and circumspection in making of the laws, that they be good in themselves and for the general benefit.

DEATH OF THE PRESIDENT-GENERAL.

That, in case of the death of the President-General, the Speaker of the Grand Council for the time being shall succeed, and be vested with the same powers and authorities, to continue till the King's pleasure be known.

It might be better, perhaps, as was said before, if the crown appointed a vice-president, to take place on the death or absence of the president-general; for so we should be more sure of a suitable person at the head of the colonies. On the death or absence of both, the speaker to take place (or rather the eldest King's governor) till his Majesty's pleasure be known.

OFFICERS, HOW APPOINTED.

That all military commission officers, whether for land or sea service, to act under this general constitution, shall be nominated by the President-General; but the approbation of the Grand Council is to be obtained, before they receive their commissions. And all civil officers are to be nominated by the Grand Council, and to receive the President-General's approbation before they officiate.

It was thought it might be very prejudicial to the service, to have officers appointed unknown to the people or unacceptable, the generality of Americans serving willingly under officers they know; and not caring to engage in the service under strangers, or such as are often appointed by governors through favor or interest. The service here meant, is not the stated, settled service in standing troops; but any sudden and short service, either for defence of our colonies, or invading the enemy's country (such as the expedition to Cape Breton in the last war; in which many substantial farmers and tradesmen engaged as common soldiers, under officers of their own country, for whom they had an esteem and affection; who would not have engaged in a standing army, or under officers from England). It was therefore thought best to give the Council the power of approving the officers, which the people will look on as a great security of their being good men. And without some such provision as this, it was thought the expense of engaging men in the service on any emergency would be much greater, and the number who could be induced to engage much less; and that therefore it would be most for the King's service and the general benefit of the nation, that the prerogative should relax a little in this particular throughout all the colonies in America; as it had already done much more in the charters of some particular colonies, viz.: Connecticut and Rhode Island.

The civil officers will be chiefly treasurers and collectors of taxes; and the suitable persons are most likely to be known by the council.

VACANCIES, HOW SUPPLIED.

But, in case of vacancy by death or removal of any officer civil or military, under this constitution, the Governor of the province in which such vacancy happens, may appoint, till the pleasure of the President-General and Grand Council can be known.

The vacancies were thought best supplied by the governors in each province, till a new appointment can be regularly made; otherwise the service might suffer before the meeting of the president-general and grand council.

EACH COLONY MAY DEFEND ITSELF IN EMERGENCY, ETC.

That the particular military as well as civil establishments in each colony remain in their present state, the general constitution notwithstanding; and that on sudden emergencies any colony may defend itself, and lay the accounts of expense thence arising before the president-general and general council, who may allow and order payment of the same, as far as they judge such accounts just and reasonable.

Otherwise the union of the whole would weaken the parts, contrary to the design of the union. The accounts are to be judged of by the president-general and grand council, and allowed if found reasonable. This was thought necessary to encourage colonies to defend themselves, as the expense would be light when borne by the whole; and also to check imprudent and lavish expense in such defences.

DECLARATION OF RIGHTS—1765.

THE New York Congress, "the Day Star of the American Union," summoned by the Massachusetts legislature, met at the City Hall in New York, Oct. 7, 1765. It consisted of twenty-eight delegates from nine colonies, Virginia, New Hampshire, Georgia, and North Carolina being unrepresented. It was much debated whether to found American liberties on natural rights or on royal charters, but the former ground was finally taken. On the 25th the delegates who were so authorized (viz., those from Massachusetts, New Jersey, Rhode Island, Pennsylvania, Delaware and Maryland), signed the Declaration of Rights, and the Congress adjourned. "Perhaps the best general summary of the rights and liberties asserted by all the colonies, is contained in the celebrated declaration drawn up by the Congress of the nine colonies assembled at New York, October, 1765." (Judge Story.)

Consult *Bancroft's U. S.*, 1st ed., V., 342; cen. ed., III., 508; last, III., 154; *Hildreth's U. S.*, II., 530; *Story's Constitution*, I., 175; *Frothingham's Rise*, 186; *Bryant and Gay's U. S.*, II., 340; *Greene's Historical View*, 72; *Pitkin's U. S.*, I., 178.

RESOLVES OF THE CONVENTION OF THE ENGLISH COLONIES AT NEW YORK, OCTOBER 19, 1765.

THE Congress upon mature deliberation, agreed to the following declarations of the rights and grievances of the colonists in America:

The members of this congress, sincerely devoted, with the warmest sentiments of affection and duty, to His Majesty's person and government, inviolably attached to the present happy establishment of the Protestant succession, and with minds deeply impressed by a sense of the present and impending misfortunes of the British colonies on this continent; having considered as maturely as time will permit, the circumstances of the said colonies, esteem it our indispensable duty to make the following declarations of our humble opinion respecting the most essential rights and liberties of the colonists and of the grievances under which they labor by reason of the several late acts of Parliament.

1. That His Majesty's subjects in these colonies, owe the same allegiance to the crown of Great Britain, that is owing from his subjects born within the realm; and all due subordination to that august body, the Parliament of Great Britain.

2. That His Majesty's liege subjects, in these colonies, are entitled to all the inherent rights and liberties of his natural born subjects within the kingdom of Great Britain.

3. That it is inseparably essential to the freedom of a people, and the undoubted right of Englishmen, that no taxes be imposed on them but with their own consent, given personally, or by their representatives.

4. That the people of these colonies are not, and from their local circumstances cannot be, represented in the House of Commons, in Great Britain.

5. That the only representatives of the people of these colonies, are persons chosen therein by themselves ; and that no taxes ever have been, or can be constitutionally imposed on them, but by their respective legislatures.

6. That all supplies to the crown, being the free gifts of the people, it is unreasonable and inconsistent with the principles and spirit of the British constitution, for the people of Great Britain to grant to His Majesty, the property of the colonists.

7. That trial by jury is the inherent and invaluable right of every British subject in these colonies.

8. That the late act of Parliament, entitled "An act for granting and applying certain stamp duties, and other duties in the British colonies and plantations, in America, etc.," by imposing taxes on the inhabitants of these colonies, and the said act, and several other acts, by extending the jurisdiction of the courts of admiralty beyond its ancient limits, have a manifest tendency to subvert the rights and liberties of the colonists.

9. That the duties imposed by several late acts of Parliament, from the peculiar circumstances of these colonies, will be extremely burthensome and grievous, and from the scarcity of specie, the payment of them absolutely impracticable.

10. That as the profits of the trade of these colonies ultimately centre in Great Britain, to pay for the manufactures which they are obliged to take from thence, they eventually contribute very largely to all supplies granted there to the crown.

11. That the restrictions imposed by several late acts of Parliament on the trade of these colonies, will render them unable to purchase the manufactures of Great Britain.

12. That the increase, prosperity, and happiness of these colonies depend on the full and free enjoyments of their rights and liberties, and an intercourse with Great Britain, mutually affectionate and advantageous.

13. That it is the right of the British subjects in these colonies to petition the King, or either house of Parliament.

Lastly. That it is the indispensable duty of these colonies, to the best of sovereigns, to the mother country, and to themselves, to endeavour by a loyal and dutiful address to His Majesty, and humble applications to both houses of Parliament, to procure the repeal of the act for granting and applying certain stamp duties, of all clauses of any other acts of Parliament, whereby the jurisdiction of the admiralty is extended, as aforesaid, and of the other late acts for the restriction of American commerce.

DECLARATION OF RIGHTS AND NON-IMPORTATION AGREEMENT—1774.

THE congress of 1774 met at Philadelphia, Sept. 5th. On the second day of the session, it was "Resolved, unanimously that a committee be appointed to state the rights of the colonies in general, the several instances in which these rights are violated or infringed, and the means most proper to be pursued for obtaining a restoration of them." The report of the committee (presented Sept. 21) provoked much discussion, and it was not till Congress had limited the field to rights infringed by acts of parliament since 1763, previous violations having been considered by the Congress of 1765, that the Declaration was agreed upon, Oct. 14.

Congress also decided on commercial non-intercourse with England, thus returning to the policy first adopted in opposition to the Stamp Act in 1765, and revived in the early days of the republic by the embargoes of Washington and Jefferson. This non-importation agreement was signed Oct. 20, by fifty members, who thus formed what John Adams called, "the memorable league of the continent in 1774, which first expressed the sovereign will of a free nation in America." Equally emphatic is the verdict of Hildreth: "the signature of the association by the members of congress may be considered as the commencement of the American Union."

Consult *Bancroft's, U. S.*, 1st. ed., VI., 146; cen. ed., IV., 406; last ed., IV., 65 *et seq.; Hildreth's, U. S.*, III., 43; *Frothingham's Rise*, 371; *Story's Constitution*, I., 179; *Bryant and Gay's U. S.*, III., 341; *Greene's Historical View*, 83; *Curtis' Constitution*, I., 22; *Pitkin's, U. S.*, I., 283.

DECLARATION OF RIGHTS—1774.

WHEREAS, since the close of the last war, the British parliament claiming a power of right, to bind the people of America by statutes in all cases whatsoever, hath, in some acts, expressly imposed taxes on them, and in others, under various pretences, but in fact for the purpose of raising a revenue, hath imposed rates and duties payable in these colonies, established a board of commissioners, with unconstitutional powers, and extended the jurisdiction of courts of admiralty, not only for collecting the said duties, but for the trial of causes merely arising within the body of a county.

And whereas, in consequence of other statutes, judges, who before held only estates at will in their offices, have been made dependent on the crown alone for their salaries, and standing armies kept in time of peace: And whereas it has lately been resolved in parliament, that by force of a statute, made in the thirty-fifth year of the reign of King Henry the Eighth, colonists may be transported to England, and tried there upon accusations for treasons, and misprisions, or concealments of treasons committed in the colonies, and by a late statute, such trials have been directed in cases therein mentioned.

And whereas, in the last session of parliament, three statutes were made; one, entitled "An act to discontinue, in such manner, and for such time as are therein mentioned, the landing and discharging, lading or shipping of goods, wares and merchandise, at the town, and within the harbour of Boston, in the province of Massachusetts-Bay, in North America;" another, entitled, "An act for the better regulating the government of the province of Massachusetts-Bay in New England;" and another, entitled, "An act for the impartial administration of justice, in the cases of persons questioned for any act done by them in the execution of the law, or for the suppression of riots and tumults, in the province of Massachusetts-Bay in New England;" and another statute was then made, "for making more effectual provision for the government of the province of Quebec, etc." All which statutes are impolitic, unjust, and cruel, as well as unconstitutional, and most dangerous and destructive of American rights.

And whereas, assemblies have been frequently dissolved, contrary to the rights of the people, when they attempted to deliberate on grievances, and their dutiful, humble, loyal, and reasonable petitions to the crown for redress, have been repeatedly treated with contempt by his majesty's ministers of state:

The good people of the several colonies of New-Hampshire, Massachussetts-Bay, Rhode-Island and Providence Plantations, Connecticut, New-York, New-Jersey, Pennsylvania, New-Castle, Kent and Sussex, on Delaware, Maryland, Virginia, North-Carolina, and South-Carolina justly alarmed at these arbitrary proceedings of parliament and administration, have severally elected, constituted and appointed deputies to meet, and sit in General Congress, in the city of Philadelphia, in order to obtain such establishment, as that their religion, laws, and liberties, may not be subverted. Whereupon the deputies so appointed being now assembled, in a full and free representation of these colonies, taking into their most serious consideration, the best means of attaining the ends aforesaid, do, in the first place, as Englishmen, their ancestors in like cases have usually done, for effecting and vindicating their rights and liberties, DECLARE,

That the inhabitants of the English colonies in North-America, by the immutable laws of nature, the principles of the English constitution, and the several charters or compacts, have the following RIGHTS:

Resolved, N. C. D. 1. That they are entitled to life, liberty, and property, and that they have never ceded to any sovereign power whatever, a right to dispose of either without their consent.

Resolved, N. C. D. 2. That our ancestors, who first settled these colonies, were at the time of their emigration from the mother country, entitled to all the rights, liberties, and immunities of free and natural-born subjects, within the realm of England.

Resolved, N. C. D. 3. That by such emigration, they by no means forfeited, surrendered, or lost any of those rights, but that they were, and their descendants now are, entitled to the exercise and enjoyment of all such of them, as their local and other circumstances enable them to exercise and enjoy.

Resolved, 4. That the foundation of English liberty, and of all free government, is a right in the people to participate in their legislative council: and as the English colonists are not represented, and from their local and other circumstances, cannot properly in the British parliament, they are entitled to a free and exclusive power of legislation in their several provincial legislatures, where their right of representation can alone be preserved, in all cases of taxation and internal polity, subject only to the negative of their sovereign, in such manner as has been heretofore used and accustomed. But, from the necessity of the case, and a regard to the mutual interest of both countries, we cheerfully consent to the operation of such acts of the British parliament; as are bona fide, restrained to the regulation of our external commerce, for the purpose of securing the commercial advantages of the whole empire to the mother country, and the commercial benefits of its respective members; excluding every idea of taxation internal or external, for raising a revenue on the subjects in America, without their consent.

Resolved, N. C. D. 5. That the respective colonies are entitled to the common law of England, and more especially to the great and inestimable privilege of being tried by their peers of the vicinage, according to the course of that law.

Resolved, 6. That they are entitled to the benefit of such of the English statutes, as existed at the time of their colonization; and which they have, by experience, respectively found to be applicable to their several local and other circumstances.

Resolved, N. C. D. 7. That these, his majesties colonies, are likewise entitled to all the immunities and privileges granted and conformed to them by royal charters, as secured by their several codes of provincial laws.

Resolved, N. C. D. 8. That they have a right peaceable to assemble, consider of their grievances, and petition the king; and that all prosecutions, prohibiting proclamations, and commitments for the same are illegal.

Resolved, N. C. D. 9. That the keeping a standing army in these colonies, in times of peace, without the consent of the legislature of that colony, in which such army is kept, is against law.

Resolved, N. C. D. 10. It is indispensably necessary to good government, and rendered essential by the English constitution, that the constituent branches of the legislature be independent of each other; that, therefore, the exercise of legislative power in several colonies, by a counsel appointed, during pleasure, by the crown, is unconstitutional, dangerous and destructive to the freedom of American legislation.

All and each of which the aforesaid deputies, in behalf of themselves, and their constituents, do claim, demand, and insist on, as their indubitable rights and liberties; which cannot be legally taken from them, altered or abridged by any power whatever, without their own consent, by their representatives in their several provincial legislatures.

In the course of our inquiry, we find many infringements and violations of the foregoing rights, which from an ardent desire, that harmony and mutual intercourse of affection and interest may be restored, we pass over for the present, and proceed to state such acts and measures as have been adopted since the late war, which demonstrate a system formed to enslave America.

Resolved, N. C. D. The following acts of parliament are infringements and violations of the rights of the colonists; and that the repeal of them is essentially necessary, in order to restore harmony between Great Britain and the American colonies, viz.:

The several acts of 4 Geo. III. ch. 15, and ch. 34.—5 Geo. III. ch. 25.—6 Geo. III. ch. 52.—7 Geo. III. ch. 41, and ch. 46.—8 Geo. III. ch. 22, which impose duties for the purpose of raising a revenue in America, extend the power of the admiralty courts beyond their ancient limits, deprive the American subject of trial by jury, authorize the judges' certificate to indemnify the prosecutor from damages, that he might otherwise be liable to, requiring oppressive security from a claimant of ships and goods seized, before he shall be allowed to defend his property, and are subservient of American rights.

Also 12 Geo. III. ch. 24, entitled "An act for the better securing his majesty's dock-yards, magazines, ships, ammunition, and stores," which declares a new offence in America, and deprives the American subject of a constitutional trial by jury of the vicinage, by authorizing the trial of any person, charged with the committing any offence described in the said act, out of the realm, to be indicted and tried for the same in any shire or county within the realm.

Also the three acts passed in the last session of parliament, for stopping the port and blocking the harbour of Boston, for altering the charter and government of Massachusetts-Bay, and that which is entitled "An act for the better administration of Justice, etc."

Also the act passed in the same session for establishing the Roman Catholic religion, in the province of Quebec, abolishing the equitable system of English laws, and erecting a tyranny there, to the great danger (from so total a dissimilarity of religion, law and government) of the neighboring British Colonies, by the assistance of whose blood and treasure the said country was conquered from France.

Also, the act passed in the same session, for the better providing suitable quarters for officers and soldiers in his majesty's service, in North-America.

Also, that the keeping a standing army in several of these colonies, in time of peace, without the consent of the legislature of that colony, in which such army is kept, is against law.

To these grievous acts and measures, Americans cannot submit, but in hopes their fellow-subjects in Great Britain will, on a revision of them, restore us to that state, in which both countries found happiness and prosperity, we have for the present, only resolved to pursue the following peaceable measures: 1. To enter into a non-importation, non-consumption, and non-exportation agreement or association. 2. To prepare an address to the people of Great Britain, and a memorial to the inhabitants of British America: and 3. To prepare a loyal address to his majesty, agreeable to resolutions already entered into.

THE ASSOCIATION OF 1774.

WE, his Majesty's most loyal subjects, the Delegates of the several Colonies of New Hampshire, Massachusetts Bay, Rhode Island, Connecticut, New York, New Jersey, Pennsylvania, the three Lower Counties of New-Castle, Kent, and Sussex, on Delaware, Maryland, Virginia, North Carolina, and South Carolina, deputed to represent them in a Continental Congress, held in the City of Philadelphia, on the fifth day of September, 1774, avowing our allegiance to his Majesty, our affection and regard for our fellow subjects in Great Britain and elsewhere, affected with the deepest anxiety; and most alarming apprehensions at those grievances and distresses, with which his Majesty's American subjects are oppressed, and having taken under our most serious deliberation, the state of the whole Continent, find, that the present unhappy situation of our affairs, is occasioned by a ruinous system of Colony Administration adopted by the British Ministry about the year 1763, evidently calculated for enslaving these Colonies, and, with them, the British Empire.

In prosecution of which system, various Acts of Parliament have been passed for raising a Revenue in America, for depriving the American subjects, in many instances, of the constitutional trial by jury, exposing their lives to danger, by directing a new and illegal trial beyond the seas, for crimes alledged to have been committed in America: and in prosecution of the same system, several late, cruel, and oppressive Acts have been passed respecting the Town of Boston and the Massachusetts Bay, and also an Act for extending the Province of Quebec, so as to border on the Western Frontiers of these Colonies, establishing an arbitrary government therein, and discouraging the settlement of British subjects in that wide extended country; thus, by the influence of civil principles and ancient prejudices, to dispose the inhabitants to act with hostility against the free Protestant Colonies, whenever a wicked Ministry shall chuse to direct them.

To obtain redress of these Grievances, which threaten destruction to the Lives, Liberty, and Property of his Majesty's subjects in North-America, we are of opinion, that a Non-Importation, Non-Consumption, and Non-Exportation Agreement, faithfully adhered to, will prove the most speedy, effectual, and peaceable measure; and, therefore, we do, for ourselves, and the inhabitants of the several Colonies, whom we represent, firmly agree and associate, under the sacred ties of Virtue, Honor and Love of our Country, as follows:

First. That from and after the first day of December next, we will not import into British America, from Great-Britain or Ireland, any Goods, Wares, or Merchandise whatsoever, or from any other place, any such goods, wares, or merchandise, as shall have been exported from Great-Britain or Ireland; nor will we, after that day, import any East India Tea from any part of the World; nor any Molasses, Syrups, Paneles, Coffee or Pimento, from the British Plantations or from Dominica; nor Wines from Madeira, or the Western Islands; nor Foreign Indigo.

Second. We will neither import nor purchase any Slave imported, after the first day of December next; after which time we will wholly discontinue the Slave Trade, and will neither be concerned in it ourselves, nor will we hire our vessels, nor sell our Commodities or Manufactures to those who are concerned in it.

Third. As a Non-Consumption Agreement, strictly adhered to, will be an effectual security for the observance of the Non-Importation, we, as above, solemnly agree and associate, that from this day we will not purchase or use any Tea imported on account of the East India Company, or any on which a Duty hath been or shall be paid;

and from and after the first day of March next, we will not purchase or use any East India Tea whatever; nor will we, nor shall any person for or under us, purchase or use any of those Goods, Wares, or Merchandises, we have agreed not to import, which we shall know, or have cause to suspect, were imported after the first day of December, except such as come under the rules and regulations of the tenth article hereafter mentioned.

Fourth. The earnest desire we have, not to injure our fellow-subjects in Great Britain, Ireland or the West-Indies, induces us to suspend a Non-Exportation, until the tenth day of September, 1775; at which time, if the said Acts and parts of Acts of the British Parliament hereinafter mentioned, are not repealed, we will not, directly or indirectly, export any Merchandise or Commodity whatsoever to Great Britain, Ireland or the West-Indies, except Rice to Europe.

Fifth. Such as are Merchants and use the British and Irish Trade, will give orders, as soon as possible to their Factors, Agents and Correspondents, in Great Britain and Ireland, not to ship any Goods to them, on any pretence whatsoever as they cannot be received in America; and if any Merchant, residing in Great Britain or Ireland, shall directly or indirectly ship any Goods, Wares, or Merchandises, for America, in order to break the said Non-Importation Agreement, or in any manner contravene the same, on such unworthy conduct being well attested, it ought to be made publick; and, on the same being so done, we will not from thenceforth have any commercial connexion, with any such Merchant.

Sixth. That such as are Owners of vessels will give positive orders to their Captains, or Masters, not to receive on board their vessel any Goods prohibited by the said Non-Importation Agreement, on pain of immediate dismission from their service.

Seventh. We will use our utmost endeavors to improve the breed of Sheep, and increase their number to the greatest extent; and to that end, we will kill them as sparingly as may be, especially those of the most profitable kind; nor will we export any to the West-Indies or elsewhere; and those of us who are or may become overstocked with, or can conveniently spare any sheep, will dispose of them to our neighbours, especially to the poorer sort, upon moderate terms.

Eighth. That we will, in our several stations encourage Frugality, Economy, and Industry; and promote Agriculture, Arts, and the Manufactures of this Country, especially that of Wool; and will discountenance and discourage, every species of extravagance and dissipation, especially all horse racing, and all kinds of gaming, cock fighting, exhibitions of plays, shews, and other expensive diversions and entertainments; and on the death of any relation or friend, none of us, or any of our families will go into any further mourning dress, than a black crape or ribbon on the arm or hat for gentlemen, and a black ribbon and necklace for ladies, and we will discountenance the giving of gloves and scarfs at funerals.

Ninth. That such as are venders of Goods or Merchandises, will not take advantage of the scarcity of Goods that may be occasioned by this Association, but will sell the same at the rates we have been respectively accustomed to do, for twelve months last past. And if any vender of Goods or Merchandises shall sell any such Goods on higher terms, or shall in any manner, or by any device whatsoever violate or depart from this Agreement, no person ought, nor will any of us deal with any such person, or his or her Factor or Agent, at any time thereafter for any commodity whatever.

Tenth. In case any Merchant, Trader, or other person, shall import any Goods or Merchandise, after the first day of December, and before the first day of February next, the same ought forthwith, at the election of the owner, to be either re-shiped or delivered up to the Committee of the County or Town wherein they shall be imported, to be stored at the wish of the importer, until the Non-Importation Agreement shall cease, or be sold under the direction of the Committee aforesaid; and in the last mentioned case, the owner or owners of such Goods shall be re-imbursed out of the sales the first cost and charges; the profit, if any, to be applied towards relieving and employing such poor inhabitants of the Town of Boston as are immediate sufferers by the Boston Port Bill; and a particular account of all Goods so returned, stored, or sold, to be inserted in the publick papers, and if any Goods or Merchandises shall be imported after the said first day of February, the same ought forthwith to be sent back again, without breaking any of the packages thereof.

Eleventh. That a Committee be chosen in every County, City, and Town, by those who are qualified to vote for Representatives in the Legislature, whose business it shall be attentively to observe the conduct of all persons touching this Association; and when it shall be made to appear to the satisfaction of the majority of any such Committee, that any person within the limits of their appointment has violated this Association, that such a majority do forthwith cause the truth of the case to be published in the Gazette, to the end that all such foes to the rights of British America may be publickly known, and universally contemned as the enemies of American Liberty; and thenceforth we respectively will break off all dealings with him or her.

Twelfth. That the Committee of Correspondence in the respective Colonies, do frequently inspect the Entries of their Custom Houses, and inform each other, from time to time, of the true state thereof, and of every other material circumstance that may occur relative to this association.

Thirteenth. That all Manufactures of this country be sold at reasonable prices, so that no undue advantage be taken of a future scarcity of Goods.

Fourteenth. And we do further agree and resolve that we will have no Trade, Commerce, Dealings, or Intercourse whatsoever with any Colony or Province in North America, which shall not accede to, or which shall hereafter violate this Association, but will hold them as unworthy of the right of freemen, and as inimical to the liberties of this country.

And we do solemnly bind ourselves and our constituents under the ties aforesaid, to adhere to this Association until such parts of the several Acts of Parliament passed since the close of the last war, as impose or continue duties on Tea, Wine, Molasses, Syrups, Paneles, Coffee, Sugar, Pimento, Indigo, Foreign Paper, Glass, and Painters' Colours, imported into America, and extend the powers of the Admiralty Courts beyond their ancient limits, deprive the American subjects of Trial by Jury, authorize the judge's certificate to indemnify the prosecutor from damages that he might otherwise be liable to from a trial by his peers, require oppressive security from a claimant of Ships or Goods seized, before he shall be allowed to defend his property, are repealed.——And until that part of the act of the 12th George III. ch. 24, entitled, "An act for the better securing his majesty's Dock-Yards, Magazines, Ships, Ammunition, and Stores," by which any person charged with committing any of the offences therein described, in America, may be tried in any Shire or County within the realm, is repealed—and until the four Acts passed in the last session of Parliament, viz.: that for stopping the Port and blocking up the Harbour of Boston—that for altering the Charter of Government of the Massachusetts Bay—and that which is entitled "An Act for the better Administration of Justice," etc.—and that for extending the Limits of Quebec, etc., are repealed. And we recommend it to the Provincial Conventions, and to the Committees in the respective Colonies, to establish such farther Regulations as they may think proper for carrying into execution this Association.

The foregoing Association being determined upon by the Congress, was ordered to be subscribed by the several Members thereof; and thereupon, we have hereunto set our respective names accordingly.

In Congress, Philadelphia, October 20, 1774,

PEYTON RANDOLPH, *President.*

VIRGINIA BILL OF RIGHTS—JUNE 12, 1776.

This was adopted by a convention that met at Williamsburg, May 6, 1776. The Bill was drafted by George Mason and was slightly changed in one clause at the instance of James Madison. "Other colonies had framed bills of rights in reference to their relations with Britain; Virginia moved from charters and customs to primal principles; from a narrow altercation about facts to the contemplation of immutable truth. She summoned the eternal laws of man's being to protest against all tyranny." (Bancroft.) This bill of rights was inserted unchanged in the Virginia State constitution of 1830, 1850–51, 1864, and, with some modification, in that of 1870.

Consult *Bancroft's U. S.*, 1st ed., VIII., 378; cen. ed., V., 254; last ed., IV., 416; *Frothingham's Rise*, 511; *Cooke's Va.*, 439.

A DECLARATION OF RIGHTS,

Made by the Representatives of the good People of Virginia, assembled in full and free Convention, which rights do pertain to them and their posterity as the basis and foundation of government.

I. That all men are by nature equally free and independent, and have certain inherent rights, of which, when they enter into a state of society, they cannot by any compact, deprive or divest their posterity; namely, the enjoyment of life and liberty, with the means of acquiring and possessing property, and pursuing and obtaining happiness and safety.

II. That all power is vested in, and consequently derived from, the people; that magistrates are their trustees and servants, and at all times amenable to them.

III. That government is, or ought to be, instituted for the common benefit, protection and security of the people, nation or community; of all the various modes and forms of government, that is best which is capable of producing the greatest degree of happiness and safety, and is most effectually secured against the danger of maladministration; and that, when a government shall be found inadequate or contrary to these purposes, a majority of the community hath an indubitable, unalienable and indefeasible right to reform, alter or abolish it, in such manner as shall be judged most conducive to the public weal.

IV. That no man, or set of men, are entitled to exclusive or separate emoluments or privileges from the community but in consideration of public services, which not being descendible, neither ought the offices of magistrate, legislator or judge to be hereditary.

V. That the legislative, executive and judicial powers should be separate and distinct; and that the members thereof may be restrained from oppression, by feeling and participating the burthens of the people, they should, at fixed periods, be reduced to a private station, return into that body from which they were originally taken, and the vacancies be supplied by frequent, certain and regular elections, in which all, or any part of the former members to be again eligible or ineligible, as the laws shall direct.

VI. That all elections ought to be free, and that all men having sufficient evidence of permanent common interest with, and attachment to the community, have the right of suffrage, and cannot be taxed, or deprived of their property for public uses, without their own consent, or that of their representatives so elected, nor bound by any law to which they have not in like manner assented, for the public good.

VII. That all power of suspending laws, or the execution of laws, by any authority, without consent of the representatives of the people, is injurious to their rights, and ought not to be exercised.

VIII. That in all capital or criminal prosecutions, a man hath a right to demand the cause and nature of his accusation, to be confronted with the accusers and witnesses, to call for evidence in his favor, and to a speedy trial by an impartial jury of twelve men of his vicinage, without whose unanimous consent he cannot be found guilty; nor can he be compelled to give evidence against himself; that no man be deprived of his liberty, except by the law of the land or the judgment of his peers.

IX. That excessive bail ought not to be required, nor excessive fines imposed, nor cruel and unusual punishments inflicted.

X. That general warrants, whereby an officer or messenger may be commanded to search suspected places without evidence of a fact committed, or to seize any person or persons not named, or whose offence is not particularly described and supported by evidence, are grievous and oppressive, and ought not to be granted.

XI. That in controversies respecting property, and in suits between man and man, the ancient trial by jury of twelve men is preferable to any other, and ought to be held sacred.

XII. That the freedom of the press is one of the great bulwarks of liberty, and can never be restrained but by despotic governments.

XIII. That a well regulated militia, composed of the body of the people, trained to arms, is the proper, natural and safe defence of a free State; that standing armies in time of peace, should be avoided as dangerous to liberty; and that in all cases the military should be under strict subordination to, and governed by, the civil power.

XIV. That the people have a right to uniform government; and therefore, that no government separate from or independent of the government of Virginia, ought to be erected or established within the limits thereof.

XV. That no free government, or the blessing of liberty, can be preserved to any people, but by a firm adherence to justice, moderation, temperance, frugality and virtue, and by a frequent recurrence to fundamental principles.

XVI. That religion, or the duty which we owe to our Creator, and the manner of discharging it, can be directed only by reason and conviction, not by force or violence; and therefore all men are equally entitled to the free exercise of religion, according to the dictates of conscience; and that it is the duty of all to practice Christian forbearance, love and charity towards each other.

DECLARATION OF INDEPENDENCE—1776.

THE preamble of the famous resolution of May 15, 1776, of the Continental Congress, declared that the exercise of every kind of authority under the crown of Great Britain should be totally suppressed.

On June 7th Richard Henry Lee, for Virginia, submitted the following resolutions which were seconded by John Adams.

"That these United Colonies are, and of right ought to be, free and independent States, that they are absolved from all allegiance to the British Crown, and that all political connection between them and the State of Great Britain is, and ought to be, totally dissolved.

"That it is expedient forthwith to take the most effectual measures for forming foreign alliances.

"That a plan of confederation be prepared and transmitted to the respective colonies for their consideration and approbation."

These resolutions were discussed June 8th and 10th, when a committee was appointed to draft a declaration in conformity with the first resolution, and further discussion was postponed to July 1. The resolution was adopted July 2d, and two days later (July 4th) the declaration reported by the committee was agreed upon. It was engrossed and signed by the members August 2, 1776.

Consult *Bancroft's U. S.* 1st ed., VIII., chaps. 59 and 60; cen. ed., V., chaps. 69 and 70; last ed., IV., chap. 28; *Hildreth's U. S.*, III., 137; *Frothingham's Rise*, 539; *Story's Constitution*, I., 191; *Bryant and Gay's U. S.*, III., 470; *Greene's Historical View*, 100; *Judge Chamberlin's Authentification of the Declaration; Mass. Hist. Soc. Proc., 2d Series, Vol.* I., 272–298; *Harper's Magazine*, III., 145.

THE DECLARATION OF INDEPENDENCE–1776.

IN CONGRESS, JULY 4, 1776.

The unanimous Declaration of the thirteen united States of America.

WHEN in the Course of human events, it becomes necessary for one people to dissolve the political bands which have connected them with another, and to assume among the Powers of the earth, the separate and equal station to which the Laws of Nature and of Nature's God entitle them, a decent respect to the opinions of mankind requires that they should declare the causes which impel them to the separation.

We hold these truths to be self-evident, that all men are created equal, that they are endowed by their Creator with certain unalienable Rights, that among these are Life, Liberty and the pursuit of Happiness. That to secure these rights, Governments are instituted among Men, deriving their just powers from the consent of the governed, That whenever any Form of Government becomes destructive of these ends, it is the Right of the People to alter or to abolish it, and to institute new Government, laying its foundation on such principles and organizing its powers in such form, as to them shall seem most likely to effect their Safety and Happiness. Prudence, indeed, will dictate that Governments long established should not be changed for light and transient causes; and accordingly all experience hath shown, that mankind are more disposed to suffer, while evils are sufferable, than to right themselves by abolishing the forms to which they are accustomed. But when a long train of abuses and usurpations, pursuing invariably the same Object, evinces a design to reduce them under absolute Despotism, it is their right, it is their duty, to throw off such Government, and to provide new Guards for their future security.—Such has been the patient sufferance of these Colonies; and such is now the necessity which constrains them to alter their former Systems of Government. The history of the present King of Great Britain is a history of repeated injuries and usurpations, all having in direct object the establishment of an absolute Tyranny over these States. To prove this, let Facts be submitted to a candid world.

He has refused his Assent to Laws, the most wholesome and necessary for the public good.

He has forbidden his Governors to pass Laws of immediate and pressing importance, unless suspended in their operation till his Assent should be obtained; and when so suspended, he has utterly neglected to attend to them.

He has refused to pass other Laws for the accommodation of large districts of people, unless those people would relinquish the right of Representation in the Legislature, a right inestimable to them and formidable to tyrants only.

He has called together legislative bodies at places unusual, uncomfortable, and distant from the depository of their Public Records, for the sole purpose of fatiguing them into compliance with his measures.

He has dissolved Representative Houses repeatedly,

for opposing with manly firmness his invasions on the rights of the people.

He has refused for a long time, after such dissolutions to cause others to be elected; whereby the Legislative Powers, incapable of Annihilation, have returned to the People at large for their exercise; the State remaining in the mean time exposed to all the dangers of invasion from without, and convulsions within.

He has endeavoured to prevent the population of these States; for that purpose obstructing the Laws for Naturalization of Foreigners; refusing to pass others to encourage their migration hither, and raising the conditions of new Appropriations of Lands.

He has obstructed the Administration of Justice, by refusing his Assent to Laws for establishing Judiciary Powers.

He has made Judges dependent on his Will alone, for the tenure of their offices, and the amount and payment of their salaries.

He has erected a multitude of New Offices, and sent hither swarms of Officers to harass our People, and eat out their substance.

He has kept among us, in times of peace, Standing Armies without the Consent of our legislature.

He has affected to render the Military independent of and superior to the Civil Power.

He has combined with others to subject us to a jurisdiction foreign to our constitution, and unacknowledged by our laws; giving his Assent to their Acts of pretended Legislation:

For quartering large bodies of armed troops among us:

For protecting them, by a mock Trial, from Punishment for any Murders which they should commit on the Inhabitants of these States:

For cutting off our Trade with all parts of the world:

For imposing taxes on us without our Consent:

For depriving us in many cases, of the benefits of Trial by Jury:

For transporting us beyond Seas to be tried for pretended offences:

For abolishing the free System of English Laws in a neighboring Province, establishing therein an Arbitrary government, and enlarging its Boundaries so as to render it at once an example and fit instrument for introducing the same absolute rule into these Colonies:

For taking away our Charters, abolishing our most valuable Laws, and altering fundamentally the Forms of our Governments:

For suspending our own Legislatures, and declaring themselves invested with Power to legislate for us in all cases whatsoever.

He has abdicated Government here, by declaring us out of his Protection and waging War against us.

He has plundered our seas, ravaged our Coasts, burnt our towns, and destroyed the lives of our people.

He is at this time transporting large armies of foreign mercenaries to compleat the works of death, desolation and tyranny, already begun with circumstances of Cruelty, & perfidy scarcely paralleled in the most barbarous ages, and totally unworthy the Head of a civilized nation.

He has constrained our fellow Citizens taken Captive on the high Seas to bear Arms against their Country, to become the executioners of their friends and Brethren, or to fall themselves by their Hands.

He has excited domestic insurrections amongst us, and has endeavoured to bring on the inhabitants of our frontiers, the merciless Indian Savages, whose known rule of warfare, is an undistinguished destruction of all ages, sexes and conditions.

In every stage of these Oppressions We have Petitioned for Redress in the most humble terms: Our repeated Petitions have been answered only by repeated injury. A Prince, whose character is thus marked by every act which may define a Tyrant, is unfit to be the ruler of a free People.

Nor have We been wanting in attention to our British brethren. We have warned them from time to time of attempts by their legislature to extend an unwarrantable jurisdiction over us. We have reminded them of the circumstances of our emigration and settlement here. We have appealed to their native justice and magnanimity, and we have conjured them by the ties of our common kindred to disavow these usurpations, which, would inevitably interrupt our connections and correspondence. They too have been deaf to the voice of justice and of consanguinity. We must, therefore, acquiesce in the necessity which denounces our Separation, and hold them, as we hold the rest of mankind, Enemies in War, in Peace Friends.

We, therefore, the Representatives of the united States of America, in General Congress, Assembled, appealing to the Supreme Judge of the world for the rectitude of our intentions, do, in the Name, and by Authority of the good People of these Colonies, solemnly publish and declare, That these United Colonies are, and of Right ought to be Free and Independent States; that they are Absolved from all Allegiance to the British Crown, and that all political connection between them and the State of Great Britain, is and ought to be totally dissolved; and that as Free and Independent States, they have full Power to levy War, conclude Peace, contract Alliances, establish Commerce, and to do all other Acts and Things which Independent States may of right do. And for the support of this Declaration, with a firm reliance on the Protection of Divine Providence, we mutually pledge to each other our Lives, our Fortunes and our sacred Honor.

JOHN HANCOCK.

New Hampshire.

JOSIAH BARTLETT,
WM. WHIPPLE,
MATTHEW THORNTON.

Massachusetts Bay.

SAML. ADAMS,
JOHN ADAMS,
ROBT. TREAT PAINE,
ELBRIDGE GERRY.

Rhode Island.

STEP. HOPKINS,
WILLIAM ELLERY.

Connecticut.

ROGER SHERMAN,
SAM'EL HUNTINGTON,
WM. WILLIAMS,
OLIVER WOLCOTT.

New York.

WM. FLOYD,
PHIL. LIVINGSTON,
FRANS. LEWIS,
LEWIS MORRIS.

New Jersey.

RICHD. STOCKTON,
JNO. WITHERSPOON,
FRAS. HOPKINSON,
JOHN HART,
ABRA. CLARK.

Pennsylvania.

ROBT. MORRIS,
BENJAMIN RUSH,
BENJA. FRANKLIN,
JOHN MORTON,
GEO. CLYMER,
JAS. SMITH,
GEORGE TAYLOR,
JAMES WILSON,
GEO. ROSS.

Delaware.

CÆSAR RODNEY,
GEO. READ,
THO. M'KEAN.

Maryland.

SAMUEL CHASE,
WM. PACA,
THOS. STONE,
CHARLES CARROLL of Carrollton.

Virginia.

GEORGE WYTHE,
RICHARD HENRY LEE,
TH JEFFERSON,
BENJA. HARRISON,
THOS. NELSON, jr.,
FRANCIS LIGHTFOOT LEE,
CARTER BRAXTON.

North Carolina.

WM. HOOPER, JOHN PENN.
JOSEPH HEWES,

South Carolina.

EDWARD RUTLEDGE, THOMAS LYNCH, Junr.,
THOS. HEYWARD, Junr., ARTHUR MIDDLETON.

Georgia.

BUTTON GWINNETT, GEO. WALTON.
LYMAN HALL,

ARTICLES OF CONFEDERATION—1777.

THE necessity of some provision for a general government was early felt. A committee, appointed by Congress June 11, 1776, "to prepare and digest the form of a confederation to be entered into between these colonies," reported July 12, articles drawn up by John Dickinson. These were not approved, and the matter dropped for the time. At length, Nov. 15, 1777, Congress agreed upon the Articles of Confederation, and ordered them forwarded to the several states that they might instruct their delegates to ratify them in congress. The dates of ratification were—Massachusetts, Rhode Island, Connecticut, New York, Pennsylvania, Virginia, and South Carolina, July 9, 1778—North Carolina, July 21, 1778—Georgia, July 24, 1778—New Jersey, Nov. 26, 1778—Delaware, Feb. 22, 1779—Maryland, March 1, 1781. "Until the adoption of the articles of confederation by all the states, congress continued a revolutionary body, which was recognized by all the colonies as *de jure* and *de facto* the national government and which, as such, came in contact with foreign powers and entered into engagements, the binding force of which on the whole people has never been called in question." (Von Holst.) The principal defects are well summarized by Schouler. I. Want of power to enforce obedience. II. Operation of the fundamental law not upon individuals but upon states. III. Large vote requisite in congress for passage of important measures. IV. Want of right to regulate foreign Commerce. V. Virtual omission of power to alter the existing articles.

Consult *Bancroft's U. S.*, 1st ed., IX., 436; cen. ed., VI., 25; last ed., V., 200; *Hildreth's U. S.*, III. 266; *Frothingham's Rise, etc.*, 569; *Story's Cons. U. S*, I., 209–251; *Curtis' Constitution*, I., 114; *Prince's The Articles of Confederation vs. the Constitution.*

ARTICLES OF CONFEDERATION—1777.

To all to whom these Presents shall come, we the undersigned Delegates of the States affixed to our Names, send greeting.

WHEREAS the Delegates of the United States of America in Congress assembled did on the fifteenth day of November in the Year of our Lord One Thousand Seven Hundred and Seventyseven, and in the Second Year of the Independence of America agree to certain articles of Confederation and perpetual Union between the States of Newhampshire, Massachusetts-bay, Rhodeisland and Providence Plantations, Connecticut, New York, New Jersey, Pennsylvania, Delaware, Maryland, Virginia, North-Carolina, South-Carolina and Georgia in the Words following, viz.

"*Articles of Confederation and perpetual Union between the States of Newhampshire, Massachusetts-bay, Rhodeisland and Providence Plantations, Connecticut, New-York, New-Jersey, Pennsylvania, Delaware, Maryland, Virginia, North-Carolina, South-Carolina and Georgia.*

ARTICLE I. The stile of this confederacy shall be "The United States of America."

ARTICLE II. Each State retains its sovereignty, freedom and independence, and every power, jurisdiction and right, which is not by this confederation expressly delegated to the United States, in Congress assembled.

ARTICLE III. The said States hereby severally enter into a firm league of friendship with each other, for their common defence, the security of their liberties, and their mutual and general welfare, binding themselves to assist each other, against all force offered to, or attacks made upon them, or any of them, on account of religion, sovereignty, trade, or any other pretence whatever.

ARTICLE IV. The better to secure and perpetuate mutual friendship and intercourse among the people of the different States in this Union, the free inhabitants of each of these States, paupers, vagabonds and fugitives from justice excepted, shall be entitled to all privileges and immunities of free citizens in the several States; and the people of each State shall have free ingress and regress to and from any other State, and shall enjoy therein all the privileges of trade and commerce, subject to the same duties, impositions and restrictions as the inhabitants thereof respectively, provided that such restrictions shall not extend so far as to prevent the removal of property imported into any State, to any other State of which the owner is an inhabitant; provided also that no imposition, duties or restriction shall be laid by any State, on the property of the United States, or either of them.

If any person guilty of, or charged with treason, felony, or other high misdemeanor in any State, shall flee from justice, and be found in any of the United States, he shall upon demand of the Governor or Executive power, of the State from which he fled, be delivered up and removed to the State having jurisdiction of his offence.

Full faith and credit shall be given in each of these

States to the records, acts and judicial proceedings of the courts and magistrates of every other State.

ARTICLE V. For the more convenient management of the general interests of the United States, delegates shall be annually appointed in such manner as the legislature of each State shall direct, to meet in Congress on the first Monday in November, in every year, with a power reserved to each State, to recall its delegates, or any of them, at any time within the year, and to send others in their stead, for the remainder of the year.

No State shall be represented in Congress by less than two, nor by more than seven members; and no person shall be capable of being a delegate for more than three years in any term of six years; nor shall any person, being a delegate, be capable of holding any office under the United States, for which he, or another for his benefit receives any salary, fees or emolument of any kind.

Each State shall maintain its own delegates in a meeting of the States, and while they act as members of the committee of the States.

In determining questions in the United States, in Congress assembled, each State shall have one vote.

Freedom of speech and debate in Congress shall not be impeached or questioned in any court, or place out of Congress, and the members of Congress shall be protected in their persons from arrests and imprisonments, during the time of their going to and from, and attendance on Congress, except for treason, felony, or breach of the peace.

ARTICLE VI. No State without the consent of the United States in Congress assembled, shall send any embassy to, or receive any embassy from, or enter into any conferrence, agreement, alliance or treaty with any king prince or state; nor shall any person holding any office of profit or trust under the United States, or any of them, accept of any present, emolument, office or title of any kind whatever from any king, prince or foreign state; nor shall the United States in Congress assembled, or any of them, grant any title of nobility.

No two or more States shall enter into any treaty, confederation or alliance whatever between them, without the consent of the United States in Congress assembled, specifying accurately the purposes for which the same is to be entered into, and how long it shall continue.

No State shall lay any imposts or duties, which may interfere with any stipulations in treaties, entered into by the United States in Congress assembled, with any king, prince or state, in pursuance of any treaties already proposed by Congress, to the courts of France and Spain.

No vessels of war shall be kept up in time of peace by any State, except such number only, as shall be deemed necessary by the United States in Congress assembled, for the defence of such State, or its trade; nor shall any body of forces be kept up by any State, in time of peace, except such number only, as in the judgment of the United States, in Congress assembled, shall be deemed requisite to garrison the forts necessary for the defence of such State; but every State shall always keep up a well regulated and disciplined militia, sufficiently armed and accoutred, and shall provide and constantly have ready for use, in public stores, a due number of field pieces and tents, and a proper quantity of arms, ammunition and camp equipage.

No State shall engage in any war without the consent of the United States in Congress assembled, unless such State be actually invaded by enemies, or shall have received certain advice of a resolution being formed by some nation of Indians to invade such State, and the danger is so imminent as not to admit of a delay, till the United States in Congress assembled can be consulted: nor shall any State grant commissions to any ships or vessels of war, nor letters of marque or reprisal, except it be after a declaration of war by the United States in

Congress assembled, and then only against the kingdom or state and the subjects thereof, against which war has been so declared, and under such regulations as shall be established by the United States in Congress assembled, unless such State be infested by pirates, in which case vessels of war may be fitted out for that occasion, and kept so long as the danger shall continue, or until the United States in Congress assembled shall determine otherwise.

ARTICLE VII. When land-forces are raised by any State for the common defence, all officers of or under the rank of colonel, shall be appointed by the Legislature of each State respectively by whom such forces shall be raised, or in such manner as such State shall direct, and all vacancies shall be filled up by the State which first made the appointment.

ARTICLE VIII. All charges of war, and all other expenses that shall be incurred for the common defence or general welfare, and allowed by the United States in Congress assembled, shall be defrayed out of a common treasury, which shall be supplied by the several States, in proportion to the value of all land within each State, granted to or surveyed for any person, as such land and the buildings and improvements thereon shall be estimated according to such mode as the United States in Congress assembled, shall from time to time direct and appoint.

The taxes for paying that proportion shall be laid and levied by the authority and direction of the Legislatures of the several States within the time agreed upon by the United States in Congress assembled.

ARTICLE IX. The United States in Congress assembled, shall have the sole and exclusive right and power of determining on peace and war, except in the cases mentioned in the sixth article—of sending and receiving ambassadors—entering into treaties and alliances, provided that no treaty of commerce shall be made whereby the legislative power of the respective States shall be restrained from imposing such imposts and duties on foreigners, as their own people are subjected to, or from prohibiting the exportation or importation of any species of goods or commodities whatsoever—of establishing rules for deciding in all cases, what captures on land or water shall be legal, and in what manner prizes taken by land or naval forces in the service of the United States shall be divided or appropriated—of granting letters of marque and reprisal in times of peace—appointing courts for the trial of piracies and felonies committed on the high seas and establishing courts for receiving and determining finally appeals in all cases of captures, provided that no member of Congress shall be appointed a judge of any of the said courts.

The United States in Congress assembled shall also be the last resort on appeal in all disputes and differences now subsisting or that hereafter may arise between two or more States concerning boundary, jurisdiction or any other cause whatever; which authority shall always be exercised in the manner following. Whenever the legislative or executive authority or lawful agent of any State in controversy with another shall present a petition to Congress, stating the matter in question and praying for a hearing, notice thereof shall be given by order of Congress to the legislative or executive authority of the other State in controversy, and a day assigned for the appearance of the parties by their lawful agents, who shall then be directed to appoint by joint consent, commissioners or judges to constitute a court for hearing and determining the matter in question: but if they cannot agree, Congress shall name three persons out of each of the United States, and from the list of such persons each party shall alternately strike out one, the petitioners beginning, until the number shall be reduced to thirteen; and from that number not less than seven, nor more than nine names as Congress shall direct, shall in the presence of Congress be drawn out by lot, and the persons whose names shall be so drawn or any five of them, shall be commissioners or judges, to hear and finally determine the controversy, so always as a major part of the judges who shall hear the cause shall agree in the determination: and if either party shall neglect to attend at the day appointed, without showing reasons, which Congress shall judge sufficient, or being present shall refuse to strike, the Congress shall proceed to nominate three persons out of each State, and the Secretary of Congress shall strike in behalf of such party absent or refusing; and the judgment and sentence of the court to be appointed, in the manner before prescribed, shall be final and conclusive; and if any of the parties shall refuse to submit to the authority of such court, or to appear or defend their claim or cause, the court shall nevertheless proceed to pronounce sentence, or judgment, which shall in like manner be final and decisive, the judgment or sentence and other proceedings being in either case transmitted to Congress, and lodged among the acts of Congress for the security of the parties concerned: provided that every commissioner, before he sits in judgment, shall take an oath to be administered by one of the judges of the supreme or superior court of the State where the cause shall be tried, "well and truly to hear and determine the matter in question, according to the best of his judgment, without favour, affection or hope of reward:" provided also that no State shall be deprived of territory for the benefit of the United States.

All controversies concerning the private right of soil claimed under different grants of two or more States, whose jurisdiction as they may respect such lands, and the States which passed such grants are adjusted, the said grants or either of them being at the same time claimed to have originated antecedent to such settlement of jurisdiction, shall on the petition of either party

15

to the Congress of the United States, be finally determined as near as may be in the same manner as is before prescribed for deciding disputes respecting territorial jurisdiction between different States.

The United States in Congress assembled shall also have the sole and exclusive right and power of regulating the alloy and value of coin struck by their own authority, or by that of the respective States.—fixing the standard of weights and measures throughout the United States—regulating the trade and managing all affairs with the Indians, not members of any of the States, provided that the legislative right of any State within its own limits be not infringed or violated—establishing and regulating post-offices from one State to another, throughout all the United States, and exacting such postage on the papers passing thro' the same as may be requisite to defray the expenses of the said office—appointing all officers of the land forces, in the service of the United States, excepting regimental officers—appointing all the officers of the naval forces, and commissioning all officers whatever in the service of the United States—making rules for the government and regulation of the said land and naval forces, and directing their operations.

The United States in Congress assembled shall have authority to appoint a committee, to sit in the recess of Congress, to be denominated "a Committee of the States," and to consist of one delegate from each State; and to appoint such other committees and civil officers as may be necessary for managing the general affairs of the United States under their direction—to appoint one of their number to preside, provided that no person be allowed to serve in the office of president more than one year in any term of three years; to ascertain the necessary sums of money to be raised for the service of the United States, and to appropriate and apply the same for defraying the public expenses—to borrow money, or emit bills on the credit of the United States, transmitting every half year to the respective States an account of the sums of money so borrowed or emitted,—to build and equip a navy—to agree upon the number of land forces, and to make requisitions from each State for its quota, in proportion to the number of white inhabitants in such State; which requisition shall be binding, and thereupon the Legislature of each State shall appoint the regimental officers, raise the men and cloath, arm and equip them in a soldier like manner, at the expense of the United States; and the officers and men so cloathed, armed and equipped shall march to the place appointed, and within the time agreed on by the United States in Congress assembled: but if the United States in Congress assembled shall, on consideration of circumstances judge proper that any State should not raise men, or should raise a smaller number than its quota, and that any other State should raise a greater number of men than the quota thereof, such extra number shall be raised, officered, cloathed, armed and equipped in the same manner as the quota of such State, unless the legislature of such State shall judge that such extra number cannot be safely spared out of the same, in which case they shall raise officer, cloath, arm and equip as many of such extra number as they judge can be safely spared. And the officers and men so cloathed, armed and equipped, shall march to the place appointed, and within the time agreed on by the United States in Congress assembled.

The United States in Congress assembled shall never engage in a war, nor grant letters of marque and reprisal in time of peace, nor enter into any treaties or alliances, nor coin money, nor regulate the value thereof, nor ascertain the sums and expenses necessary for the defence and welfare of the United States, or any of them, nor emit bills, nor borrow money on the credit of the United States, nor appropriate money, nor agree upon the number of vessels of war, to be built or purchased, or the number of land or sea forces to be raised, nor appoint a commander in chief of the army or navy, unless nine States assent to the same: nor shall a question on any other point, except for adjourning from day to day be determined, unless by the votes of a majority of the United States in Congress assembled.

The Congress of the United States shall have power to adjourn to any time within the year, and to any place within the United States, so that no period of adjournment be for a longer duration than the space of six months, and shall publish the journal of their proceedings monthly, except such parts thereof relating to treaties, alliances or military operations, as in their judgment require secresy; and the yeas and nays of the delegates of each State on any question shall be entered on the journal, when it is desired by any delegate; and the delegates of a State, or any of them, at his or their request shall be furnished with a transcript of the said journal, except such parts as are above excepted, to lay before the Legislatures of the several States.

ARTICLE X. The committee of the States, or any nine of them, shall be authorized to execute, in the recess of Congress, such of the powers of Congress as the United States in Congress assembled, by the consent of nine States, shall from time to time think expedient to vest them with; provided that no power be delegated to the said committee, for the exercise of which, by the articles of confederation, the voice of nine States in the Congress of the United States assembled is requisite.

ARTICLE XI. Canada acceding to this confederation, and joining in the measures of the United States, shall be admitted into, and entitled to all the advantages of this Union: but no other colony shall be admitted into the same, unless such admission be agreed to by nine States.

ARTICLE XII. All bills of credit emitted, monies borrowed and debts contracted by, or under the authority of Congress, before the assembling of the United States, in pursuance of the present confederation, shall be deemed and considered as a charge against the United States, for payment and satisfaction whereof the said United States, and the public faith are hereby solemnly pledged.

ARTICLE XIII. Every State shall abide by the determinations of the United States in Congress assembled, on all questions which by this confederation are submitted to them. And the articles of this confederation shall be inviolably observed by every State, and the Union shall be perpetual; nor shall any alteration at any time hereafter be made in any of them; unless such alteration be agreed to in a Congress of the United States, and be afterwards confirmed by the Legislatures of every State.

And whereas it has pleased the Great Governor of the world to incline the hearts of the Legislatures we respectively represent in Congress, to approve of, and to authorize us to ratify the said articles of confederation and perpetual union. Know ye that we the undersigned delegates, by virtue of the power and authority to us given for that purpose, do by these presents, in the name and in behalf of our respective constituents, fully and entirely ratify and confirm each and every of the said articles of confederation and perpetual union, and all and singular the matters and things therein contained: and we do further solemnly plight and engage the faith of our respective constituents, that they shall abide by the determinations of the United States in Congress assembled, on all questions, which by the said confederation are submitted to them. And that the articles thereof shall be inviolably observed by the States we re[s]pectively represent, and that the Union shall be perpetual.

In witness whereof we have hereunto set our hands in Congress. Done at Philadelphia in the State of Pennsylvania the ninth day of July in the year of our Lord one thousand seven hundred and seventy-eight, and in the third year of the independence of America.

On the part & behalf of the State of New Hampshire.

JOSIAH BARTLETT, JOHN WENTWORTH, Junr., August 8th, 1778.

On the part and behalf of the State of Massachusetts Bay.

JOHN HANCOCK, SAMUEL ADAMS, ELBRIDGE GERRY, FRANCIS DANA, JAMES LOVELL, SAMUEL HOLTEN.

On the part and behalf of the State of Rhode Island and Providence Plantations.

WILLIAM ELLERY, HENRY MARCHANT, JOHN COLLINS.

On the part and behalf of the State of Connecticut.

ROGER SHERMAN, SAMUEL HUNTINGTON, OLIVER WOLCOTT, TITUS HOSMER, ANDREW ADAMS.

On the part and behalf of the State of New York.

JAS. DUANE, FRA. LEWIS, WM. DUER, GOUV. MORRIS.

On the part and in behalf of the State of New Jersey, Novr. 26, 1778.

JNO. WITHERSPOON, NATH. SCUDDER.

On the part and behalf of the State of Pennsylvania.

ROBT. MORRIS, DANIEL ROBERDEAU, JONA. BAYARD SMITH, WILLIAM CLINGAN, JOSEPH REED, 22d July, 1778.

On the part & behalf of the State of Delaware.

THO. M'KEAN,
Feby. 12, 1779.
JOHN DICKINSON, May 5th, 1779.
NICHOLAS VAN DYKE.

On the part and behalf of the State of Maryland.

JOHN HANSON,
March 1, 1781.
DANIEL CARROLL,
Mar. 1, 1781.

On the part and behalf of the State of Virginia.

RICHARD HENRY LEE,
JOHN BANISTER,
THOMAS ADAMS,
JNO. HARVIE,
FRANCIS LIGHTFOOT LEE.

On the part and behalf of the State of No. Carolina.

JOHN PENN, July 21, 1778.
CORNS. HARNETT,
JNO. WILLIAMS.

On the part & behalf of the State of South Carolina.

HENRY LAURENS,
WILLIAM HENRY DRAYTON,
JNO. MATHEWS,
RICHD. HUTSON.
THOS. HEYWARD, Junr.

On the part & behalf of the State of Georgia.

JNO. WALTON,
24th July, 1778.
EDWD. TELFAIR,
EDWD. LANGWORTHY.

TREATY OF PEACE—1783.

CORNWALLIS surrendered Oct. 19, 1781, and Feb. 27, 1782, Parliament voted against continuing the American War. Lord North's ministry went out and the new administration dispatched Richard Oswald to negotiate peace with Franklin at Paris. The negotiations extended from April till Nov. 30, 1782, when the provisional or preliminary articles of peace were signed. These articles were "to be inserted in and constitute the treaty of peace" which should be concluded when Great Britain and France should have arranged terms of peace. The definitive treaty was signed as below, Sept. 3, 1783.

Consult *Bancroft's U. S.*, last ed., VI., 36; cen. ed., VI., 434; *Bryant and Gay*, IV., 89; *Hildreth*, III., 418; *Fiske*, "*Political Consequences of Cornwallis' Surrender*," *in Atlantic Monthly*; Jan., 1886; *Curtis, in Harper's Mag.*, April and May, 1883; *Treaties and Conventions* (Sen. ex. Doc. No. 36, 43d Cong. 3d. Sess.), 1009.

DEFINITIVE TREATY OF PEACE BETWEEN THE UNITED STATES OF AMERICA AND HIS BRITANNIC MAJESTY. CONCLUDED SEPTEMBER 3, 1783.

In the name of the Most Holy and Undivided Trinity.

It having pleased the Divine Providence to dispose

the heart of the most serene and most potent Prince George the Third, by the Grace of God King of Great Britain, France and Ireland, Defender of the Faith, Duke of Brunswick and Luneburg, Arch-Treasurer and Prince Elector of the Holy Roman Empire, &ca., and of the United States of America, to forget all past misunderstandings and differences that have unhappily interrupted the good correspondence and friendship which they mutually wish to restore; and to establish such a beneficial and satisfactory intercourse between the two countries, upon the ground of reciprocal advantages and mutual convenience, as may promote and secure to both perpetual peace and harmony: And having for this desirable end already laid the foundation of peace and reconciliation, by the provisional articles, signed at Paris on the 30th of Nov'r, 1782, by the commissioners empowered on each part, which articles were agreed to be inserted in and to constitute the treaty of peace proposed to be concluded between the Crown of Great Britain and the said United States, but which treaty was not to be concluded until terms of peace should be agreed upon between Great Britain and France, and His Britannic Majesty should be ready to conclude such treaty accordingly; and the treaty between Great Britain and France having since been concluded, His Britannic Majesty and the United States of America, in order to carry into full effect the provisional articles above mentioned, according to the tenor thereof, have constituted and appointed, that is to say, His Britannic Majesty on his part, David Hartley, esqr., member of the Parliament of Great Britain; and the said United States on their part, John Adams, esqr., late a commissioner of the United States of America at the Court of Versailles, late Delegate in Congress from the State of Massachusetts, and chief justice of the said State, and Minister Plenipotentiary of the said United States to their High Mightinesses the States General of the United Netherlands; Benjamin Franklin, esq're, late Delegate in

Congress, from the State of Pennsylvania, president of the convention of the said State, and Minister Plenipotentiary from the United States of America at the Court of Versailles; John Jay, esq're, late president of Congress, and chief justice of the State of New York, and Minister Plenipotentiary from the said United States at the Court of Madrid, to be the Plenipotentiaries for the concluding and signing the present definitive treaty; who, after having reciprocally communicated their respective full powers, have agreed upon and confirmed the following articles:

ARTICLE I.

HIS Britannic Majesty acknowledges the said United States, viz. New Hampshire, Massachusetts Bay, Rhode Island, and Providence Plantations, Connecticut, New York, New Jersey, Pennsylvania, Delaware, Maryland, Virginia, North Carolina, South Carolina, and Georgia, to be free, sovereign and independent States; that he treats with them as such, and for himself, his heirs and successors, relinquishes all claims to the Government, propriety and territorial rights of the same, and every part thereof.

ARTICLE II.

AND that all disputes which might arise in future, on the subject of the boundaries of the United States may be prevented, it is hereby agreed and declared, that the following are, and shall be their boundaries, viz: From the north-west angle of Nova Scotia, viz. that angle which is formed by a line drawn due north from the source of Saint Croix River to the Highlands; along the said Highlands which divide those rivers that empty themselves into the river St. Lawrence, from those which fall into the Atlantic Ocean, to the northwesternmost head of Connecticut River; thence down along the middle of that river, to the forty-fifth degree of north latitude; from thence, by a line due west on the said latitude, until it strikes the river Iroquois or Cataraquy; thence along the middle of said river into Lake Ontario, through the middle of said lake until it strikes the communication by water between that lake and Lake Erie; thence along the middle of said communication into Lake Erie, through the middle of said lake until it arrives at the water communication between that lake and Lake Huron; thence along the middle of said water communication into the Lake Huron; thence through the middle of said lake to the water communication between that lake and Lake Superior; thence through Lake Superior northward of the Isles Royal and Philipeaux, to the Long Lake; thence through the middle of said Long Lake, and the water communication between it and the Lake of the Woods, to the said Lake of the Woods; thence through the said lake to the most northwestern point thereof, and from thence on a due west course to the river Mississippi; thence by a line to be drawn along the middle of the said river Mississippi until it shall intersect the northernmost part of the thirty-first degree of north latitude. South, by a line to be drawn due east from the determination of the line last mentioned, in the latitude of thirty-one degrees north of the Equator, to the middle of the river Apalachicola or Catahouche; thence along the middle thereof to its junction with the Flint River; thence strait to the head of St. Mary's River; and thence down along the middle of St. Mary's River to the Atlantic Ocean. East, by a line to be drawn along the middle of the river St. Croix, from its mouth in the Bay of Fundy to its source, and from its source directly north to the aforesaid Highlands, which divide the rivers that fall into the Atlantic Ocean from those which fall into the river St. Lawrence; comprehending all islands within twenty leagues of any part of the shores of the United States, and lying between lines to be drawn due east from the points where the aforesaid boundaries between Nova Scotia on the one part, and East Florida on the other, shall respectively touch the Bay of Fundy and the Atlantic Ocean; excepting such islands as now are, or heretofore have been, within the limits of the said province of Nova Scotia.

ARTICLE III.

It is agreed that the people of the United States shall continue to enjoy unmolested the right to take fish of every kind on the Grand Bank, and on all the other banks of Newfoundland; also in the Gulph of Saint Lawrence, and at all other places in the sea where the inhabitants of both countries used at any time heretofore to fish. And also that the inhabitants of the United States shall have liberty to take fish of every kind on such part of the coast of Newfoundland as British fishermen shall use (but not to dry or cure the same on that island) and also on the coasts, bays, and creeks of all other of His Britannic Majesty's dominions in America; and that the American fishermen shall have liberty to dry and cure fish in any of the unsettled bays, harbours, and creeks of Nova Scotia, Magdalen Islands, and Labrador, so long as the same shall remain unsettled; but so soon as the same or either of them shall be settled, it shall not be lawful for the said fishermen to dry or cure fish at such settlement, without a previous agreement for that purpose with the inhabitants, proprietors, or possessors of the ground.

ARTICLE IV.

It is agreed that creditors on either side shall meet with no lawful impediment to the recovery of the full value in sterling money, of all bona fide debts heretofore contracted.

ARTICLE V.

It is agreed that the Congress shall earnestly recommend it to the legislatures of the respective States, to provide for the restitution of all estates, rights, and properties which have been confiscated, belonging to real British subjects, and also of the estates, rights, and properties of persons resident in districts in the possession of His Majesty's arms, and who have not borne arms against the said United States. And that persons of any other description shall have free liberty to go to any part or parts of any of the thirteen United States, and therein to remain twelve months, unmolested in their endeavors to obtain the restitution of such of their estates, rights, and properties as may have been confiscated ; and that Congress shall also earnestly recommend to the several States a reconsideration and revision of all acts or laws regarding the premises, so as to render the said laws or acts perfectly consistent, not only with justice and equity but with that spirit of conciliation which, on the return of the blessings of peace, should universally prevail. And that Congress shall also earnestly recommend to the several States, that the estates, rights, and properties of such last mentioned persons, shall be restored to them, they refunding to any persons who may be now in possession, the bona fide price (where any has been given) which such persons may have paid on purchasing any of the said lands, rights, or properties, since the confiscation. And it is agreed, that all persons who have any interest in confiscated lands, either by debts, marriage settlements, or otherwise, shall meet with no lawful impediment in the prosecution of their just rights.

ARTICLE VI.

That there shall be no future confiscations made, nor any prosecutions commenc'd, against any person or persons for, or by reason of the part which he or they may have taken in the present war; and that no person shall, on that account, suffer any future loss or damage, either in his person, liberty or property; and that those who may be in confinement on such charges, at the time of the ratification of the treaty in America, shall be immediately set at liberty, and the prosecutions so commenced be discontinued.

ARTICLE VII.

THERE shall be a firm and perpetual peace between His Britannic Majesty and the said States, and between the subjects of the one and the citizens of the other, wherefore all hostilities, both by sea and land, shall from henceforth cease: All prisoners on both sides shall be set at liberty, and His Britannic Majesty shall, with all convenient speed, and without causing any destruction, or carrying away any negroes or other property of the American inhabitants, withdraw all his armies, garrisons, and fleets from the said United States, and from every port, place, and harbour within the same; leaving in all fortifications the American artillery that may be therein: And shall also order and cause all archives, records, deeds, and papers, belonging to any of the said States, or their citizens, which in the course of the war, may have fallen into the hands of his officers, to be forthwith restored and deliver'd to the proper States and persons to whom they belong.

ARTICLE VIII.

THE navigation of the river Mississippi, from its source to the ocean, shall forever remain free and open to the subjects of Great Britain, and the citizens of the United States.

ARTICLE IX.

In case it should so happen that any place or territory belonging to Great Britain or to the United States, should have been conquer'd by the arms of either from the other, before the arrival of the said provisional articles in America, it is agreed, that the same shall be restored without difficulty, and without requiring any compensation.

ARTICLE X.

The solemn ratifications of the present treaty, expedited in good and due form, shall be exchanged between the contracting parties, in the space of six months, or sooner if possible, to be computed from the day of the signature of the present treaty. In witness whereof, we the undersigned, their Ministers Plenipotentiary, have in their name and in virtue of our full powers, signed with our hands the present definitive treaty, and caused the seals of our arms to be affix'd thereto.

Done at Paris, this third day of September, in the year of our Lord one thousand seven hundred and eighty-three.

D. Hartley. [L. S.]
John Adams. [L. S.]
B. Franklin. [L. S.]
John Jay. [L. S.]

NORTHWEST ORDINANCE—1787.

On the same day (March 1, 1784) that Virginia ceded her western territory to Congress, Thomas Jefferson reported in Congress a plan for the temporary government of this newly acquired territory. Among its provisions was the prohibition of slavery after 1800, but this clause was cancelled. The measure passed April 23, 1784. From this time many plans were reported by various committees, but no definite action was taken till 1787, when, on July 13, the "Ordinance for the Government of the Territory of the United States north-west of the river Ohio" was passed. This ordinance, even when ordered to a third reading, did not contain "those great principles for which it has since been distinguished as one of the greatest monuments of civil jurisprudence," above all the prohibition of slavery, which Mr. Dane, of Massachusetts, offered as an amendment, July 12.

"The ordinance of 1787, in particular, deserves to rank among immortal parchments both for what it accomplished and what it inspired. Nor would it be wild hyperbole to opine that save for the adoption and unflinching execution of that ordinance by Congress in early times, the American Union would ere to-day have found a grave."

In 1790 this ordinance, excepting certain clauses,

was extended to the territory south of the river Ohio.

Consult *Donaldson's Public Domain*, chap. I., (Mis. Doc., 45, 47, Cong. Ina. Sess.); *Bancroft's U. S.*, last ed., II., 277; *Poole's article on Cutter's Influence, North American Review*, vol. 53, p. 334; *Bryant and Gay's U. S.*, IV.; *Harper's Magazine*, vol. 71, 554; *Burnet's Northwestern Territory*, 37.

THE NORTHWEST TERRITORIAL GOVERNMENT—1787.

[THE CONFEDERATE CONGRESS, JULY 13, 1787.]

An Ordinance for the government of the territory of the United States northwest of the river Ohio.

SECTION 1. *Be it ordained by the United States in Congress assembled*, That the said Territory, for the purpose of temporary government, be one district, subject, however, to be divided into two districts, as future circumstances may, in the opinion of Congress, make it expedient.

SEC. 2. *Be it ordained by the authority aforesaid*, That the estates both of resident and non-resident proprietors in the said territory, dying intestate, shall descend to, and be distributed among, their children and the descendants of a deceased child in equal parts, the descendants of a deceased child or grandchild to take the share of their deceased parent in equal parts among them; and where there shall be no children or descendants, then in equal parts to the next of kin, in equal degree; and among collaterals, the children of a deceased brother or sister of the intestate shall have, in equal parts among them, their deceased parent's share; and there shall, in no case, be a distinction between kindred of the whole and half blood; saving in all cases to the widow of the intestate, her third

16

part of the real estate for life, and one-third part of the personal estate; and this law relative to descents and dower, shall remain in full force until altered by the legislature of the district. And until the governor and judges shall adopt laws as hereinafter mentioned, estates in the said territory may be devised or bequeathed by wills in writing, signed and sealed by him or her in whom the estate may be, (being of full age,) and attested by three witnesses; and real estates may be conveyed by lease and release, or bargain and sale, signed, sealed, and delivered by the person, being of full age, in whom the estate may be, and attested by two witnesses, provided such wills be duly proved, and such conveyances be acknowledged, or the execution thereof duly proved, and be recorded within one year after proper magistrates, courts, and registers, shall be appointed for that purpose; and personal property may be transferred by delivery, saving, however, to the French and Canadian inhabitants, and other settlers of the Kaskaskies, Saint Vincents, and the neighboring villages, who have heretofore professed themselves citizens of Virginia, their laws and customs now in force among them, relative to the descent and conveyance of property.

SEC. 3. *Be it ordained by the authority aforesaid*, That there shall be appointed, from time to time, by Congress, a governor, whose commission shall continue in force for the term of three years, unless sooner revoked by Congress; he shall reside in the district, and have a freehold estate therein, in one thousand acres of land, while in the exercise of his office.

SEC. 4. There shall be appointed from time to time, by Congress, a secretary, whose commission shall continue in force for four years, unless sooner revoked; he shall reside in the district, and have a freehold estate therein, in five hundred acres of land, while in the exercise of his office. It shall be his duty to keep and preserve the acts and laws passed by the legislature, and the public records of the district, and the proceedings of the governor in his executive department, and transmit authentic copies of such acts and proceedings every six months to the Secretary of Congress. There shall also be appointed a court, to consist of three judges, any two of whom to form a court, who shall have a common-law jurisdiction and reside in the district, and have each therein a freehold estate, in five hundred acres of land, while in the exercise of their offices; and their commissions shall continue in force during good behavior.

SEC. 5. The governor and judges, or a majority of them, shall adopt and publish in the district such laws of the original States, criminal and civil, as may be necessary, and best suited to the circumstances of the district, and report them to Congress from time to time, which laws shall be in force in the district until the organization of the general assembly therein, unless disapproved of by Congress; but afterwards the legislature shall have authority to alter them as they shall think fit.

SEC. 6. The governor, for the time being, shall be commander-in-chief of the militia, appoint and commission all officers in the same below the rank of general officers; all general officers shall be appointed and commissioned by Congress.

SEC. 7. Previous to the organization of the general assembly the governor shall appoint such magistrates, and other civil officers, in each county or township, as he shall find necessary for the preservation of the peace and good order in the same. After the general assembly shall be organized the powers and duties of magistrates and other civil officers shall be regulated and defined by the said assembly; but all magistrates and other civil officers, not herein otherwise directed, shall, during the continuance of this temporary government, be appointed by the governor.

SEC. 8. For the prevention of crimes, and injuries, the laws to be adopted or made shall have force in all parts of the district, and for the execution of process, criminal and civil, the governor shall make proper divisions thereof; and he shall proceed, from time to time, as circumstances may require, to lay out the parts of the district in which the Indian titles shall have been extinguished, into counties and townships, subject, however, to such alterations as may thereafter be made by the legislature.

SEC. 9. So soon as there shall be five thousand free male inhabitants, of full age, in the district, upon giving proof thereof to the governor, they shall receive authority, with time and place, to elect representatives from their counties or townships, to represent them in the general assembly: *Provided*, That for every five hundred free male inhabitants there shall be one representative, and so on, progressively, with the number of free male inhabitants, shall the right of representation increase, until the number of representatives shall amount to twenty-five; after which the number and proportion of representatives shall be regulated by the legislature; *Provided*, That no person be eligible or qualified to act as a representative, unless he shall have been a citizen of one of the United States three years, and be a resident in the district, or unless he shall have resided in the district three years; and, in either case, shall likewise hold in his own right, in fee-simple, two hundred acres of land within the same: *Provided also*, That a freehold in fifty acres of land in the district, having been a citizen of one of the States, and being resident in the district, or the like freehold and two years' residence in the district, shall be necessary to qualify a man as an elector of a representative.

SEC. 10. The representatives thus elected shall serve for the term of two years; and in case of the death of a representative, or removal from office, the governor shall issue a writ to the county or township, for which he was a member, to elect another in his stead, to serve for the residue of the term.

SEC. 11. The general assembly, or legislature, shall consist of the governor, legislative council, and a house of representatives. The legislative council shall consist of five members, to continue in office five years, unless sooner removed by Congress; any three of whom to be a quorum; and the members of the council shall be nominated and appointed in the following manner, to wit: As soon as representatives shall be elected the governor shall appoint a time and place for them to meet together, and when met they shall nominate ten persons, resident in the district, and each possessed of a freehold in five hundred acres of land, and return their names to Congress, five of whom Congress shall appoint and commission to serve as aforesaid; and whenever a vacancy shall happen in the council, by death or removal from office, the house of representatives shall nominate two persons, qualified as aforesaid, for each vacancy, and return their names to Congress, one of whom Congress shall appoint and commission for the residue of the term; and every five years, four months at least before the expiration of the time of service of the members of the council, the said house shall nominate ten persons, qualified as aforesaid, and return their names to Congress, five of whom Congress shall appoint and commission to serve as members of the council five years, unless sooner removed. And the governor, legislative council, and house of representatives shall have authority to make laws in all cases for the good government of the district, not repugnant to the principles and articles in this ordinance established and declared. And all bills, having passed by a majority in the house, and by a majority in the council, shall be referred to the governor for his assent; but no bill, or legislative act whatever, shall be of any force without his assent. The governor shall have power to convene, prorogue, and dissolve the general assembly when, in his opinion, it shall be expedient.

SEC. 12. The governor, judges, legislative council, secretary, and such other officers as Congress shall appoint in the district, shall take an oath or affirmation of fidelity, and of office ; the governor before the President of Congress, and all other officers before the governor. As soon as a legislature shall be formed in the district, the council and house assembled, in one room, shall have authority, by joint ballot, to elect a delegate to Congress, who shall have a seat in Congress, with a right of debating, but not of voting, during this temporary government.

SEC. 13. And for extending the fundamental principles of civil and religious liberty, which form the basis whereon these republics, their laws and constitutions, are erected ; to fix and establish those principles as the basis of all laws, constitutions, and governments, which forever hereafter shall be formed in the said territory ; to provide, also, for the establishment of States, and permanent government therein, and for their admission to a share in the Federal councils on an equal footing with the original States, at as early periods as may be consistent with the general interest :

SEC. 14. It is hereby ordained and declared, by the authority aforesaid, that the following articles shall be considered as articles of compact, between the original States and the people and States in the said territory, and forever remain unalterable, unless by common consent, to wit :

ARTICLE I.

No person, demeaning himself in a peaceable and orderly manner, shall ever be molested on account of his mode of worship, or religious sentiments, in the said territory.

ARTICLE II.

The inhabitants of the said territory shall always be entitled to the benefits of the writs of *habeas corpus*, and of the trial by jury ; of a proportionate representation of the people in the legislature, and of judicial proceedings according to the course of the common law. All persons shall be bailable, unless for capital offences, where the proof shall be evident, or the presumption great. All fines shall be moderate ; and no cruel or unusual punishments shall be inflicted. No man shall be deprived of his liberty or property, but by the judgment of his peers, or the law of the land, and should the public exigencies make it necessary, for the common preservation, to take any person's property, or to demand his particular services, full compensation shall be made for the same. And, in the just preservation of rights and property, it is understood and declared, that no law ought ever to be made or have force in the said territory, that shall, in any manner whatever, interfere with or affect private contracts, or engagements, *bona fide*, and without fraud previously formed.

ARTICLE III.

Religion, morality, and knowledge being necessary to good government and the happiness of mankind, schools and the means of education shall forever be encouraged. The utmost good faith shall always be observed towards the Indians; their lands and property shall never be taken from them without their consent ; and in their property, rights, and liberty they never shall be invaded or disturbed, unless in just and lawful wars authorized by Congress ; but laws founded in justice and humanity shall, from time to time, be made, for preventing wrongs being done to them, and for preserving peace and friendship with them.

ARTICLE IV.

The said territory, and the States which may be formed therein, shall forever remain a part of this confederacy of the United States of America, subject to the articles of Confederation, and to such alterations therein as shall be constitutionally made; and to all the acts and ordinances of the United States in Congress assembled, conformable thereto. The inhabitants and settlers in the said territory shall be subject to pay a part of the Federal debts, contracted, or to be contracted, and a proportional part of the expenses of government to be apportioned on them by Congress, according to the same common rule and measure by which apportionments thereof shall be made on the other States; and the taxes for paying their proportion shall be laid and levied by the authority and direction of the legislatures of the district, or districts, or new States, as in the original States, within the time agreed upon by the United States in Congress assembled. The legislatures of those districts, or new States, shall never interfere with the primary disposal of the soil by the United States in Congress assembled, nor with any regulations Congress may find necessary for securing the title in such soil to the *bona-fide* purchasers. No tax shall be imposed on lands the property of the United States; and in no case shall non-resident proprietors be taxed higher than residents. The navigable waters leading into the Mississippi and Saint Lawrence, and the carrying places between the same, shall be common highways, and forever free, as well to the inhabitants of the said territory as to the citizens of the United States, and those of any other States that may be admitted into the confederacy, without any tax, impost, or duty therefor.

ARTICLE V.

There shall be formed in the said territory not less than three nor more than five States; and the boundaries of the States, as soon as Virginia shall alter her act of cession and consent to the same, shall become fixed and established as follows, to wit: The western State, in the said territory, shall be bounded by the Mississippi, the Ohio, and the Wabash Rivers; a direct line drawn from the Wabash and Post Vincents, due north, to the territorial line between the United States and Canada; and by the said territorial line to the Lake of the Woods and Mississippi. The middle State shall be bounded by the said direct line, the Wabash from Post Vincents to the Ohio, by the Ohio, by a direct line drawn due north from the mouth of the Great Miami to the said territorial line, and by the said territorial line. The eastern State shall be bounded by the last-mentioned direct line, the Ohio, Pennsylvania, and the said territorial line: *Provided, however*, And it is further understood and declared, that the boundaries of these three States shall be subject so far to be altered, that, if Congress shall hereafter find it expedient, they shall have authority to form one or two States in that part of the said territory which lies north of an east and west line drawn through the southerly bend or extreme of Lake Michigan. And whenever any of the said States shall have sixty thousand free inhabitants therein, such State shall be admitted by its delegates, into the Congress of the United States, on an equal footing with the original States, in all respects whatever; and shall be at liberty to form a permanent constitution and State government: *Provided*, The constitution and government, so to be formed, shall be republican, and in conformity to the principles contained in these articles, and, so far as it can be consistent with the general interest of the confederacy, such admission shall be allowed at an earlier period, and when there may be a less number of free inhabitants in the State than sixty thousand.

ARTICLE VI.

There shall be neither slavery nor involuntary servitude in the said territory, otherwise than in the punishment of crimes, whereof the party shall have been duly convicted: *Provided always,* That any person escaping into the same, from whom labor or service is lawfully claimed in any one of the original States, such fugitive may be lawfully reclaimed, and conveyed to the person claiming his or her labor or service as aforesaid.

Be it ordained by the authority aforesaid, That the resolutions of the 23d of April, 1784, relative to the subject of this ordinance, be, and the same are hereby, repealed, and declared null and void.

Done by the United States, in Congress assembled, the 13th day of July, in the year of our Lord 1787, and of their sovereignty and independence the twelfth.

CONSTITUTION OF THE UNITED STATES.

At the close of the revolution it was evident that the Articles of Confederation were not suited to the exigencies of the nation. Suggestions of a convention to revise the Articles came from various quarters, but led to no result till the Virginia Legislature, in January, 1786, appointed commissioners to meet such as might be appointed by other states "to take into consideration the trade of the United States; to examine the relative situations and trade of the said states; to consider how far a uniform system in their commercial regulations may be necessary to their common interest and their permanent harmony; and to report to the several states such an act relative to this great object as, when unanimously ratified by them, will enable the United States in Congress assembled effectually to provide for the same." Accordingly twelve commissioners from the five states of New York, New Jersey, Pennsylvania, Delaware and Virginia met at Annapolis, September 11, 1786, and, after a short session, adjourned, recommending that a full convention of delegates from all the states be held at Philadelphia, May 2d next, to mature plans for adapting the federal government "to the exigency of the union." The Congress of the Confederation, Feb. 21, 1787, recommended to the several states that a convention be held at Philadelphia "for the sole and express purpose of revising the Articles of Confederation, and reporting to Congress and the several legislatures, such alterations and provisions therein as shall, when agreed to in Congress and confirmed by the States, render the Federal Constitution adequate to the exigencies of Government and the preservation of the union." How *closely* the convention followed these instructions is well known.

The convention, consisting of fifty delegates, from twelve states (all but Rhode Island), met at Philadelphia, May 14, 1787, and sat with closed doors till September 17, 1787, when Washington transmitted, as the result of their labors, the Constitution to Congress.

Congress transmitted the Constitution to the several legislatures, and, September 13, 1788, eleven states having ratified it, passed resolutions providing for the choosing of electors for President and Vice-President.

The dates of the ratification of the Constitution by the several states are as follows:—Delaware, December 7, 1787; Pennsylvania, December 12, 1787; New Jersey, December 18, 1787; Georgia, January 2, 1788; Connecticut, January 9, 1788; Massachusetts, February 6, 1788; Maryland, April 28, 1788; South Carolina, May 23, 1788; New Hampshire, June 21, 1788; Virginia, June 26, 1788; New York, July 26, 1788; North Carolina, November 21, 1789; Rhode Island, May 29, 1790.

Consult *Bancroft's Hist. of the Constitution; Bancroft's U. S.*, last ed., vol. VI.; *Story's Commentary on the Constitution*, especially vol. I., book III., chaps. i. and ii.; *Hildreth's U. S.*, III., 482; *Bryant and Gay's U. S.*, vol. IV., *Curtis' Hist. Constitution; Frothingham's Rise of the Republie*, 589; *Towle's Constitution; Elliott's Debates; Schouler's U. S.*, I., 36–78 *McMaster's, U. S.*, I., 43

CONSTITUTION OF THE UNITED STATES—1787.

WE THE PEOPLE of the United States, in Order to form a more perfect Union, establish Justice, insure domestic Tranquillity, provide for the common defence, promote the general Welfare, and secure the Blessings of Liberty to ourselves and our Posterity, do ordain and establish this CONSTITUTION for the United States of America.

ARTICLE I.

SECTION 1. All legislative Powers herein granted shall be vested in a Congress of the United States, which shall consist of a Senate and House of Representatives.

SECTION 2. The House of Representatives shall be composed of Members chosen every second Year by the People of the several States, and the Electors in each State shall have the Qualifications requisite for Electors of the most numerous Branch of the State Legislature.

No Person shall be a Representative who shall not have attained to the Age of twenty-five Years, and been seven Years a Citizen of the United States, and who shall not, when elected, be an Inhabitant of that State in which he shall be chosen.

Representatives and direct Taxes shall be apportioned among the several States which may be included within this Union, according to their respective Numbers, which shall be determined by adding to the whole Number of Free persons, including those bound to Service for a Term of Years, and excluding Indians not taxed, three fifths of all other Persons. The actual Enumeration shall be made within three Years after the first Meeting of the Congress of the United States, and within every subsequent Term of ten Years, in such Manner as they shall by Law direct. The Number of Representatives shall not exceed one for every thirty Thousand, but each State shall have at Least one Representative; and until such enumeration shall be made, the State of New Hampshire shall be entitled to chuse three, Massachusetts eight, Rhode Island and Providence Plantations one, Connecticut five, New York six, New Jersey four, Pennsylvania eight, Delaware one, Maryland six, Virginia ten, North Carolina five, South Carolina five, and Georgia three.

When vacancies happen in the Representation from any State, the Executive Authority thereof shall issue Writs of Election to fill such Vacancies.

The House of Representatives shall chuse their Speaker and other Officers; and shall have the sole Power of Impeachment.

SECTION 3. The Senate of the United States shall be composed of two Senators from each State, chosen by the Legislature thereof, for six Years; and each Senator shall have one Vote.

Immediately after they shall be assembled in Consequence of the first Election, they shall be divided as equally as may be into three Classes. The seats of the Senators of the first Class shall be vacated at the Expiration of the second Year, of the second Class at the Expiration of the fourth Year, and of the third Class at the Expiration of the sixth Year, so that one-third may be chosen every second Year; and if Vacancies happen by Resignation, or otherwise, during the Recess of the Legislature of any State, the Executive thereof may make temporary Appointments until the next Meeting of the Legislature, which shall then fill such Vacancies.

No Person shall be a Senator who shall not have attained to the Age of thirty Years, and been nine Years a Citizen of the United States, and who shall not, when elected, be an Inhabitant of that State for which he shall be chosen.

The Vice President of the United States shall be President of the Senate, but shall have no Vote, unless they be equally divided.

The Senate shall chuse their other Officers, and also a President pro tempore, in the Absence of the Vice President, or when he shall exercise the Office of President of the United States.

The Senate shall have the sole Power to try all Impeachments. When sitting for that Purpose, they shall be on Oath or Affirmation. When the President of the United States is tried, the Chief Justice shall preside: and no Person shall be convicted without the Concurrence of two thirds of the Members present.

Judgment in Cases of Impeachment shall not extend further than to removal from Office, and disqualification to hold and enjoy any Office of honor, Trust or Profit under the United States: but the Party convicted shall nevertheless be liable and subject to Indictment, Trial, Judgment and Punishment, according to Law.

SECTION 4. The Times, Places and manner of holding Elections for Senators and Representatives, shall be prescribed in each State by the Legislature thereof; but the Congress may at any time by Law make or alter such Regulations, except as to the Places of chusing Senators.

The Congress shall assemble at least once in every Year, and such Meeting shall be on the first Monday in

December, unless they shall by Law appoint a different Day.

SECTION 5. Each House shall be the Judge of the Elections, Returns and Qualifications of its own Members, and a Majority of each shall constitute a Quorum to do Business; but a smaller Number may adjourn from day to day, and may be authorized to compel the Attendance of absent Members, in such Manner, and under such Penalties as each House may provide.

Each House may determine the Rules of its Proceedings, punish its Members for disorderly Behaviour, and, with the Concurrence of two thirds, expel a Member.

Each House shall keep a Journal of its Proceedings, and from time to time publish the same, excepting such Parts as may in their Judgment require Secrecy; and the Yeas and Nays of the Members of either House on any question shall, at the Desire of one fifth of those present, be entered on the Journal.

Neither House, during the Session of Congress, shall, without the Consent of the other, adjourn for more than three days, nor to any other Place than that in which the two Houses shall be sitting.

SECTION 6. The Senators and Representatives shall receive a Compensation for their services, to be ascertained by Law, and paid out of the Treasury of the United States. They shall in all Cases, except Treason, Felony and Breach of the Peace, be privileged from Arrest during their Attendance at the Session of their respective Houses, and in going to and returning from the same; and for any Speech or Debate in either House, they shall not be questioned in any other Place.

No Senator or Representative shall, during the Time for which he was elected, be appointed to any civil Office under the Authority of the United States, which shall have been created, or the Emoluments whereof shall have been encreased during such time; and no Person holding any Office under the United States, shall be a Member of either House during his Continuance in Office.

SECTION 7. All bills for raising Revenue shall originate in the House of Representatives; but the Senate may propose or concur with Amendments as on other Bills.

Every Bill which shall have passed the House of Representatives and the Senate, shall, before it become a Law, be presented to the President of the United States; if he approve he shall sign it, but if not he shall return it, with his Objections to that House in which it shall have originated, who shall enter the Objections at large on their Journal, and proceed to reconsider it. If after such Reconsideration two thirds of that House shall agree to pass the Bill, it shall be sent, together with the Objections, to the other House, by which it shall likewise be reconsidered, and if approved by two thirds of that House, it shall become a Law. But in all such Cases the Votes of both Houses shall be determined by yeas and Nays, and the Names of the Persons voting for and against the Bill shall be entered on the Journal of each House respectively. If any Bill shall not be returned by the President within ten Days (Sundays excepted) after it shall have been presented to him, the Same shall be a Law, in like Manner as if he had signed it, unless the Congress by their Adjournment prevent its Return, in which Case it shall not be a Law.

Every Order, Resolution, or Vote to which the Concurrence of the Senate and House of Representatives may be necessary (except on a question of Adjournment) shall be presented to the President of the United States; and before the Same shall take Effect, shall be approved by him, or being disapproved by him, shall be repassed by two thirds of the Senate and House of Representatives, according to the Rules and Limitations prescribed in the Case of a Bill.

SECTION 8. The Congress shall have Power to lay and

collect Taxes, Duties, Imposts and Excises, to pay the Debts and provide for the common Defence and general Welfare of the United States; but all Duties, Imposts and Excises shall be uniform throughout the United States;

To borrow Money on the credit of the United States;

To regulate Commerce with foreign Nations, and among the several States, and with the Indian Tribes;

To establish an uniform Rule of Naturalization, and uniform Laws on the subject of Bankruptcies throughout the United States;

To coin Money, regulate the Value thereof, and of foreign Coin, and fix the Standard of Weights and Measures;

To provide for the Punishment of counterfeiting the Securities and current Coin of the United States;

To establish Post Offices and post Roads;

To promote the Progress of Science and useful Arts, by securing for limited Times to Authors and Inventors the exclusive Right to their respective Writings and Discoveries;

To constitute Tribunals inferior to the supreme Court;

To define and punish Piracies and Felonies committed on the high Seas, and Offences against the Law of Nations;

To declare War, grant Letters of Marque and Reprisal, and make Rules concerning Captures on Land and Water;

To raise and support Armies, but no Appropriation of Money to that Use shall be for a longer Term than two Years;

To provide and maintain a Navy;

To make Rules for the Government and Regulation of the land and naval Forces;

To provide for calling forth the Militia to execute the Laws of the Union, suppress Insurrections and repel Invasions;

To provide for organizing, arming, and disciplining the Militia, and for governing such Part of them as may be employed in the Service of the United States, reserving to the States respectively, the Appointment of the Officers, and the Authority of training the Militia according to the discipline prescribed by Congress;

To exercise exclusive Legislation in all Cases whatsoever, over such District (not exceeding ten Miles square) as may, by Cession of particular States, and the Acceptance of Congress, become the Seat of the Government of the United States, and to exercise like Authority over all Places purchased by the Consent of the Legislature of the State in which the Same shall be, for the Erection of Forts, Magazines, Arsenals, dock-Yards, and other needful Buildings;—And

To make all Laws which shall be necessary and proper for carrying into Execution the foregoing Powers, and all other Powers vested by this Constitution in the Government of the United States, or in any Department or Officer thereof.

SECTION 9. The Migration or Importation of such Persons as any of the States now existing shall think proper to admit, shall not be prohibited by the Congress prior to the Year one thousand eight hundred and eight, but a Tax or duty may be imposed on such Importation, not exceeding ten dollars for each Person.

The Privilege of the Writ of Habeas Corpus shall not be suspended, unless when in Cases of Rebellion or Invasion the public Safety may require it.

No Bill of Attainder or ex post facto Law shall be passed.

No Capitation, or other direct, tax shall be laid, unless in Proportion to the Census or Enumeration herein before directed to be taken.

No Tax or Duty shall be laid on Articles exported from any State.

No Preference shall be given by any Regulation of

Commerce or Revenue to the Ports of one State over those of another: nor shall Vessels bound to, or from, one State, be obliged to enter, clear, or pay Duties in another.

No Money shall be drawn from the Treasury, but in Consequence of Appropriations made by Law; and a regular Statement and Account of the Receipts and Expenditures of all public Money shall be published from time to time.

No Title of Nobility shall be granted by the United States: And no Person holding any Office of Profit or Trust under them, shall, without the Consent of the Congress, accept of any present, Emolument, Office, or Title, of any kind whatever, from any King, Prince, or foreign State.

SECTION 10. No State shall enter into any Treaty, Alliance, or Confederation; grant Letters of Marque and Reprisal; coin Money; emit Bills of Credit; make any Thing but gold and silver Coin a Tender in Payment of Debts; pass any Bill of Attainder, ex post facto Law, or Law impairing the Obligation of Contracts, or grant any Title of Nobility.

No State shall, without the Consent of the Congress, lay any Imposts or Duties on Imports or Exports, except what may be absolutely necessary for executing it's inspection Laws: and the net Produce of all Duties and Imposts, laid by any State on Imports or Exports, shall be for the Use of the Treasury of the United States; and all such Laws shall be subject to the Revision and Controul of the Congress.

No State shall, without the Consent of Congress, lay any Duty of Tonnage, keep Troops, or Ships of War in time of Peace, enter into any Agreement or Compact with another State, or with a foreign Power, or engage in War, unless actually invaded, or in such imminent Danger as will not admit of delay.

ARTICLE II.

SECTION 1. The executive Power shall be vested in a President of the United States of America. He shall hold his Office during the Term of four Years, and, together with the Vice President, chosen for the same Term, be elected, as follows

Each State shall appoint, in such Manner as the Legislature thereof may direct, a Number of Electors, equal to the whole Number of Senators and Representatives to which the State may be entitled in the Congress: but no Senator or Representative, or Person holding an Office of Trust or Profit under the United States, shall be appointed an Elector.

The electors shall meet in their respective States, and vote by ballot for two persons, of whom one at least shall not be an inhabitant of the same State with themselves. And they shall make a list of all the persons voted for, and of the number of votes for each; which list they shall sign and certify, and transmit sealed to the seat of the Government of the United States, directed to the President of the Senate. The President of the Senate shall, in the presence of the Senate and House of Representatives, open all the certificates, and the votes shall then be counted. The person having the greatest number of votes shall be the President, if such number be a majority of the whole number of electors appointed; and if there be more than one who have such majority, and have an equal number of votes, then the House of Representatives shall immediately chuse by ballot one of them for President; and if no person have a majority, then from the five highest on the list the said House shall in like manner chuse the President. But in chusing the President, the votes shall be taken by States, the representation from each State having one vote; a quorum for this purpose shall consist of a member or members from two-thirds of the States, and a majority of all the States shall be necessary to a choice. In every case, after the choice of the President, the person having the greatest number of votes of the electors shall be the Vice President. But if there should remain two or more who have equal votes, the Senate shall chuse from them by ballot the Vice-President.

The Congress may determine the Time of chusing the Electors, and the Day on which they shall give their Votes; which Day shall be the same throughout the United States.

No person except a natural born Citizen, or a Citizen of the United States, at the time of the Adoption of this Constitution, shall be eligible to the Office of President; neither shall any Person be eligible to that office who shall not have attained to the Age of thirty five Years, and been fourteen Years a Resident within the United States.

In Case of the Removal of the President from Office, or of his Death, Resignation or Inability to discharge the Powers and Duties of the said Office, the Same shall devolve on the Vice President, and the Congress may by Law provide for the Case of Removal, Death, Resignation or Inability, both of the President and Vice President, declaring what Officer shall then act as President, and such Officer shall act accordingly, until the Disability be removed, or a President shall be elected.

The President shall, at stated Times, receive for his Services, a Compensation, which shall neither be encreased nor diminished during the Period for which he shall have been elected, and he shall not receive within that Period any other Emolument from the United States, or any of them.

Before he enter on the Execution of his Office, he shall take the following Oath or Affirmation:—"I do solemnly swear (or affirm) that I will faithfully execute the Office of President of the United States, and will to the best of my Ability, preserve, protect and defend the Constitution of the United States."

SECTION 2. The President shall be Commander in Chief of the Army and Navy of the United States, and of the Militia of the several States, when called into the actual Service of the United States; he may require the Opinion, in writing, of the principal Officer in each of the executive Departments, upon any Subject relating to the Duties of their respective Offices, and he shall have Power to grant Reprieves and Pardons for Offences against the United States, except in Cases of Impeachment.

He shall have Power, by and with the Advice and Consent of the Senate, to make Treaties, provided two thirds of the Senators present concur; and he shall nominate, and by and with the Advice and Consent of the Senate, shall appoint Ambassadors, other public Ministers and Consuls, Judges of the supreme Court, and all other Officers of the United States, whose Appointments are not herein otherwise provided for, and which shall be established by Law: but the Congress may by Law vest the Appointment of such inferior Officers, as they think proper, in the President alone, in the Courts of Law, or in the Heads of Departments.

The President shall have Power to fill up all Vacancies that may happen during the recess of the Senate, by granting Commissions which shall expire at the End of their next Session.

SECTION 3. He shall from time to time give to the Congress Information of the state of the Union, and recommend to their Consideration such Measures as he shall judge necessary and expedient; he may, on extraordinary Occasions, convene both Houses, or either of them, and, in Case of Disagreement between them, with Respect to the Time of Adjournment, he may adjourn them to such Time as he shall think proper; he shall receive Ambassadors and other public Ministers; he shall take Care that the Laws be faithfully executed, and shall Commission all the Officers of the United States.

SECTION 4. The President, Vice President and all civil Officers of the United States, shall be removed from Office on Impeachment for, and Conviction of, Treason, Bribery, or other high Crimes and Misdemeanors.

ARTICLE III.

SECTION 1. The judicial Power of the United States, shall be vested in one supreme Court, and in such inferior Courts as the Congress may from time to time ordain and establish. The Judges, both of the supreme and inferior Courts, shall hold their Offices during good Behaviour, and shall, at stated Times, receive for their Services, a Compensation, which shall not be diminished during their Continuance in Office.

SECTION 2. The judicial Power shall extend to all Cases, in Law and Equity, arising under this Constitution, the Laws of the United States, and Treaties made, or which shall be made, under their Authority;—to all Cases affecting Ambassadors, other public Ministers and Consuls;—to all Cases of admiralty and maritime Jurisdiction;—to Controversies to which the United States shall be a Party;—to Controversies between two or more States;—between a State and Citizens of another State;—between Citizens of different States,—between Citizens of the same State claiming Lands under Grants of different States, and between a State, or the Citizens thereof, and foreign States, Citizens or Subjects.

In all Cases affecting Ambassadors, other public Ministers and Consuls, and those in which a State shall be Party, the supreme Court shall have original Jurisdiction. In all the other Cases before mentioned, the supreme Court shall have appellate Jurisdiction, both as to Law and Fact, with such Exceptions, and under such Regulations as the Congress shall make.

The Trial of all Crimes, except in Cases of Impeachment, shall be by Jury; and such Trial shall be held in the State where the said Crimes shall have been committed; but when not committed within any State, the Trial shall be at such Place or Places as the Congress may by Law have directed.

SECTION 3. Treason against the United States, shall consist only in levying War against them, or in adhering to their Enemies, giving them Aid and Comfort. No Person shall be convicted of Treason unless on the Testimony of two Witnesses to the same overt Act, or on Confession in open Court.

The Congress shall have Power to declare the Punishment of Treason, but no Attainder of Treason shall work Corruption of Blood, or Forfeiture except during the Life of the Person attainted.

ARTICLE IV.

SECTION 1. Full Faith and Credit shall be given in each State to the public Acts, Records, and judicial Proceedings of every other State. And the Congress may by general Laws prescribe the Manner in which such Acts, Records and Proceedings shall be proved, and the Effect thereof.

SECTION 2. The Citizens of each State shall be entitled to all Privileges and immunities of Citizens in the several States.

A person charged in any State with Treason, Felony, or other Crime, who shall flee from Justice, and be found in another State, shall on Demand of the executive Authority of the State from which he fled, be delivered up to be removed to the State having Jurisdiction of the Crime.

No Person held to Service or Labour in one State, under the Laws thereof, escaping into another, shall, in Consequence of any Law or Regulation therein, be discharged from such Service or Labour, but shall be delivered up on Claim of the Party to whom such Service or Labour may be due.

SECTION 3. New States may be admitted by the Congress into this Union; but no new State shall be formed or erected within the Jurisdiction of any other State; nor any State be formed by the Junction of two or more States, or Parts of States, without the Consent of the Legislatures of the States concerned as well as of the Congress.

The Congress shall have Power to dispose of and make all needful Rules and Regulations respecting the Territory or other Property belonging to the United States; and nothing in this Constitution shall be so construed as to Prejudice any Claims of the United States, or of any particular State.

SECTION 4. The United States shall guarantee to every State in this Union a Republican Form of Government, and shall protect each of them against Invasion; and on Application of the Legislature, or of the Executive (when the Legislature cannot be convened) against domestic Violence.

ARTICLE V.

The Congress, whenever two thirds of both Houses shall deem it necessary, shall propose Amendments to this Constitution, or, on the Application of the Legislatures of two thirds of the several States, shall call a Convention for proposing Amendments, which, in either Case, shall be valid to all Intents and Purposes, as Part of this Constitution, when ratified by the Legislatures of three fourths of the several States, or by Conventions in three fourths thereof, as the one or the other Mode of Ratification may be proposed by the Congress; Provided that no Amendment which may be made prior to the Year One thousand eight hundred and eight shall in any

Manner affect the first and fourth Clauses in the Ninth Section of the first Article; and that no State, without its Consent, shall be deprived of its equal Suffrage in the Senate.

ARTICLE VI.

All Debts contracted and Engagements entered into, before the Adoption of this Constitution, shall be as valid against the United States under this Constitution, as under the Confederation.

This Constitution, and the Laws of the United States which shall be made in Pursuance thereof; and all Treaties made, or which shall be made, under the Authority of the United States, shall be the supreme Law of the Land; and the Judges in every State shall be bound thereby, any Thing in the Constitution or Laws of any State to the Contrary notwithstanding.

The Senators and Representatives before mentioned, and the Members of the several State Legislatures, and all executive and judicial Officers, both of the United States and of the several States, shall be bound by Oath or Affirmation, to support this Constitution; but no religious Test shall ever be required as a Qualification to any Office or public Trust under the United States.

ARTICLE VII.

The ratification of the Conventions of nine States, shall be sufficient for the Establishment of this Constitution between the States so ratifying the Same.

DONE in Convention by the Unanimous Consent of the States present the Seventeenth Day of September in the Year of our Lord one thousand seven hundred and Eighty seven, and of the Independance of the United

States of America the Twelfth. **In witness** whereof We have hereunto subscribed our Names,

G° : WASHINGTON—
Presidt., and Deputy from Virginia.

New Hampshire.

JOHN LANGDON, NICHOLAS GILMAN.

Massachusetts.

NATHANIEL GORHAM, RUFUS KING.

Connecticut.

WM. SAML. JOHNSON, ROGER SHERMAN.

New York.

ALEXANDER HAMILTON.

New Jersey.

WIL: LIVINGSTON, WM. PATERSON,
DAVID BREARLEY, JONA. DAYTON.

Pennsylvania.

B. FRANKLIN, THOS. FITZSIMONS,
THOMAS MIFFLIN, JARED INGERSOLL,
ROBT. MORRIS, JAMES WILSON,
GEO. CLYMER, GOUV. MORRIS.

Delaware.

GEO. READ, RICHARD BASSETT,
GUNNING BEDFORD, Jun., JACO: BROOM.
JOHN DICKINSON,

Maryland.

JAMES MCHENRY, DAN. CARROLL.
DAN. JENIFER, of St. Thomas,

Virginia.

JOHN BLAIR, JAMES MADISON, Jr.

North Carolina.

WM. BLOUNT, HUGH WILLIAMSON.
RICH'D DOBBS SPEIGHT,

South Carolina.

J. RUTLEDGE, CHARLES PINCKNEY,
CHARLES COTESWORTH PINCKNEY, PIERCE BUTLER.

Georgia.

WILLIAM FEW, ABR. BALDWIN.

Attest: WILLIAM JACKSON, *Secretary.*

ARTICLES IN ADDITION TO, AND AMENDMENT OF, THE CONSTITUTION OF THE UNITED STATES OF AMERICA, PROPOSED BY CONGRESS, AND RATIFIED BY THE LEGISLATURES OF THE SEVERAL STATES PURSUANT TO THE FIFTH ARTICLE OF THE ORIGINAL CONSTITUTION.

[ARTICLE I.]*

Congress shall make no law respecting an establishment of religion, or prohibiting the free exercise thereof; or abridging the freedom of speech, or of the press; or the right of the people peaceably to assemble, and to petition the Government for a redress of grievances.

[ARTICLE II.]

A well regulated Militia, being necessary to the security of a free State, the right of the people to keep and bear Arms, shall not be infringed.

[ARTICLE III.]

No Soldier shall, in time of peace, be quartered in any house, without the consent of the Owner, nor in time of war, but in a manner to be prescribed by law.

[ARTICLE IV.]

The right of the people to be secure in their persons, houses, papers, and effects, against unreasonable searches

* The first ten amendments to the Constitution of the United States were proposed to the legislatures of the several States by the First Congress, on the 25th September, 1789.

and seizures, shall not be violated, and no Warrants shall issue, but upon probable cause, supported by Oath or affirmation, and particularly describing the place to be searched, and the persons or things to be seized.

[ARTICLE V.]

No person shall be held to answer for a capital, or otherwise infamous crime, unless on a presentment or indictment of a Grand Jury, except in cases arising in the land or naval forces, or in the Militia, when in actual service in time of War or public danger; nor shall any person be subject for the same offence to be twice put in jeopardy of life or limb; nor shall be compelled in any Criminal Case to be a witness against himself, nor be deprived of life, liberty, or property, without due process of law; nor shall private property be taken for public use, without just compensation.

[ARTICLE VI.]

In all criminal prosecutions, the accused shall enjoy the right to a speedy and public trial, by an impartial jury of the State and district wherein the crime shall have been committed, which district shall have been previously ascertained by law, and to be informed of the nature and cause of the accusation; to be confronted with the witnesses against him; to have compulsory process for obtaining witnesses in his favor, and to have the Assistance of Counsel for his defence.

[ARTICLE VII.]

In suits at common law, where the value in controversy shall exceed twenty dollars, the right of trial by jury shall be preserved, and no fact tried by a jury shall be otherwise re-examined in any Court of the United States, than according to the rules of the common law.

[ARTICLE VIII.]

Excessive bail shall not be required, nor excessive fines imposed, nor cruel and unusual punishments inflicted.

[ARTICLE IX.]

The enumeration in the Constitution, of certain rights, shall not be construed to deny or disparage others retained by the people.

[ARTICLE X.]

The powers not delegated to the United States by the Constitution, nor prohibited by it to the States, are reserved to the States respectively, or to the people.

[ARTICLE XI.]*

The Judicial power of the United States shall not be construed to extend to any suit in law or equity, commenced or prosecuted against one of the United States by Citizens of another State, or by Citizens or Subjects of any Foreign State.

[ARTICLE XII.]†

The Electors shall meet in their respective States, and vote by ballot for President and Vice-President, one of

* The eleventh amendment to the Constitution of the United States was proposed to the legislatures of the several States by the Third Congress, on the 5th of September, 1794; and was declared in a message from the President to Congress, dated the 8th of January, 1798, to have been ratified by the legislatures of three-fourths of the States. [POORE.]

† The twelfth amendment to the Constitution of the United States was proposed to the legislatures of the several States by the Eighth Congress, on the 12th of December, 1803, in lieu of the third paragraph of the first section of the third article; and was declared in a proclamation of the Secretary of State, dated the 25th of September, 1804, to have been ratified by the legislatures of three-fourths of the States. [POORE.]

whom, at least, shall not be an inhabitant of the same State with themselves; they shall name in their ballots the person voted for as President, and in distinct ballots the person voted for as Vice-President, and they shall make distinct lists of all persons voted for as President, and of all persons voted for as Vice-President, and of the number of votes for each, which lists they shall sign and certify, and transmit sealed to the seat of the Government of the United States, directed to the President of the Senate;—The President of the Senate shall, in the presence of the Senate and House of Representatives, open all the certificates and the votes shall then be counted;—The person having the greatest number of votes for President, shall be the President, if such number be a majority of the whole number of Electors appointed; and if no person have such majority, then from the persons having the highest numbers not exceeding three on the list of those voted for as President, the House of Representatives shall choose immediately, by ballot, the President. But in choosing the President, the votes shall be taken by states, the representation from each state having one vote; a quorum for this purpose shall consist of a member or members from two thirds of the states, and a majority of all the states shall be necessary to a choice. And if the House of Representatives shall not choose a President whenever the right of choice shall devolve upon them, before the fourth day of March next following, then the Vice-President shall act as President, as in the case of the death or other constitutional disability of the President. The person having the greatest number of votes as Vice-president, shall be the Vice-President, if such number be a majority of the whole number of Electors appointed, and if no person have a majority, then from the two highest numbers on the list, the Senate shall choose the Vice-President; a quorum for the purpose shall consist of two-thirds of the whole number of Senators, and a majority of the whole number shall be necessary to a choice. But no person constitutionally ineligible to the office of President shall be eligible to that of Vice-President of the United States.

[ARTICLE XIII.] *

SECTION I. Neither slavery nor involuntary servitude, except as a punishment for crime whereof the party shall have been duly convicted, shall exist within the United States, or any place subject to their jurisdiction.

SECTION 2. Congress shall have power to enforce this article by appropriate legislation.

[ARTICLE XIV.] †

SECTION I. All persons born or naturalized in the United States, and subject to the jurisdiction thereof, are

* The thirteenth amendment to the Constitution of the United States was proposed to the legislatures of the several States by the Thirty-eighth Congress, on the first of February, 1865; and was declared, in a proclamation of the Secretary of State, dated the 18th of December, 1865, to have been ratified by the legislatures of twenty-seven of the thirty-six States viz.: Illinois, Rhode Island, Michigan, Maryland, New York, West Virginia, Maine, Kansas, Massachusetts, Pennsylvania, Virginia, Ohio, Missouri, Nevada, Indiana, Louisiana, Minnesota, Wisconsin, Vermont, Tennessee, Arkansas, Connecticut, New Hampshire, South Carolina, Alabama, North Carolina, and Georgia. [POORE.]

† The fourteenth amendment to the Constitution of the United States was proposed to the legislatures of the several States by the Thirty-ninth Congress, on the 16th of June, 1866. On the 21st of July, 1868, Congress adopted and transmitted to the Department of State a concurrent resolution, declaring that "the legislatures of the States of Connecticut, Tennessee, New Jersey, Oregon, Vermont, New York, Ohio, Illinois, West Virginia, Kansas, Maine, Nevada, Missouri, Indiana, Minnesota, New Hampshire, Massachusetts, Nebraska, Iowa, Arkansas, Florida, North Carolina, Alabama, South Carolina, and Louisiana, being three-fourths and more of the several States of the Union, have ratified the fourteenth article of amendment to the Constitution of the United States, duly proposed by two-thirds of each House of the Thirty-ninth Congress: Therefore, *Resolved*, That said fourteenth article is hereby declared to be a part of the Constitution of the United States, and it shall be duly promulgated as such by the Secretary of State." [POORE.]

citizens of the United States and of the State wherein they reside. No State shall make or enforce any law which shall abridge the privileges or immunities of citizens of the United States; nor shall any State deprive any person of life, liberty, or property, without due process of law; nor deny to any person within its jurisdiction the equal protection of the laws.

SECTION 2. Representatives shall be apportioned among the several States according to their respective numbers, counting the whole number of persons in each State, excluding Indians not taxed. But when the right to vote at any election for the choice of electors for President and Vice President of the United States, Representatives in Congress, the Executive and Judicial officers of a State, or the members of the Legislature thereof, is denied to any of the male inhabitants of such State, being twenty-one years of age, and citizens of the United States, or in any way abridged, except for participation in rebellion, or other crime, the basis of representation therein shall be reduced in the proportion which the number of such male citizens shall bear to the whole number of male citizens twenty-one years of age in such State.

SECTION 3. No person shall be a Senator or Representative in Congress, or elector of President and Vice-President, or hold any office, civil, or military, under the United States, or under any State, who, having previously taken an oath, as a member of Congress, or as an officer of the United States, or as a member of any State Legislature, or as an executive or judicial officer of any State, to support the Constitution of the United States, shall have engaged in insurrection or rebellion against the same, or given aid or comfort to the enemies thereof. But Congress may by a vote of two-thirds of each House, remove such disability.

SECTION 4. The validity of the public debt of the United States, authorized by law, including debts incurred for payment of pensions and bounties for services in suppressing insurrection or rebellion, shall not be questioned. But neither the United States nor any State shall assume or pay any debt or obligation incurred in aid of insurrection or rebellion against the United States, or any claim for the loss or emancipation of any slave; but all such debts, obligations and claims shall be held illegal and void.

SECTION 5. The Congress shall have power to enforce, by appropriate legislation, the provisions of this article.

[ARTICLE XV.]*

SECTION 1. The right of citizens of the United States to vote shall not be denied or abridged by the United States or by any State on account of race, color, or previous condition of servitude.

SECTION 2. The Congress shall have power to enforce this article by appropriate legislation.

ARTICLES IN ADDITION TO, AND AMENDMENT OF, THE CONSTITUTION OF THE UNITED STATES, PROPOSED BY CONGRESS, BUT NOT RATIFIED BY THE LEGISLATURES OF THE SEVERAL STATES, PURSUANT TO THE FIFTH ARTICLE OF THE ORIGINAL CONSTITUTION.

PROPOSED BY THE FIRST CONGRESS, FIRST SESSION, MARCH 4, 1789.

ARTICLE I. After the first enumeration required by the first article of the Constitution, there shall be one Representative for every thirty thousand, until the num-

* The fifteenth amendment to the Constitution of the United States was proposed to the legislatures of the several States by the Fortieth Congress, on the 27th of February, 1869, and was declared, in a proclamation of the Secretary of State, dated March 30, 1870, to have been ratified by the legislatures of twenty-nine of the thirty-seven States. [POORE.]

ber shall amount to one hundred, after which, the proportion shall be so regulated by Congress, that there shall be not less than one hundred Representatives, nor less than one Representative for every forty thousand persons, until the number of Representatives shall amount to two hundred, after which the proportion shall be so regulated by Congress, that there shall not be less than two hundred Representatives, nor more than one Representative for every fifty thousand persons.

ART. II. No law, varying the compensation for the services of the Senators and Representatives, shall take effect, until an election of Representatives shall have intervened.

PROPOSED BY THE ELEVENTH CONGRESS, SECOND SESSION, NOVEMBER 27, 1809.

If any citizen of the United States shall accept, claim, receive or retain any title of nobility or honor, or shall, without the consent of Congress, accept and retain any present, pension, office or emolument of any kind whatever, from any emperor, king, prince, or foreign power, such person shall cease to be a citizen of the United States, and shall be incapable of holding any office of trust or profit under them, or either of them.

PROPOSED BY THE THIRTY-SIXTH CONGRESS, SECOND SESSION, MARCH 2, 1861.

ARTICLE XIII. No amendment shall be made to the Constitution which will authorize or give to Congress the power to abolish or interfere, within any State, with the domestic institutions thereof, including that of persons held to labor or service by the laws of said State.

ALIEN AND SEDITION LAWS—1798.

During the French excitement the Federalists pushed through Congress two acts which proved the ruin of their party. The Alien Act of June 25, 1795, "which stands without a parallel in American legislation," was followed, July 6, by a second act directed against "Alien Enemies." The Alien Act passed the house by a close vote of 46 to 40. The Sedition Act of July 14, 1798, passed the house by a still closer vote of 44 to 41. Five years before (1792) England had passed an alien act followed by other acts of similar tenor.

The first prosecution under the Sedition Act was peculiar. Matthew Lyon, M.C., from Vermont, was tried, convicted and sentenced to four months' imprisonment and $1000 fine. In 1840, long after Lyon's death, Congress restored to his heirs the fine paid, with the accrued interest.

The opposition to these acts formulated itself in numerous petitions from all sections, north as well as south, and finally in the Virginia and Kentucky Revolutions.

Consult *Schouler's U. S.*, I., 393; *Stevens' Albert Gallatin*, 156; *Von Holst's Cons. Hist. U.S.*, I., 142; *Bryant and Gay's U. S.*, IV., 129; *McMaster's U. S.*, II., 393; *Hildreth's U. S.*, V., 216 and 225; *Gibbs' Washington and Adams*, II., 73; *Hamilton's Republic*, VII., 156, 276, 341.

AN ACT CONCERNING ALIENS.

SECTION 1. *Be it enacted by the Senate and House of Representatives of the United States of America in Congress assembled*, That it shall be lawful for the President of the United States at any time during the continuance of this act to *order* all such *aliens* as he shall judge dangerous to the peace and safety of the United States, or shall have reasonable grounds to suspect are concerned in any treasonable or secret machinations against the government thereof, to depart out of the territory of the United States, within such time as shall be expressed in such order, which order shall be served on such alien by delivering him a copy thereof, or leaving the same at his usual abode, and returned to the office of the Secretary of State, by the marshal or other person to whom the same shall be directed. And in case any alien, so ordered to depart, shall be found at large within the United States after the time limited in such order for his departure, and not having obtained a *licence* from the President to reside therein, or having obtained such *licence* shall not have conformed thereto, every such alien shall, on conviction thereof, be imprisoned for a term not exceeding three years, and shall never after be admitted to become a citizen of the United States. *Provided always, and be it further enacted*, that if any alien so ordered to depart shall prove to the satisfaction of the President, by evidence to be taken before such person or persons as the President shall direct, who are for that purpose hereby authorized to administer oaths, that no injury or danger to the United States will arise from suffering such alien to reside therein, the President of the United States may grant a *licence* to such alien to remain within the United States for such time as he shall judge proper, and at such place as he may designate. And the President may also require of such alien to enter into a bond to the United States, in such penal sum as he may direct, with one or more sufficient sureties to the satisfaction of the person authorized by the President to take the same, conditioned for the good behavior of such alien during his residence in the United States, and not violating his licence, which licence the President may revoke whenever he shall think proper.

SEC. 2. *And be it further enacted*, That it shall be lawful for the President of the United States, whenever he may deem it necessary for the public safety, to order to be removed out of the territory thereof, any alien, who may or shall be in prison in pursuance of this act; and to cause to be arrested and sent out of the United States such of those aliens as shall have been ordered to depart therefrom and shall not have obtained a licence as aforesaid, in all cases where, in the opinion of the President, the public safety requires a speedy removal. And if any alien so removed or sent out of the United States by the President, shall voluntarily return thereto, unless by permission of the President of the United States, such alien on conviction thereof, shall be imprisoned so long as, in the opinion of the President, the public safety may require.

SEC. 3. *And be it further enacted*, That every master or commander of any ship or vessel which shall come into any port of the United States after the first day of July next, shall immediately on his arrival make report in writing to the collector or other chief officer of the customs of such port, of all aliens, if any, on board his vessel, specifying their names, age, the place of nativity, the country from which they shall have come, the nation to which they belong and owe allegiance, their occupation and a description of their persons, as far as he shall be informed thereof, and on failure, every such master and commander shall forfeit and pay three hundred dollars, for the payment whereof on default of such master or commander, such vessel shall also be holden, and may by such collector or other officer of the customs be de-tained. And it shall be the duty of such collector or other officer of the customs, forthwith to transmit to the office of the department of State true copies of all such returns.

SEC. 4. *And be it further enacted*, That the circuit and district courts of the United States, shall respectively have cognizance of all crimes and offences against this act. And all marshalls and other officers of the United States are required to execute all precepts and orders of the President of the United States issued in pursuance or by virtue of this act.

SEC. 5. *And be it further enacted*, That it shall be lawful for any alien who may be ordered to be removed from the United States, by virtue of this act, to take with him such part of his goods, chattels, or other property as he may find convenient; and all property left in the United States by any alien, who may be removed, as aforesaid, shall be, and remain subject to his order and disposal, in the same manner as if this act had not been passed.

SEC. 6. *And be it further enacted*, That this act shall continue and be in force for and during the term of two years from the passing thereof.

Approved June 25, 1798.

AN ACT IN ADDITION TO THE ACT ENTITLED "AN ACT FOR THE PUNISHMENT OF CERTAIN CRIMES AGAINST THE UNITED STATES.

SECTION I. *Be it enacted by the Senate and House of Representatives of the United States of America assembled*, That if any persons shall unlawfully combine or conspire together, with intent to oppose any measure or measures of the government of the United States, which are or shall be directed by proper authority, or to impede the operation of any law of the United States, or to intimidate or prevent any person holding a place or office in or under the government of the United States, from undertaking, performing or executing his trust or duty; and if any person or persons, with intent as aforesaid, shall counsel, advise or attempt to procure any insurrection, riot, unlawful assembly, or combination, whether such conspiracy, threatening, counsel, advice, or attempt shall have the proposed effect or not, he or they shall be deemed guilty of a high misdemeanor, and on conviction, before any court of the United States having jurisdiction thereof, shall be punished by a fine not exceeding five thousand dollars and by imprisonment during a term not less than six months nor exceeding five years; and further at the discretion of the court may be holden to find sureties for his good behavior in such sum, and for such time, as the said court may direct.

SEC. 2. *And be it further enacted*, That if any person shall write, print, utter or publish, or shall cause or procure to be written, printed, uttered or published or shall knowingly and willingly assist or aid in writing, printing, uttering or publishing any false, scandalous and malicious writing or writings against the government of the United States, or either house of the Congress of the United States, or the President of the United States, with intent to defame the said government, or either house of the said Congress, or the said President, or to bring them or either of them, into contempt or disrepute; or to excite against them, or either, or any of them, the hatred of the good people of the United States, or to stir up sedition within the United States, or to excite any unlawful combinations therein, for opposing or resisting any law of the United States, or any act of the President of the United States, and one in pursuance of any such law, or of the powers in him vested by the constitution of the United States, or to resist, oppose, or defeat any such law or act, or to aid, encourage or abet any hostile designs of any foreign nation against the United States, their people or government, then such person, being thereof convicted before any court of the United States having jurisdiction thereof, shall be punished by a fine not exceeding two thousand dollars, and by imprisonment not exceeding two years.

SEC. 3. *And be it further enacted, and declared*, That if any person shall be prosecuted under this act, for the writing or publishing any libel aforesaid, it shall be lawful for the defendant, upon the trial of the cause, to give in evidence in his defence, the truth of the matter contained in the publication charged as a libel. And the jury who shall try the cause, shall have a right to determine the law and the fact, under the direction of the court, as in other cases.

SEC. 4. *And be it further enacted*, That this act shall continue and be in force until the third day of March, one thousand eight hundred and one, and no longer: *Provided*, that the expiration of the act shall not prevent or defeat a prosecution and punishment of any offence against the law, during the time it shall be in force.

Approved, July 14, 1798.

THE VIRGINIA AND KENTUCKY RESOLUTIONS.

The Virginia and Kentucky Resolutions, the expression of the opposition to the Alien and Sedition laws originated in a conference at Monticello between Thos. Jefferson and two brothers, Geo. Nicholas, of Kentucky, and Wm. C. Nicholas, of Virginia, while Madison may have been present. As a result, Jefferson drafted the Kentucky resolutions and Madison, the Virginia. Jefferson's resolutions were passed by the Kentucky legislature November 10, 1798, and Madison's, by the Virginia legislature December 21, 1798. These resolutions were forwarded to the legislatures of the several states and elicited decidedly unfavorable replies from the states north of the Potomac. In answer to these replies the Kentucky resolutions of 1799 were adopted.

Jefferson's latest biographer, John T. Morse, says the Kentucky Resolutions "remained a foundation and sufficient precedent and authority for all the subsequent secession doctrines of the Eastern states, for the nullification proceedings of South Carolina, almost, if not quite, for the Rebellion of 1861."

The Kentucky legislature somewhat modified Jefferson's draft, striking out the nullification clause, which, however, appeared in the final resolution in the next year, 1799.

Consult *Schouler's U. S.*, I., 423; *Bryant and Gay's U. S.*, IV., 130; *Von Holst's Const. Hist. U. S.*, I., 143; *Hildreth's U. S.*, V., 272; *McMaster's U. S.*, II., 419; *Morse's Jefferson*, 193. The original draft of the Kentucky Resolution is in *Jefferson's Works*, IX., 494. The replies of the States to the Resolutions, together with Madison's Report in the replies, are in *Elliot's Debates*, vol. IV.

VIRGINIA RESOLUTIONS OF 1798.

VIRGINIA *to wit*,

IN THE HOUSE OF DELEGATES,

Friday, December 21st, 1798.

Resolved, that the General Assembly of Virginia doth unequivocally express a firm resolution to maintain and defend the constitution of the United States, and the constitution of this state, against every aggression, either foreign or domestic, and that they will support the government of the United States in all measures, warranted by the former.

That this Assembly most solemnly declares a warm attachment to the union of the states, to maintain which, it pledges its powers; and that for this end, it is their duty, to watch over and oppose every infraction of those principles, which constitute the only basis of that union, because a faithful observance of them, can alone secure its existence, and the public happiness.

That this Assembly doth explicitly and peremptorily declare, that it views the powers of the Federal Government, as resulting from the compact, to which the states are parties; as limited by the plain sense and intention of the instrument constituting that compact; as no farther valid than they are authorized by the grants enumerated in that compact, and that in case of a deliberate, palpable and dangerous exercise of other powers not granted by the said compact, the states who are parties thereto have the right, and are in duty bound, to interpose for arresting the progress of the evil, and for maintaining, within their respective limits, the authorities, rights, and liberties appertaining to them.

That the General Assembly doth also express its deep regret, that a spirit has, in sundry instances, been manifested by the Federal Government, to enlarge its powers by forced constructions of the constitutional charter which defines them; and that indications have appeared of a design to expound certain general phrases (which having been copied from the very limited grant of powers in the former articles of confederation were the less liable to be misconstrued) so as to destroy the meaning and effect of the particular enumeration, which necessarily explains and limits the general phrases; and so as to consolidate the states by degrees into one sovereignty, the obvious tendency and inevitable consequence of which would be, to transform the present republican system of the United States, into an absolute, or at best a mixed monarchy.

That the General Assembly doth particularly protest against the palpable and alarming infractions of the constitution, in the two late cases of the "Alien and Sedition acts," passed at the last session of Congress; the first of which exercises a power nowhere delegated to the Federal Government; and which by uniting legislative and judicial powers, to those of executive, subverts the general principles of free government, as well as the particular organization and positive provisions of the federal constitution: and the other of which acts, exercises in like manner a power not delegated by the constitution, but on the contrary expressly and positively forbidden by one of the amendments thereto; a power which more than any other ought to produce universal alarm, because it is levelled against that right of freely examining public characters and measures, and of free communication among the people thereon, which has ever been justly deemed, the only effectual guardian of every other right.

That this state having, by its convention which ratified the federal constitution, expressly declared, "that among other essential rights, the liberty of conscience and the press cannot be cancelled, abridged, restrained or modified by any authority of the United States," and from its extreme anxiety to guard these rights from every possible attack of sophistry and ambition, having with other states recommended an amendment for that purpose, which amendment was in due time annexed to the constitution, it would mark a reproachful inconsistency and criminal degeneracy, if an indifference were now shewn to the most palpable violation of one of the rights thus declared and secured, and to the establishment of a precedent which may be fatal to the other.

That the good people of this Commonwealth having ever felt and continuing to feel the most sincere affection for their brethren of the other states, the truest anxiety for establishing and perpetuating the union of all, and the most scrupulous fidelity to that constitution which is the pledge of mutual friendship, and the instrument of mutual happiness: the General Assembly doth solemnly appeal to the like dispositions of the other states, in confidence that they will concur with this commonwealth in declaring, as it does hereby declare, that the acts aforesaid are unconstitutional, and that the necessary and proper measures will be taken by each for coöperating with this state, in maintaining unimpaired the authorities, rights, and liberties, reserved to the states respectively, or to the people.

That the Governor be desired to transmit a copy of the

foregoing resolutions to the executive authority of each of the other states, with a request, that the same may be communicated to the legislature thereof.

And that a copy be furnished to each of the Senators and Representatives representing this state in the Congress of the United States.

Attest, JOHN STEWART, *C. H. D.*

1798, December the 24th.

Agreed to by the Senate. H. BROOKE, *C. S.*

KENTUCKY RESOLUTIONS OF 1798.

I. *Resolved*, that the several states composing the United States of America, are not united on the principle of unlimited submission to their General Government; but that by compact under the style and title of a Constitution for the United States and of amendments thereto, they constituted a General Government for special purposes, delegated to that Government certain definite powers, reserving each state to itself, the residuary mass of right to their own self-Government; and that whensoever the General Government assumes undelegated powers, its acts are unauthoritative, void, and of no force: That to this compact each state acceded as a state, and is an integral party, its co-states forming as to itself, the other party: That the Government created by this compact was not made the exclusive or final *judge* of the extent of the powers delegated to itself; since that would have made its discretion, and not the constitution, the measure of its powers; but that as in all other cases of compact among parties having no common Judge, each party has an equal right to judge for itself, as well of infractions as of the mode and measure of redress.

II. Resolved, that the Constitution of the United States having delegated to Congress a power to punish treason, counterfeiting the securities and current coin of the

United States, piracies and felonies committed on the High Seas, and offences against the laws of nations, and no other crimes whatever, and it being true as a general principle, and one of the amendments to the Constitution having also declared, "that the powers not delegated to the United States by the Constitution, nor prohibited by it to the states, are reserved to the states respectively, or to the people," therefore also the same act of Congress passed on the 14th day of July, 1798, and entitled "An act in addition to the act entitled an act for the punishment of certain crimes against the United States;" as also the act passed by them on the 27th day of June, 1798, entitled "An act to punish frauds committed on the Bank of the United States" (and all other their acts which assume to create, define, or punish crimes other than those enumerated in the constitution) are altogether void and of no force, and that the power to create, define, and punish such other crimes is reserved, and of right appertains solely and exclusively to the respective states, each within its own Territory.

III. Resolved, that it is true as a general principle, and is also expressly declared by one of the amendments to the Constitution that "the powers not delegated to the United States by the Constitution, nor prohibited by it to the states, are reserved to the states respectively or to the people;" and that no power over the freedom of religion, freedom of speech, or freedom of the press being delegated to the United States by the Constitution, nor prohibited by it to the states, all lawful powers respecting the same did of right remain, and were reserved to the states, or to the people: That thus was manifested their determination to retain to themselves the right of judging how far the licentiousness of speech and of the press may be abridged without lessening their useful freedom, and how far those abuses which cannot be separated from their use, should be tolerated rather than the use be destroyed; and thus also they guarded against all abridgement by the United States of the freedom of religious opinions and exercises, and retained to themselves the right of protecting the same, as this state, by a Law passed on the general demand of its Citizens, had already protected them from all human restraint or interference: And that in addition to this general principle and express declaration, another and more special provision has been made by one of the amendments to the Constitution which expressly declares, that "Congress shall make no laws respecting an Establishment of religion, or prohibiting the free exercise thereof, or abridging the freedom of speech, or of the press," thereby guarding in the same sentence, and under the same words, the freedom of religion, of speech, and of the press, insomuch, that whatever violates either, throws down the sanctuary which covers the others, and that libels, falsehoods, defamation, equally with heresy and false religion, are withheld from the cognizance of federal tribunals. That therefore the act of the Congress of the United States passed on the 14th day of July, 1798, entitled "An act in addition to the act for the punishment of certain crimes against the United States," which does abridge the freedom of the press, is not law, but is altogether void and of no effect.

IV. Resolved, that alien friends are under the jurisdiction and protection of the laws of the state wherein they are; that no power over them has been delegated to the United States, nor prohibited to the individual states distinct from their power over citizens; and it being true as a general principle, and one of the amendments to the Constitution having also declared, that "the powers not delegated to the United States by the Constitution, nor prohibited to the states are reserved to the states respectively or to the people," the act of the Congress of the United States passed on the 22d day of June, 1798, entitled "An act concerning aliens," which assumes power over alien friends not delegated by the Constitution, is not law, but is altogether void and of no force.

V. Resolved, that in addition to the general principle as well as the express declaration, that powers not delegated are reserved, another and more special provision inserted in the Constitution from abundant caution has declared, "that the *migration* or importation of such persons as any of the states now existing shall think proper to admit, shall not be prohibited by the Congress prior to the year 1808." That this Commonwealth does admit the migration of alien friends described as the subject of the said act concerning aliens; that a provision against prohibiting their migration, is a provision against all acts equivalent thereto, or it would be nugatory; that to remove them when migrated is equivalent to a prohibition of their migration, and is, therefore contrary to the said provision of the Constitution, and void.

VI. Resolved, that the imprisonment of a person under the protection of the Laws of this Commonwealth on his failure to obey the simple *order* of the President to depart out of the United States, as is undertaken by the said act entitled "An act concerning Aliens," is contrary to the Constitution, one amendment to which has provided, that "no person shall be deprived of liberty without due process of law," and that another having provided "that in all criminal prosecutions, the accused shall enjoy the right to a public trial by an impartial jury, to be informed of the nature and cause of the accusation, to be confronted with the witnesses against him, to have compulsory process for obtaining witnesses in his favour, and to have the assistance of counsel for his defence," the same act undertaking to authorize the President to remove a person out of the United States who is under the protection of the Law, on his own suspicion, without accusation, without jury, without public trial, without confrontation of the witnesses against him, without having witnesses in his favour, without defence, without counsel, is contrary to these provisions also of the Constitution, is therefore not law but utterly void and of no force.

That transferring the power of judging any person who is under the protection of the laws, from the Courts to the President of the United States, as is undertaken by the same act concerning Aliens, is against the article of the Constitution which provides, that "the judicial power of the United States shall be vested in the Courts, the Judges of which shall hold their offices during good behaviour," and that the said act is void for that reason also; and it is further to be noted, that this transfer of Judiciary power is to that magistrate of the General Government who already possesses all the Executive, and a qualified negative in all the Legislative powers.

VII. Resolved, that the construction applied by the General Government (as is evidenced by sundry of their proceedings) to those parts of the Constitution of the United States which delegate to Congress a power to lay and collect taxes, duties, imposts, and excises; to pay the debts, and provide for the common defence, and general welfare of the United States, and to make all laws which shall be necessary and proper for carrying into execution the powers vested by the Constitution in the Government of the United States, or any department thereof, goes to the destruction of all the limits prescribed to their power by the Constitution—That words meant by that instrument to be subsidiary only to the execution of the limited powers, ought not to be so construed as themselves to give unlimited powers, nor a part so to be taken, as to destroy the whole residue of the instrument: That the proceedings of the General Government under colour of these articles, will be a fit and necessary subject for revisal and correction at a time of greater tranquillity, while those specified in the preceding resolutions call for immediate redress.

VIII. Resolved, that the preceding Resolutions be

transmitted to the Senators and Representatives in Congress from this Commonwealth, who are hereby enjoined to present the same to their respective Houses, and to use their best endeavours to procure at the next session of Congress, a repeal of the aforesaid unconstitutional and obnoxious acts.

IX. Resolved lastly, that the Governor of this Commonwealth be, and is hereby authorized and requested to communicate the preceding Resolutions to the Legislatures of the several States, to assure them that this Commonwealth considers Union for specified National purposes, and particularly for those specified in their late Federal Compact, to be friendly to the peace, happiness, and prosperity of all the states: that faithful to that compact according to the plain intent and meaning in which it was understood and acceded to by the several parties, it is sincerely anxious for its preservation: that it does also believe, that to take from the states all the powers of self government, and transfer them to a general and consolidated Government, without regard to the special delegations and reservations solemnly agreed to in that compact, is not for the peace, happiness, or prosperity of these states: And that therefore, this Commonwealth is determined, as it doubts not its Co-states are, to submit to undelegated & consequently unlimited powers in no man or body of men on earth: that if the acts before specified should stand, these conclusions would flow from them; that the General Government may place any act they think proper on the list of crimes & punish it themselves, whether enumerated or not enumerated by the Constitution as cognizable by them: that they may transfer its cognizance to the President or any other person, who may himself be the accuser, counsel, judge, and jury, whose *suspicions* may be the evidence, his order the sentence, his officer the executioner, and his breast the sole record of the transaction: that a very numerous and valuable description of the inhabitants of these states, being by this precedent reduced as outlaws, to the absolute dominion of one man and the barrier of the Constitution thus swept away from us all, no rampart now remains against the passions and the powers of a majority of Congress, to protect from a like exportation or other grievous punishment the minority of the same body, the Legislature, Judges, Governors, & Counsellors of the states, nor their other peaceable inhabitants who may venture to reclaim the constitutional rights & liberties of the state & people, or who for other causes, good or bad, may be obnoxious to the views or marked by the suspicions of the President, or be thought dangerous to his or their elections or other interests public or personal: that the friendless alien has indeed been selected as the safest subject of a first experiment: but the citizen will soon follow, or rather has already followed; for already has a Sedition Act marked him as its prey: that these and successive acts of the same character, unless arrested on the threshold, may tend to drive these states into revolution and blood, and will furnish new calumnies against Republican Governments, and new pretexts for those who wish it to be believed, that man cannot be governed but by a rod of iron: that it would be a dangerous delusion were a confidence in the men of our choice to silence our fears for the safety of our rights: that confidence is everywhere the parent of despotism: free government is founded in jealousy and not in confidence; it is jealousy and not confidence which prescribes limited Constitutions to bind down those whom we are obliged to trust with power: that our Constitution has accordingly fixed the limits to which and no further our confidence may go; and let the honest advocate of confidence read the Alien and Sedition Acts, and say if the Constitution has not been wise in fixing limits to the Government it created, and whether we should be wise in destroying those limits? Let him say what the Government is if it be not a tyranny, which the men of our choice have conferred on the President, and the President of our choice has assented to and accepted over the friendly strangers, to whom the mild spirit of our country and its laws had pledged hospitality and protection: that the men of our choice have more respected the bare suspicions of the President than the solid rights of innocence, the claims of justification, the sacred force of truth, and the forms & substance of law and justice. In questions of power then let no more be heard of confidence in man, but bind him down from mischief by the chains of the Constitution. That this Commonwealth does therefore call on its co-States for an expression of their sentiments on the acts concerning Aliens, and for the punishment of certain crimes herein before specified, plainly declaring whether these acts are or are not authorized by the Federal Compact? And it doubts not that their sense will be so announced as to prove their attachment unaltered to limited Government, whether general or particular, and that the rights and liberties of their Co-states will be exposed to no dangers by remaining embarked on a common bottom with their own: That they will concur with this Commonwealth in considering the said acts as so palpably against the Constitution as to amount to an undisguised declaration, that the Compact is not meant to be the measure of the powers of the General Government, but that it will proceed in the exercise over these states of all powers whatsoever: That they will view this as seizing the rights of the states and consolidating them in the hands of the general government with a power assumed to bind the states (not merely in cases made federal) but in all cases whatsoever, by laws made, not with their consent, but by others against their consent: That this would be to surrender the form of Government we have chosen, and live under one deriving its powers from its own will, and not from our authority; and that the Co-states, recurring to their natural right in cases not made federal, will concur in declaring these acts void and of no force, and will each unite with this Commonwealth in requesting their repeal at the next session of Congress.

EDMUND BULLOCK, *S. H. R.*
JOHN CAMPBELL, *S. S. P. T.*

Passed the House of Representatives, Nov. 10th, 1798.
Attest, THOMAS TODD, *C. H. R.*

In Senate, November 13th, 1798, unanimously concurred in,
Attest, B. THRUSTON, *Clk. Sen.*

Approved November 16th, 1798.
JAMES GARRARD, *G. K.*

By the Governor,
HARRY TOULMIN,
Secretary of State.

THE KENTUCKY RESOLUTIONS OF 1799.

HOUSE OF REPRESENTATIVES, Thursday, Nov. 14, 1799.

The house, according to the standing order of the day, resolved itself into a committee, of the whole house, on the state of the commonwealth, (Mr. Desha in the chair,) and, after some time spent therein, the speaker resumed the chair, and Mr. Desha reported that the committee had taken under consideration sundry resolutions passed by several state legislatures, on the subject of the Alien and Sedition Laws, and had come to a resolution thereupon, which he delivered in at the clerk's table, where it was read and *unanimously* agreed to by the House as follows:—

The representatives of the good people of this commonwealth, in General Assembly convened, having maturely considered the answers of sundry states in the Union to their resolutions, passed the last session, respecting certain unconstitutional laws of Congress, commonly called the Alien and Sedition Laws, would be faithless indeed to themselves, and to those they represent, were they silently to acquiesce in the principles and doctrines attempted to be maintained in all those answers, that of Virginia only accepted. To again enter the field of argument, and attempt more fully or forcibly to expose the unconstitutionality of those obnoxious laws, would, it is apprehended, be as unnecessary as unavailing. We cannot, however, but lament that, in the discussion of those interesting subjects by sundry of the legislatures of our sister states, unfounded suggestions and uncandid insinuations, derogatory to the true character and principles of this commonwealth, have been substituted in place of fair reasoning and sound argument. Our opinions of these alarming measures of the general government, together with our reasons for those opinions, were detailed with decency and with temper, and submitted to the discussion and judgment of our fellow-citizens throughout the Union. Whether the like decency and temper have been observed in the answers of most of those States who have denied or attempted to obviate the great truths contained in those resolutions, we have now only to submit to a candid world. *Faithful to the true principles of the federal Union, unconscious of any designs to disturb the harmony of that Union* and anxious only to escape the fangs of despotism, the good people of this commonwealth are regardless of censure or calumniation. Lest, however, the silence of this commonwealth should be construed into an acquiescence in the doctrines and principles advanced, and attempted to be maintained by the said answers or, at least those of our fellow-citizens, throughout the Union, who so widely differ from us on those important subjects, should be deluded by the expectation that we shall be deterred from what we conceive our duty, or shrink from the principles contained in those resolutions,—therefore,

Resolved, That this Commonwealth considers the Federal Union upon the terms and for the purposes specified in the late compact, conducive to the liberty and happiness of the several States: That it does now unequivocally declare its attachment to the Union, and to that compact, agreeably to its obvious and real intention, and will be among the last to seek its dissolution: That, if those who administer the general government be permitted to transgress the limits fixed by that compact, by a total disregard to the special delegations of power therein contained, an annihilation of the State governments, and the creation, upon their ruins of a general consolidated government, will be the inevitable consequence: That the principle and construction, contended for by sundry of the state legislatures, that the general government is the exclusive judge of the extent of the powers delegated to it, stop not short of *despotism*—since the discretion of those who administer the government, and not the *Constitution,* would be the measure of their powers: That the several States who formed that instrument, being sovereign and independent, have the unquestionable right to judge of the infraction; and, *That a nullification, by those sovereignties of all unauthorized acts done under color of that instrument, is the rightful remedy:* That this Commonwealth does, under the most deliberate reconsideration, declare, that the said Alien and Sedition Laws are, in their opinion, palpable violations of the said Constitution; and, however cheerfully it may be disposed to surrender its opinion to a majority of its sister States, in matters of ordinary or doubtful policy, yet, in momentous regulations like the present, which so vitally wound the best rights of the citizen, it would consider a silent acquiescence as highly criminal: That, although this Commonwealth, as a party to the Federal compact, *will bow to the laws of the Union,* yet it does, at the same time, declare, that it will not now, or ever hereafter, cease to oppose, in a constitutional manner, every attempt, at what quarter so ever offered, to violate that compact: And finally, in order that no pretext or arguments may be drawn from a supposed acquiescence, on the part of this Commonwealth, in the constitutionality of those laws, and be thereby used as precedents for similar future violations of the federal compact, this Commonwealth does now enter against them its solemn PROTEST.

Extract, etc. *Attest,* THOMAS TODD, *C. H. R.*

In Senate, Nov. 22, 1799.—Read and concurred in.

Attest, B. THURSTON, *C. S.*

ORDINANCE OF NULLIFICATION—1832.

The protection tariff of 1828 gave great dissatisfaction to the Southern states, some legislatures even pronouncing it unconstitutional. The tariff of 1832, though reducing the duties, failed to satisfy the South while Calhoun's development of the doctrine of nullification incited to more decided action. Accordingly a state convention assembling at Charleston, S. C., passed the following ordinance of nullification Nov. 24, 1832, to take effect the first of the ensuing February. The convention merely carried out the principles of the Virginia and Kentucky resolutions of 1798 and 1799. President Jackson promptly issued a proclamation against nullification (Dec. 10, 1832), answering the arguments of the nullifiers, and asserted his determination to maintain the Union. Congress, after heated discussion, passed a bill for enforcing the tariff; but all trouble was averted by the passage of Clay's Compromise Tariff, providing for a gradual reduction, of duties till Sep. 30, 1842, after which time duties were to be uniformly 20 per cent. The bill was signed by the President Mar. 2, 1833, and on Mar. 16, South Carolina repealed the nullification ordinance.

By this compromise harmony was restored; but the final settlement of the nullification question was merely postponed.

Consult *Bryant and Gay's U. S.*, IV.; *Von Holst's Cons. Hist. U. S.*, I., 475; *Benton's Thirty Years' View*, I., 297–361; *Sumner's Jackson*, 291; *Von Holst's Calhoun*, 104; *Parton's Jackson*, III., 457.

An ordinance to nullify certain acts of the Congress of the United States, purporting to be laws laying duties and imposts on the importation of foreign commodities.

Whereas the Congress of the United States by various acts, purporting to be acts laying duties and imposts on foreign imports, but in reality intended for the protection of domestic manufactures, and the giving of bounties to classes and individuals engaged in particular employments, at the expense and to the injury and oppression of other classes and individuals, and by wholly exempting from taxation certain foreign commodities, such as are not produced or manufactured in the United States, to afford a pretext for imposing higher and excessive duties on articles similar to those intended to be protected, hath exceeded its just powers under the constitution, which confers on it no authority to afford such protection, and hath violated the true meaning and intent of the constitution, which provides for equality in imposing the burdens of taxation upon the several States and portions of the confederacy: And whereas the said Congress, exceeding its just power to impose taxes and collect revenue for the purpose of effecting and accomplishing the specific objects and purposes which the constitution of the United States authorizes it to effect and accomplish, hath raised and collected unnecessary revenue for objects unauthorized by the constitution.

We, therefore, the people of the State of South Carolina, in convention assembled, do declare and ordain, and it is hereby declared and ordained, that the several acts and parts of acts of the Congress of the United States, purporting to be laws for the imposing of duties and imposts on the importation of foreign commodities, and now having actual operation and effect within the United States, and, more especially, an act entitled "An act in alteration of the several acts imposing duties on imports," approved on the nineteenth day of May, one thousand eight hundred and twenty-eight, and also an act entitled "An act to alter and amend the several acts imposing duties on imports," approved on the fourteenth day of July, one thousand eight hundred and thirty-two, are unauthorized by the constitution of the United States, and violate the true meaning and intent thereof and are null, void, and no law, nor binding upon this State, its officers or citizens; and all promises, contracts, and obligations, made or entered into, or to be made or entered into, with purpose to secure the duties imposed by said acts, and all judicial proceedings which shall be hereafter had in affirmance thereof, are and shall be held utterly null and void.

And it is further ordained, that it shall not be lawful for any of the constituted authorities, whether of this State or of the United States, to enforce the payment of duties imposed by the said acts within the limits of this State; but it shall be the duty of the legislature to adopt such measures and pass such acts as may be necessary to give full effect to this ordinance, and to prevent the enforcement and arrest the operation of the said acts and parts of acts of the Congress of the United States within the limits of this State, from and after the 1st day of February next, and the duty of all other constituted authorities, and of all persons residing or being within the limits of this State, and they are hereby required and enjoined to obey and give effect to this ordinance, and such acts and measures of the legislature as may be passed or adopted in obedience thereto.

And it is further ordained, that in no case of law or

equity, decided in the courts of this State, wherein shall be drawn in question the authority of this ordinance, or the validity of such act or acts of the legislature as may be passed for the purpose of giving effect thereto, or the validity of the aforesaid acts of Congress, imposing duties, shall any appeal be taken or allowed to the Supreme Court of the United States, nor shall any copy of the record be permitted or allowed for that purpose; and if any such appeal shall be attempted to be taken, the courts of this State shall proceed to execute and enforce their judgments according to the laws and usages of the State, without reference to such attempted appeal, and the person or persons attempting to take such appeal may be dealt with as for a contempt of the court.

And it is further ordained, that all persons now holding any office of honor, profit, or trust, civil or military, under this State (members of the legislature excepted), shall, within such time, and in such manner as the legislature shall prescribe, take an oath well and truly to obey, execute, and enforce this ordinance, and such act or acts of the legislature as may be passed in pursuance thereof, according to the true intent and meaning of the same; and on the neglect or omission of any such person or persons so to do, his or their office or offices shall be forthwith vacated, and shall be filled up as if such person or persons were dead or had resigned; and no person hereafter elected to any office of honor, profit, or trust, civil or military (members of the legislature excepted), shall, until the legislature shall otherwise provide and direct, enter on the execution of his office, or be in any respect competent to discharge the duties thereof until he shall, in like manner, have taken a similar oath; and no juror shall be empannelled in any of the courts of this State, in any cause in which shall be in question this ordinance, or any act of the legislature passed in pursuance thereof, unless he shall first, in addition to the usual oath, have taken an oath that he will well and truly obey, execute, and enforce this ordinance, and such act or acts of the legislature as may be passed to carry the same into operation and effect, according to the true intent and meaning thereof.

And we, the people of South Carolina, to the end that it may be fully understood by the government of the United States, and the people of the co-States, that we are determined to maintain this our ordinance and declaration, at every hazard, do further declare that we will not submit to the application of force on the part of the federal government, to reduce this State to obedience; but that we will consider the passage, by Congress, of any act authorizing the employment of a military or naval force against the State of South Carolina, her constitutional authorities or citizens; or any act abolishing or closing the ports of this State, or any of them, or otherwise obstructing the free ingress and egress of vessels to and from the said ports, or any other act on the part of the federal government, to coerce the State, shut up her ports, destroy or harass her commerce, or to enforce the acts hereby declared to be null and void, otherwise than through the civil tribunals of the country, as inconsistent with the longer continuance of South Carolina in the Union; and that the people of this State will henceforth hold themselves absolved from all further obligation to maintain or preserve their political connection with the people of the other States; and will forthwith proceed to organize a separate government, and do all other acts and things which sovereign and independent States may of right do.

Done in convention at Columbia, the twenty-fourth day of November, in the year of our Lord one thousand eight hundred and thirty-two, and in the fifty-seventh year of the declaration of the independence of the United States of America.

ORDINANCE OF SECESSION—1860.

ON receiving the news of Lincoln's election the South Carolina legislature called a convention which passed the Ordinance of Secession December 20, 1860. This was done because, as the South Carolina declaration of independence stated: "A geographical line had been drawn across the Union, and all the states north of that line have united in the election of a man to the high office of President of the United States, whose opinions and purposes are hostile to slavery." Copies of this ordinance were forwarded to the other Southern states which passed similiar ordinances, as follows: Mississippi, January 9, 1861; Florida, January 10; Alabama, January 11; Georgia, January 19; Louisiana, January 26; Texas, February 1. Delegates from the seceded states met at Montgomery, Alabama, February 4, 1861, and organized a provisional government. These states were afterwards joined by Virginia, April 17; Arkansas, May 6; and North Carolina, May 20.

Consult *Lossing's Civil War*, I., 103; *Comte de Paris' Civil War*, I., 122; *Greeley's American Conflict*, I., 344; *Draper's Civil War*, I., 514.

ORDINANCE OF SECESSION—1860.

An ordinance to dissolve the Union between the State of South Carolina and other States united with her under the compact entitled "The Constitution of the United States of America."

We, the People of the State of South Carolina, in Convention assembled, do declare and ordain, and it is hereby declared and ordained, that the Ordinance adopted by us in Convention, on the Twenty-third of May, in the year of our Lord one thousand seven hundred and eighty-eight, whereby the Constitution of the United States was ratified, and also all other Acts and parts of Acts of the General Assembly of the State ratifying amendments of the said Constitution, are hereby repealed, and the Union now subsisting between South Carolina and other States, under the name of the United States of America, is hereby dissolved.

In justification of the preceding ordinance was issued the following:

SOUTH CAROLINA DECLARATION OF INDEPENDENCE.

The State of South Carolina, having determined to resume her separate and equal place among nations, deems it due to herself, to the remaining United States of America, and to the nations of the world, that she should declare the causes which have led to this act.

In the year 1765, that portion of the British empire embracing Great Britain, undertook to make laws for the government of that portion composed of the thirteen American colonies. A struggle for the right of self-government ensued, which resulted, on the 4th of July, 1776, in a declaration by the colonies, "that they are, and of right ought to be, free and independent states, and that, as free and independent states, they have full power to levy war, to conclude peace, contract alliances, establish commerce, and do all other acts and things which independent states may of right do."

They further solemnly declared, that whenever any "form of government becomes destructive of the ends for which it was established, it is the right of that people to alter or abolish it, and to institute a new government." Deeming the government of Great Britain to have become destructive of these ends, they declared that the colonies "are absolved from all allegiance to the British crown, and that all political connection between them and the states of Great Britain is and ought to be totally dissolved."

In pursuance of this declaration of independence, each of the thirteen states proceeded to exercise its separate sovereignty; adopted for itself a constitution, and appointed officers for the administration of government in all its departments—legislative, executive, and judicial. For purpose of defense, they united their arms and their counsels; and, in 1778, they united in a league, known as the articles of confederation, whereby they agreed to intrust the administration of their external relations to a common agent, known as the Congress of the United States, expressly declaring in the first article, "that each state retains its sovereignty, freedom, and independence, and every power, jurisdiction, and right which is not, by this confederation, expressly delegated to the United States in Congress assembled."

Under this consideration the war of the Revolution was carried on, and on the 3d of September, 1783, the contest ended, and a definite treaty was signed by Great Britain, in which she acknowledged the independence of the colonies in the following terms:

Article I. His Britannic Majesty acknowledges the said United States, viz.: New Hampshire, Massachusetts Bay, Rhode Island and Providence Plantation, Connecticut, New York, New Jersey, Pennsylvania, Delaware, Maryland, Virginia, North Carolina, South Carolina, and Georgia, to be free, sovereign, and independent states; that he treats them as such; and for himself, his heirs, and successors, relinquishes all claim to the government, proprietary and territorial rights of the same, and every part thereof.

Thus was established the two great principles asserted by the colonies, namely, the right of a state to govern itself, and the right of a people to abolish a government when it becomes destructive of the ends for which it was instituted. And concurrent with the establishment of these principles was the fact, that each colony became and was recognized by the mother country as a free, sovereign, and independent state.

In 1787, deputies were appointed by the states to revise the articles of confederation, and on September 17th, 1787, the deputies recommended for the adoption of the states the articles of union known as the constitution of the United States.

The parties to whom the constitution was submitted were the several sovereign states; they were to agree or disagree, and when nine of them agreed, the compact was to take effect among those concurring; and the general government, as the common agent, was then to be invested with their authority.

If only nine of the thirteen states had concurred, the other four would have remained as they then were—separate, sovereign states, independent of any of the provisions of the constitution. In fact, two of the states did not accede to the constitution until long after it had gone into operation among the other eleven; and during that interval, they exercised the functions of an independent nation.

By this constitution, certain duties were charged on the several states, and the exercise of certain of their powers not delegated to the United States by the constitution, nor prohibited by it to the states, are reserved to the states respectively, or to the people. On the 23d of May, 1788, South Carolina, by a convention of people, passed an ordinance assenting to this constitution, and afterwards altering her own constitution to conform herself to the obligation she had undertaken.

Thus was established, by compact between the states, a government with defined objects and powers, limited to the express words of the grant, and to so much more only as was necessary to execute the power granted. The limitations left the whole remaining mass of power subject to the clause reserving it to the state or to the people, and rendered unnecessary any specification of reserved powers.

We hold that the government thus established is subject to the two great principles asserted in the declaration of independence, and we hold further that the mode of its formation subjects it to a third fundamental principle, namely—the law of compact. We maintain that in every compact between two or more parties, the obligation is mutual—that the failure of one of the contracting parties to perform a material part of the agreement entirely released the obligation of the other, and that, where no arbiter is appointed, each party is remitted to his own judgment to determine the fact of failure with all its consequences.

In the present case that fact is established with certainty. We assert that fifteen of the states have deliberately refused for years past to fulfil their constitutional obligation, and we refer to their own statutes for the proof.

The constitution of the United States, in its fourth article, provides as follows:

"No person held to service or labor in one state, under the laws thereof, escaping into another, shall, in consequence of any law or regulation therein, be discharged from any service or labor, but shall be delivered up, on claim of party to whom such service or labor may be due."

This stipulation was so material to the compact that without it that compact would not have been made. The greater number of the contracting parties held slaves, and the state of Virginia had previously declared her estimate of its value by making it the condition of cession of the territory which now compose the states north of the Ohio river.

The same article of the constitution stipulates also for the sedition by the several states of fugitives from justice from the other states.

The general government, as the common agent, passed laws to carry into effect these stipulations of the states. For many years these laws were executed. But an increasing hostility on the part of the northern states to the institution of slavery has led to a disregard of their obligations, and the laws of the general government have ceased to effect the objects of the constitution. The states of Maine, New Hampshire, Vermont, Massachusetts, Connecticut, Rhode Island, New York, Pennsylvania, Illinois, Indiana, Ohio, Michigan, Wisconsin, and Iowa have enacted laws which either nullify the acts of Congress, or render useless any attempt to execute them. In many of these states the fugitive is discharged from the service of labor claimed, and in none of them has the state government complied with the stipulation made in the constitution. The state of New Jersey, at an early day, passed a law for the rendition of fugitive slaves in conformity with her constitutional undertaking; but the current of anti-slavery feeling has led her more recently to enact laws which render imperative the remedies provided by her own law, and by the laws of Congress. In the state of New York even the right of transit for a slave has been denied by her tribunals, and the states of Ohio and Iowa have refused to surrender to justice fugitives charged with murder and inciting servile insurrection in the state of Virginia. Thus the constitutional compact has been deliberately broken and disregarded by the non-slaveholding states, and the consequence follows that South Carolina is released from its obligation.

The ends for which this constitution was framed are declared by itself to be "to form a more perfect union, establish justice, insure domestic tranquillity, provide for the common defence, protect the general welfare, and secure the blessings of liberty to ourselves and posterity."

These ends it endeavored to accomplish by a federal government, in which each state was recognized as an equal, and had separate control over its own institutions. The right of property in slaves was recognized by giving to free persons distinct political rights; by giving them the right to represent, and burdening them with direct taxes for three-fifths of their slaves; by authorizing the importation of slaves for twenty years, and by stipulating for the rendition of fugitives from labor.

We affirm that these ends for which this government was instituted have been defeated, and the government itself has been made destructive of them by the action of the non-slaveholding state. These states have assumed the right of deciding upon the propriety of our domestic institutions, and have denied the rights of property established in fifteen of the states and recognized by the constitution; they have denounced as sinful the institution of slavery; they have permitted the open establishment among them of societies whose avowed object is to disturb the peace and claim the property of the citizens of other states. They have encouraged and assisted thousands of our slaves to leave their homes, and those who remain have been incited by emissaries, books, and pictures to servile insurrection.

For twenty-five years this agitation has been steadily increasing, until it has now secured to its aid the power of the common government. Observing the forms of the constitution, a sectional party has found within that article establishing the executive department the means of subverting the constitution itself. A geographical line has been drawn across the Union, and all the states north of that line have united in the election of a man to the high office of President of the United States, whose opinions and purposes are hostile to slavery. He is to be entrusted with the administration of the common government, because he has declared that that "government cannot endure permanently half slave, half free," and that the public mind must rest in the belief that slavery is in the course of ultimate extinction.

This sectional combination for the subversion of the constitution has been aided in some of the states by elevating to citizenship persons who, by the supreme law of the land, are incapable of becoming citizens, and their votes have been used to inaugurate a new policy hostile to the south, and destructive of its peace and safety.

On the 4th of March next, this party will take possession of the government. It has announced that the south shall be excluded from the common territory; that the judicial tribunals shall be made sectional, and that a war must be waged against slavery until it shall cease throughout the United States.

The guarantees of the constitution will then no longer exist; the equal rights of the states will be lost. The slaveholding states will no longer have the power of self-government or self-protection, and the federal government will have become their enemies.

Sectional interest and animosity will deepen the irritation, and all hope of remedy is rendered vain by the fact that public opinion at the north has invested a great political error with the sanctions of a more erroneous religious belief.

We, therefore, the people of South Carolina, by our delegates in convention assembled, appealing to the Supreme Judge of the world for the rectitude of our intentions, have solemnly declared that the union heretofore existing between this state and the other states of North America is dissolved, and that the state of South Carolina has resumed her position among the nations of the world as a free, sovereign, and independent state, with full power to levy war, conclude peace, contract alliances, establish commerce, and to do all other acts and things which independent states may, of right, do.

And, for the support of this declaration, with a firm reliance on the protection of Divine Providence, we mutually pledge to each other, our lives, our fortunes, and our sacred honor.

EMANCIPATION PROCLAMATION—1863.

September 22, 1862, after the battle of Antietam, President Lincoln issued a proclamation declaring: "That on the first day of January, in the year of our Lord one thousand eight hundred and sixty-three, all persons held as slaves within any state, or designated part of a state, the people whereof shall then be in rebellion against the United States, shall be then, thenceforward, and forever free." Accordingly, January 1, 1863, the Emancipation Proclamation was issued, placing the war on its true footing. This proclamation was confirmed by the thirteenth amendment to the Constitution, adopted December 18, 1865.

Consult *Wilson's Rise and Fall of Slave Power in America*, III., 380; *Lossing's Civil War*; *Comte de Paris' Civil War*, II., 745; *Greeley's American Conflict*, II., 249; *Draper's Civil War*, II., 607; *Arnold's Lincoln*, 252.

EMANCIPATION PROCLAMATION BY ABRAHAM LINCOLN, JANUARY 1, 1863.

Whereas, On the twenty-second day of September, in the year of our Lord one thousand eight hundred and sixty-two, a proclamation was issued by the President of the United States, containing among other things the following, to wit: "That on the first day of January, in the year of our Lord one thousand eight hundred and sixty-three, all persons held as slaves within any state, or designated part of the state, the people whereof shall be in rebellion against the United States, shall be then, thenceforward, and forever free; and the executive government of the United States, including the military and naval authority thereof, will recognize and maintain the freedom of such persons, and will do no act or acts to repress such persons or any of them in any efforts they may make for their actual freedom; that the Executive will, on the first day of January aforesaid, by proclamation, designate the states, and parts of states, if any, in which the people thereof, respectively, shall then be in rebellion against the United States; and the fact that any state, or the people thereof, shall on that day be in good faith represented in the Congress of the United States by members chosen thereto at elections wherein a majority of the qualified voters of such states shall have participated, shall, in the absence of strong countervailing testimony, be deemed conclusive evidence that such state, and the people thereof, be not then in rebellion against the United States."

Now, therefore, I, Abraham Lincoln, President of the United States, by virtue of the power in me vested as commander-in-chief of the army and navy of the United States in time of actual armed rebellion against the authority and government of the United States, and as a fit and necessary war-measure for suppressing said rebellion, do, on this first day of January, in the year of our Lord one thousand eight hundred and sixty-three, and in accordance with my purpose so to do, publicly proclaimed for the full period of one hundred days from the day first above mentioned, order and designate as the states and parts of states, wherein the people thereof, respectively, are this day in rebellion against the United States, the following, to wit: Arkansas, Texas, Louisiana (except the parishes of St. Bernard, Plaquemines, Jefferson, St. John, St. Charles, St. James, Ascension, Assumption, Terre-

Bonne, Lafourche, Ste. Marie, St. Martin, and Orleans, including the city of New Orleans), Mississippi, Alabama, Florida, Georgia, South Carolina, North Carolina, and Virginia (except the forty-eight counties designated as West Virginia, and also the counties of Berkley, Accomac, Northampton, Elizabeth City, York, Princess Anna, and Norfolk, including the cities of Norfolk and Portsmouth), and which excepted parts are, for the present, left precisely as if this proclamation were not issued. And by virtue of the power, and for the purpose aforesaid, I do order and declare, that all persons held as slaves within said designated states and parts of states, are and henceforward shall be free; and that the executive government of the United States, including the military and naval authorities thereof, will recognize and maintain the freedom of said persons. And I hereby enjoin upon the people so declared to be free to abstain from all violence, unless in necessary self-defense; and I recommend to them, that in all cases, when allowed, they labor faithfully for reasonable wages. And I further declare and make known, that such persons, of suitable condition, will be received into the armed service of the United States, to garrison forts, positions, stations, and other places, and to man vessels of all sorts in said service. And upon this act, sincerely believed to be an act of justice, warranted by the constitution upon military necessity, I invoke the considerate judgment of mankind and the gracious favor of Almighty God.

In testimony whereof I have hereunto set my name, and caused the seal of the United States to be affixed. Done at the city of Washington this first day of January, in the year of our Lord one thousand eight hundred and sixty-three, and of the independence of the United States the eighty-seventh.

ABRAHAM LINCOLN.

By the President:

WILLIAM H. SEWARD,
Secretary of State.

REFERENCES.

Adams (J. Q.), N. E. Confederacy of 1643, Mass. Hist. Soc. Coll.
Arnold (I. N.), Life of Abraham Lincoln.
Arnold (S. G.), History of Rhode Island, 2 v.
Bancroft (George), History of the United States.
Barry (J. S.), History of Massachusetts, 3 v.
Benton (T. H.), Thirty Years' View, 2 v.
Bogman (J. L.), History of Maryland.
Browne (W. H.), Maryland. (American Commonwealths.)
Bryant (W. C.) and Gay (S. H.), Popular History of the U. S., 4 v.
Burnet (Jacob), Notes on Early Settlement of the North-west Territory.
Chalmers (George), Political Annals.
" " Revolt of the American Colonies, 2 v.
Chamberlin (Mellin), Authentification of the Declaration of Independence, Mass. Hist. Soc. Proc.
Cooke (J. E.), Virginia. (American Commonwealths.)
Curtis (Geo. T.), History of the Formation and Adoption of the Constitution of the United States, 2 v.
Curtis (Geo. T.), The Treaty of Peace and Independence, *Harpers' Magazine*, LXVI.
Davis (J. C. B.), Treaties and Conventions, Senate Ex. Doc. No. 36, Forty-First Congress, 3d Session.
Donaldson (Thomas), The Public Domain, H. Mis. Doc. 45, pt. 4, 47th Congress, 2d Session.
Doyle (J. A.), The English Colonies in America.
Draper (J. W.), History of the American Civil War, 3 v.
Elliot (Jonathan), Debates on the Adoption of the Federal Constitution.
Fiske (John), Political Consequences of Cornwallis' Surrender, *Atlantic Monthly*.
Frothingham (Richard), Rise of the Republic of the U. S.
Gibbs (George), Memoirs of the Administrations of Washington and Adams, 2 v.
Greeley (Horace), American Conflict, 2 v.
Greene (G. W.), Historical View of the American Revolution.
" " Short History of Rhode Island.
Hamilton (J. C.), History of the United States, 7 v.
Hildreth (Richard), History of the United States, 6 v.
Holst (H. von), Constitutional History of the United States, 5 v.
" " John C. Calhoun. (American Statesmen.)

Jefferson (Thomas), Works, 9 v.
Lossing (Benson J.), Pictorial History of the Civil War.
McMaster (John B.), History of the People of the United States, 2 v.
Morse (J. T.), Thomas Jefferson. (American Statesmen.)
Neil (E. D.), English Colonization.
" " Virginia Company.
Palfrey (J. G.), History of New England, 4 v.
Paris (Comte de), History of the Civil War in America, 3 v.
Parton (James), Life of Andrew Jackson.
Pitkin (Timothy), Political and Civil History of the United States, 2 v.
Poole (W. F.), Dr. Cutter and the Ordinance of 1787, *North American Review*, v. 122.
Poore (B. P.), Federal and State Constitution.
Prince (L. B.), The Articles of Confederation *vs.* The Constitution.
Proud (Robert), History of Pennsylvania.
Schouler (James), History of the United States under the Constitution, 3 v.
Stevens (J. A.), Albert Gallatin. (American Statesmen.)
Story (Joseph), Commentaries on the Constitution, 3 v.
Sumner (W. G.), Andrew Jackson. (American Statesmen.)
Towle (N. C.), History and Analysis of the Constitution of the United States.
Webster (Daniel), Works, 6 v.
Wilson (Henry), History of the Rise and Fall of the Slave Power in America, 3 v.
Wenser (Justin), and others, Memorial History of Boston, 4 v.

INDEX OF DOCUMENTS.

Illustrations of History, and Examples of Oratory.

AMERICAN ORATIONS, FROM THE COLONIAL PERIOD TO THE PRESENT TIME.—Selected as specimens of Eloquence, and with special reference to their value in throwing light upon the more important epochs and issues of American History. Edited, with introductions and notes, by ALEXANDER JOHNSTON, Professor of Jurisprudence and Political Economy in the College of New Jersey. Three volumes, 16mo. Uniform with "Prose Masterpieces." $3.75.

CONTENTS.—*Colonialism:* Henry, Hamilton, Washington. *Constitutional Government:* Ames, Nicholas. *Rise of Democracy:* Jefferson, Nott, Randolph, Quincy, Clay. *Rise of Nationality:* Calhoun, Hayne, Webster. *Anti-Slavery Struggle:* Phillips, Calhoun, Webster, Clay. *Abolition Movement:* Phillips. *Kansas-Nebraska Bill:* Chase, Sumner, Douglas. *Crime against Kansas:* Sumner; Preston S. Brooks' Reply to Sumner. *Defence of Massachusetts:* Burlingame. *On Debates in Congress:* Clingman. Lincoln *on his Nomination;* Douglas in reply. Breckenridge and Seward *on Slavery*. *Secession:* Crittenden, Iverson, Toombs, Hale, Stevens, Cox. *Civil War and Reconstruction:* Lincoln, Davis (Jefferson), Stevens, Douglas, Vallandigham, Schurz, Beecher, Lincoln (second inaugural address), Davis (H. W.), Pendleton, Sherman, Stevens, Garfield, Blackburn, Haygood. *Protection and Free Trade:* Clay, Hurd.

"The idea, the plan, and the execution of the work are admirable."—*Boston Advertiser.*

"The best method, in our judgment, to acquire a truly fine style either for the pen or the platform is by reading and re-reading the best specimens of English; and for the orator, whether at the bar, on the platform, or in the pulpit, a careful reading of these volumes will be an admirable education."—*Christian Union*, New York.

BRITISH ORATIONS.—A selection of the more important and representative Political Addresses of the past two centuries. Edited, with introductions and notes, by CHARLES K. ADAMS, Professor of History in the University of Michigan. Three vols., 16mo. Uniform with "American Orations." $3.75.

CONTENTS.—Eliot (Sir John), Pym, Chatham, Mansfield, Burke, Pitt, Fox, Mackintosh, Erskine, Canning, Macaulay, Cobden, Bright, Beaconsfield, Gladstone.

"Carefully selected specimens of oratorical eloquence. . . . . The volumes contain a rich store of instructive, no less entertaining material."—*Advertiser*, Boston.

"Show the great currents of political thoughts that have done much to shape the history of Great Britain."—*N. E. Journal of Education*, Boston.

"Not only of interest to the student of oratory, but to all who would trace the rise and progress of free political institutions."—*Transcript*, Portland.

G. P. PUTNAM'S SONS,

27 and 29 West 23d Street - - New York and London.